MW01640308

Gilbert A. Jarvis
Thérèse M. Bonin

Diane W. Birckbichler
Linita C. Shih

¿Y tú?

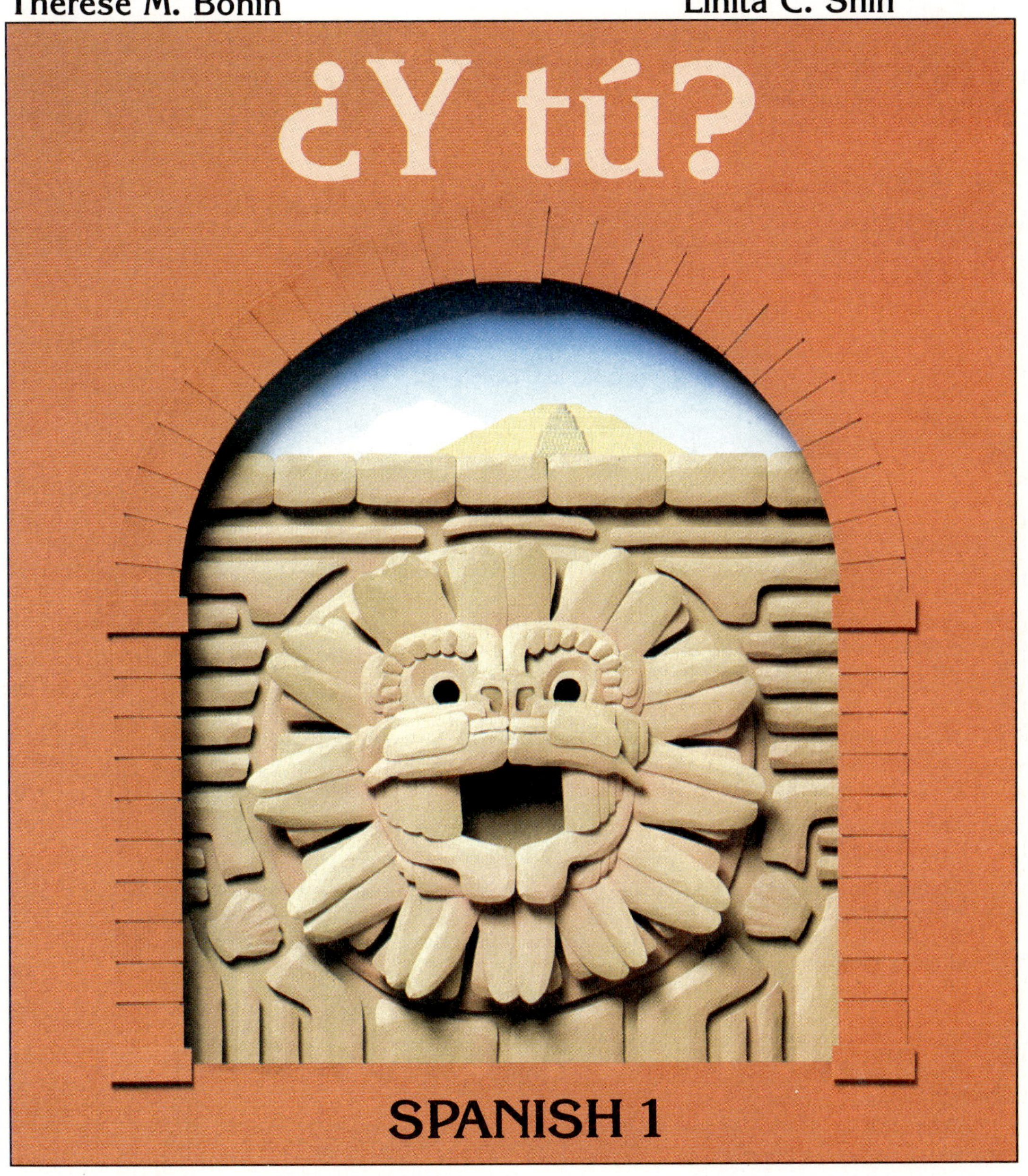

SPANISH 1

HOLT, RINEHART AND WINSTON, PUBLISHERS
New York • Toronto • Mexico City • London • Sydney • Tokyo

Cover illustration: Detail, Temple of Quetzalcóatl, "The Plumed Serpent," at the pyramids of Teotihuacán, Mexico.

Material on page 292 is adapted from *En Contacto: Lecturas Intermedias* by Mary McVey-Gill, *et al.*, pp. 24–25, Copyright © 1980 by Holt, Rinehart and Winston. Reprinted by permission of Holt, Rinehart and Winston, CBS College Publishing.

Material on pages 330–331, adapted from *Tú* magazine, is used with permission of Transworld Feature Syndicate Inc.

Material on pages 335–336 is adapted from *Spanish for Oral and Written Review* by Mario Iglesias and Walter Meiden, pp. 152–153, Copyright © 1981, 1975 by Holt, Rinehart and Winston. Reprinted by permission of Holt, Rinehart and Winston, CBS College Publishing.

Printed in the United States of America

ISBN: 0-03-057507-9
567 039 98765432

ART CREDITS

Cover art: Bill Finewood

Phillipe Carrere: pp. 25, 28

Penny Carter: pp. 3, 23, 26, 32, 40, 49, 55, 61, 62, 86, 87, 111, 138, 141, 142, 161, 184, 202, 206, 212, 221, 226, 263, 267, 279, 297, 306, 330, 331

Pam Ford Johnson: pp. 13, 14, 24, 31, 40, 49, 52, 74, 75, 76, 89, 90, 91, 99, 100, 101, 106, 147, 148, 149, 185, 191, 253, 254, 332, 337

Felipe Galindo: pp. 12, 18, 20, 27, 31, 37, 43, 56, 60, 65, 73, 75, 77, 79, 83, 90, 102, 103, 105, 110, 116, 126, 130, 133, 151, 156, 157, 160, 165, 173, 175, 181, 183, 187, 188, 199, 200, 205, 210, 215, 218, 219, 229, 230, 234, 239, 243, 256, 257, 259, 260, 261, 265, 270, 281, 286, 290, 294, 307, 311, 316, 321, 335, 336, 338

Kathie Kelleher: pp. 7, 8, 9, 35, 58, 95, 117, 127, 129, 138, 139, 140, 183, 213, 214, 220, 232, 273, 310, 314, 324, 325

Hillary Newby: pp. 114, 123, 125, 134, 146, 158, 167, 198

Daniel Tesser: p. 33

Randi Wasserman: p. 41

CONSULTANTS

We would like to thank the teachers and administrators who reviewed each chapter of the manuscript. Their enthusiastic reception of the materials was very encouraging, and their suggestions for improvements were most helpful. We are very pleased to acknowledge the important contributions of the consultants whose names appear below.

Alicia Amoss
Upper Arlington High School
Upper Arlington, Ohio

Blanche Armendáriz
Texas A & I University
Kingsville, Texas

Anthony J. Bent
Lexington Public Schools
Lexington, Massachusetts

Carla S. Brice
Richardson High School
Richardson, Texas

Judy Dozier
Meadowbrook Junior High School
Shawnee Mission, Kansas

Isaac Goldemberg
New York University
New York, New York

Robert A. Hawkins
Upper Arlington Schools
Columbus, Ohio

Ilene Davis Linssen
Oakland Unified School District
Oakland, California

Albert L. Pike, Jr.
Billerica Public Schools
Billerica, Massachusetts

Patricia Ríos
Irving Independent School District
Irving, Texas

C. Albert Rubio
Greensboro Public Schools
Greensboro, North Carolina

Evelyn Vandiver
Charlotte-Mecklenburg Schools
Charlotte, North Carolina

RINCONES CULTURALES

Topics

CONTENTS

Capítulo preliminar

LET'S LEARN SPANISH

LET'S LEARN SPANISH

Beginning to study Spanish

As you begin your study of Spanish, you will quickly become aware that learning a new language is very different from learning other subjects. The ways you study other subjects are sometimes not the best ways to learn another language. With some subjects you don't have to study every day, but with Spanish you should study and practice daily. The following suggestions will help you in learning Spanish.

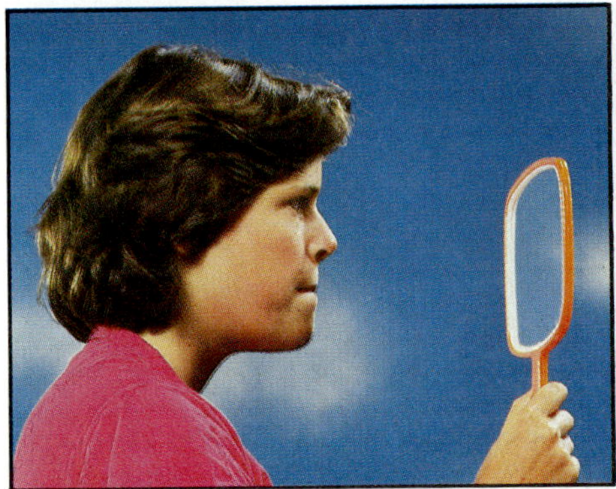

Don't be afraid of the new sounds of Spanish. You will quickly discover that some of the sounds in Spanish are different from sounds in English. At first, they may seem "strange," but as you use them, they will become very familiar, and you will become accustomed to pronouncing them. Even if your Spanish sounds are not perfect, keep practicing. Don't be concerned about having a perfect accent. Actually, you may already know some Spanish because English has borrowed from Spanish: words like **cafetería**, **chocolate**, and **patio.**

Practice Spanish whenever you can. Most of your class time will be spent practicing Spanish. Learning a language should not be viewed as memorizing new words or grammar rules but rather as using and hearing Spanish over and over in class activities until it becomes familiar. Don't be afraid to make mistakes. They are a normal part of practice, and they help you learn. Also, practice outside of class whenever you can. Get together with another student, teach a younger brother or sister, or ask a Spanish-speaking person to help.

Don't miss the basic building blocks of Spanish. Learning a language involves building upon words and grammar already learned. Learning to use the material in Chapter Two requires knowing Chapter One. The words and sentence patterns learned during the first days of Spanish will continue to be important every day.

When you are not sure of something in Spanish, go ahead and take your best guess. Sometimes you'll see or hear a word or phrase you don't understand. Think about what word you believe should be in that place. Guess the meaning. At other times you'll be unsure about how to say something. Go ahead! Try! You may be right, and, for sure, you'll learn faster.

Use what you know already

One of the nice things about learning Spanish is that it has many similarities to English. In other words, you will be able to use what you already know about English to make learning Spanish much easier.

A good example of the "head start" you have in choosing Spanish as a new language is the number of words you can recognize when you see them written, such as **problema**, **fotografía**, **conversación**, and **independencia**. These words are called cognates. Some words such as *junta*, *fiesta*, *armadillo*, and *rodeo* have been taken directly from Spanish. Others have become anglicized, that is, adapted to English: *vanilla* (**vainilla**), *coffee* (**café**), and *alligator* (**el lagarto**). You have already, probably without knowing it, developed skill in guessing the meaning of new words.

Look at the captions for the following photographs. You'll see much that looks familiar. In fact, you'll be able to understand a great deal already.

One of the first things you notice is that the alphabet Spanish uses is almost the same as the alphabet English uses. That is a tremendous head start compared to languages that have a different alphabet. You also notice that some words are spelled the same as English words.

Silvia estudia biología, álgebra y la historia de México.

You probably guessed the meaning of **estudia** and also that **y** means *and* because you expect history, biology, and algebra to be linked together like this. Your natural tendency to read past words like **la** and **de** was right because no two languages are exactly alike. (You might even have guessed the meaning of **de** because of names and expressions that are used in the United States.)

Here is another caption that you can easily understand but that shows how you need to be flexible in understanding the meaning.

The subject-verb word order is the same as English. You might recognize **mi** as similar to *my* and **es** as similar to *is*. Although **profesor** can mean *professor*, here it means *teacher*. **Simpático** looks like *sympathetic*, but it means *nice*. And you would probably translate **no** as *isn't he*? The sentence then would read: *My teacher's nice, isn't he?* Thus, rigid word-for-word translation, though it may help you to understand, does not always give you the words you would use in English. Be flexible. Think of other ways to express the meaning.

Mi profesor es simpático, ¿no?

Not all Spanish words and sentence patterns will be familiar to you. New words must be learned, and new grammar is always important. For example, you will probably be able to guess the correct meaning of **programa de televisión** and of **estudia** here. You will probably guess from the context that **mira** means *watches* but not necessarily that **mientras** means *while*.

Carlos mira un programa de televisión mientras estudia.

Have you noticed the accent marks and punctuation? Accent marks are a part of Spanish spelling and are often a clue to the pronunciation of new words: **simpático**, **televisión**, **café**.

Another mark that is a part of Spanish spelling is the tilde: **señor**, **español**. You will occasionally see the diaeresis in Spanish words such as **bilingüe**.

In Spanish, exclamation points and question marks are used at the beginning as well as at the end: **¿Habla usted español? ¡Dios mío!** You will find that the initial punctuation marks are very helpful when reading.

As you have seen, there are words and sentence patterns in Spanish that resemble those in English. Other aspects will be different and must be learned. When your teacher reads the captions aloud, you will hear sounds that may be different from what you expect.

The sounds of Spanish are often different from the sounds we use in English. At the beginning of your study of Spanish, make a special effort to recognize and to pronounce the new sounds.

Spanish is useful

One reason to choose Spanish as your second language is its practical importance. Spanish, the language of 300 million people in twenty-one countries, is one of the official languages of the United Nations and is an important language for international commerce. It is particularly vital to Americans because Spanish is a second language in many areas of the United States and because we share a common boundary and a continent with nations whose future is closely linked to ours.

With more than 20 million Spanish speakers, the United States has the fourth largest Spanish-speaking population in the world. Some of the largest cities with Spanish-speaking populations are in the United States. New York, Los Angeles, Miami, and Chicago all have over 1 million Spanish speakers.

American business recognizes the importance of Spanish both at home and abroad by asking for people with a knowledge of Spanish, as a glance at the help-wanted section of any large newspaper shows. Knowing Spanish can be the key to a rewarding career.

In addition, Hispanic peoples have made valuable contributions to our culture and to Western civilization. A knowledge of Spanish opens the doors to an appreciation of the art, music, and literature of Spain and Latin America while international travel brings these countries closer to home.

ESPAÑOL/INGLÉS
Se necesita secretaria bilingüe. Práctica en trabajos de oficina. Llame al Sr. Pérez. Tel. 32-87-60

Bilingual Bonus $20-25K
OFFICE MANAGER
Prestigious investment firm seeks person with proven exp. in office administration. Will interface with wealthy Latin American clients. Requires fluency in formal Spanish. Ideal for person with career advancement in mind.

Maps of the Hispanic world

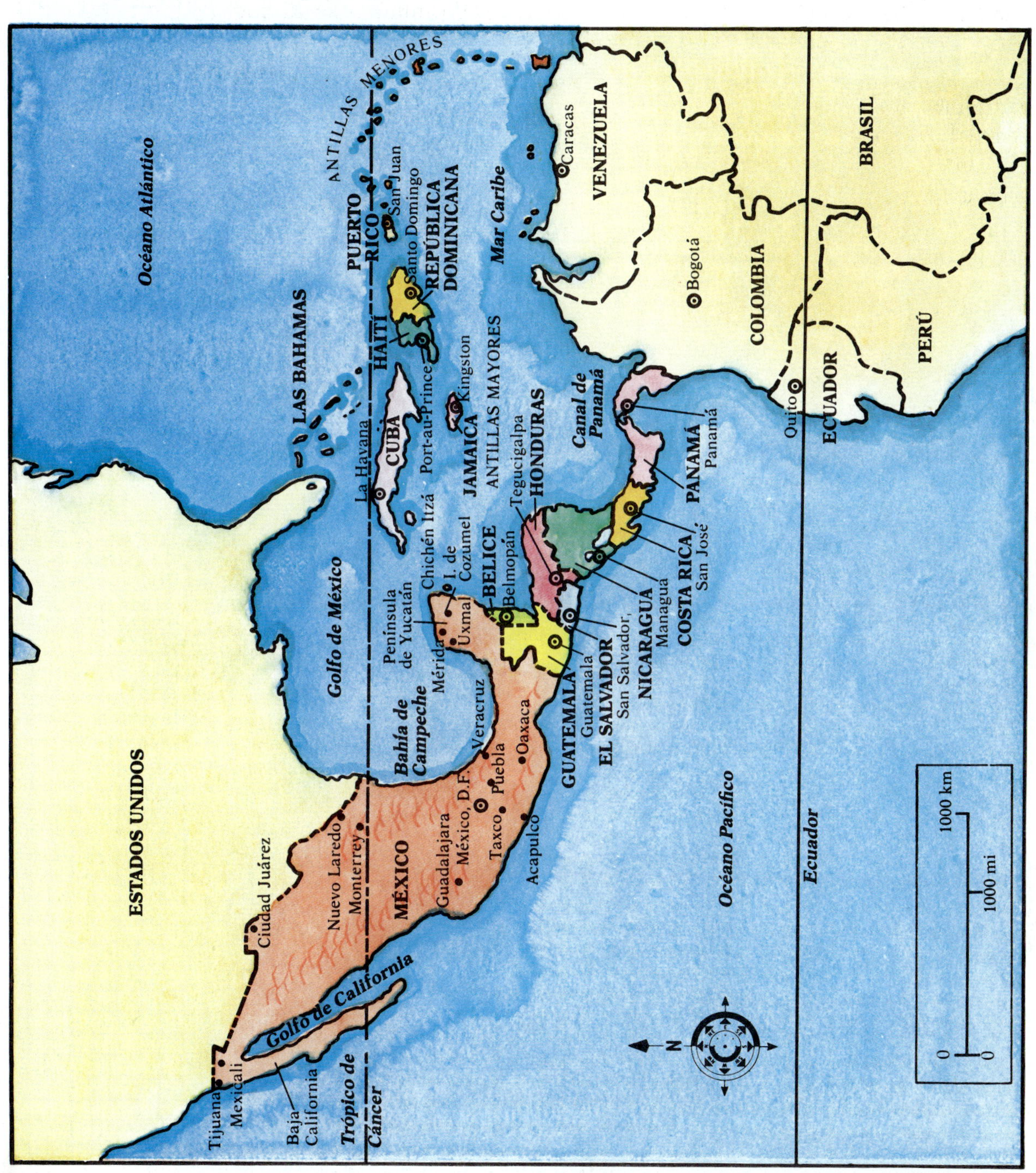

México, Centroamérica y el Caribe

Mar Caribe
NICARAGUA
Barranquilla
Maracaibo
Caracas
VENEZUELA
GUYANA
Georgetown
Océano Atlántico
COSTA RICA
PANAMÁ
Medellín
Río Magdalena
Río Orinoco
Paramaribo
Cayena
GUAYANA FRANCESA
Bogotá
Cali
COLOMBIA
SURINAM
Quito
ECUADOR
Ecuador
Iquitos
Río Amazonas
PERÚ
BRASIL
Machu Picchu
Lima
Cuzco
BOLIVIA
Lago Titicaca
La Paz
Brasilia
Sucre
Río Paraná
PARAGUAY
Río de Janeiro
São Paulo
Trópico de Capricornio
Asunción
CHILE
ARGENTINA
Océano Pacífico
Río Uruguay
Córdoba
CORDILLERA DE LOS ANDES
URUGUAY
Santiago
Buenos Aires
Punta del Este
Montevideo
Mar del Plata
Río de la Plata
N
ISLAS MALVINAS (G.B.)
0
500 km
0
500 mi
TIERRA DEL FUEGO
Estrecho de Magallanes

Sudamérica

España

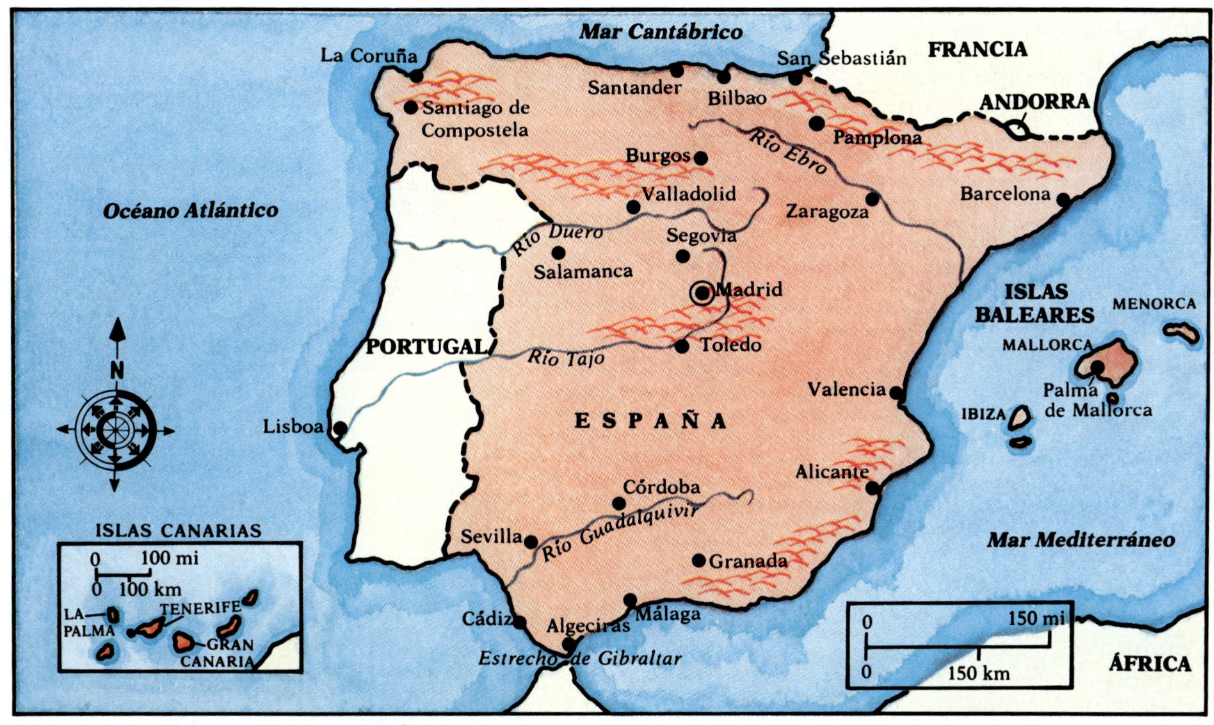

Starting to speak Spanish

Useful classroom expressions

The more you practice Spanish, the better you will be able to communicate. Routine classroom expressions can be used immediately in Spanish.

Learn to understand the following expressions your teacher will probably use often, and learn to say those that you will want to use.

El profesor o la profesora dice (*The teacher says*):

1.	Escuchen, por favor.	Please listen.
2.	Repitan, por favor.	Please repeat.
3.	Contesten, por favor.	Please answer.
4.	Abran el libro.	Open your books.
5.	Cierren el libro.	Close your books.
6.	Vayan a la pizarra, por favor.	Go to the board, please.
7.	¿Entienden?	Do you understand?
8.	Saquen papel y lápiz, por favor.	Take out paper and pencil, please.
9.	Saquen la tarea.	Take out your homework.
10.	Siéntense, por favor.	Please sit down.

Learn to say the following expressions.

Los estudiantes dicen (*The students say*):

1.	Sí, señora (profesora).	Yes.
2.	No, señor (profesor).	No.
3.	No sé, señorita (profesora).	I don't know.
4.	Repita, por favor.	Repeat, please.
5.	¿Cómo?	What?
6.	¿Cómo se dice . . . ?	How do you say . . . ?
7.	¿Qué quiere decir . . . ?	What does . . . mean?
8.	No entiendo.	I don't understand.
9.	Gracias.	Thank you.
10.	De nada.	You're welcome.

Nombres hispanos

Learn to recognize the following Spanish names when you hear them. You may also want to choose one to use in class.

Alberto	Hugo	Alicia	Gloria
Alejandro	Humberto	Amalia	Graciela
Alfonso	Javier	Ana	Inés
Alfredo	Joaquín	Andrea	Isabel
Andrés	Jorge	Bárbara	Lucía
Antonio	José	Beatriz	Luisa
Arturo	Juan	Caridad	Manuela
Bernardo	Luis	Carlota	Margarita
Camilo	Marcos	Carolina	María
Carlos	Mario	Catalina	Mariana
Cristóbal	Miguel	Cecilia	Marta
Daniel	Nicolás	Cristina	Micaela
David	Pablo	Daniela	Mónica
Edmundo	Pedro	Diana	Pilar
Eduardo	Ramón	Dorotea	Raquel
Ernesto	Raúl	Elena	Rosalía
Esteban	Ricardo	Elisa	Rosario
Eugenio	Roberto	Elsa	Silvia
Felipe	Simón	Esperanza	Teresa
Fernando	Teodoro	Estela	Verónica
Gerardo	Tomás	Eva	Victoria
Gregorio	Vicente	Francisca	Virginia
Guillermo	Víctor	Gabriela	Yolanda

Notice that some names can be either girls' names or boys' names, depending on the ending: **Mario–María**, **Antonio–Antonia**, **Luis–Luisa**, **Marcelo–Marcela**, **Víctor–Victoria**, **Eugenio–Eugenia**.

Just as in English, many Spanish names also have nicknames or **apodos**. For example, someone named Francisco might be called **Paco** or **Paquito** by his friends and family. Similarly **José** might be called **Pepe**. **Isabel** would be known as **Belita** and **Graciela** or **Marcela** as **Chela**.

Another very common way to form nicknames in Spanish is to add a diminutive ending to the name. One common diminutive ending in Spanish is **ito** or **ita**. **Juan**, for example, might be called **Juanito** or **Juanín** (Johnny), and **Eva** would probably be called **Evita** (Evie) by friends and family.

El alfabeto español

The Spanish alphabet is slightly different from the English alphabet because it has four letters that do not occur in English as separate letters: *ch* (**che**), *ll* (**elle**), *ñ* (**eñe**), and *rr* (**erre**).

Note that in a dictionary you would look for **che** after **ce**, **elle** after **ele**, **eñe** after **ene,** and **erre** after **ere**.

a	a	j	jota	r	ere
b	be	k*	ka	rr	erre
c	ce	l	ele	s	ese
ch	che	ll	elle	t	te
d	de	m	eme	u	u
e	e	n	ene	v	ve, uve
f	efe	ñ	eñe	w*	doble ve
g	ge	o	o	x	equis
h	hache	p	pe	y	i griega
i	i	q	cu	z	zeta

*The letters *k* and *w* are usually not considered part of the Spanish alphabet because they are used in words borrowed from other languages. One example of such a word is *kilo*, which comes from Classical Greek.

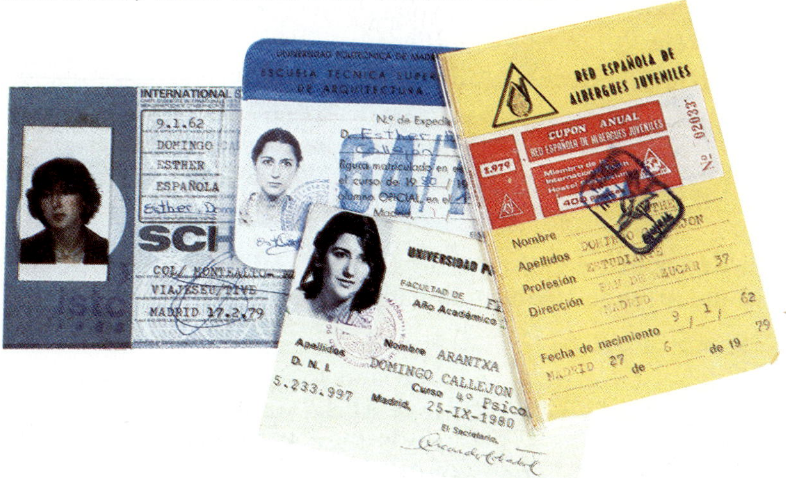

Actividades

A. Oculista. Imagine you're on vacation in Mexico and have to go to the eye doctor. How would you read the letters on his chart?

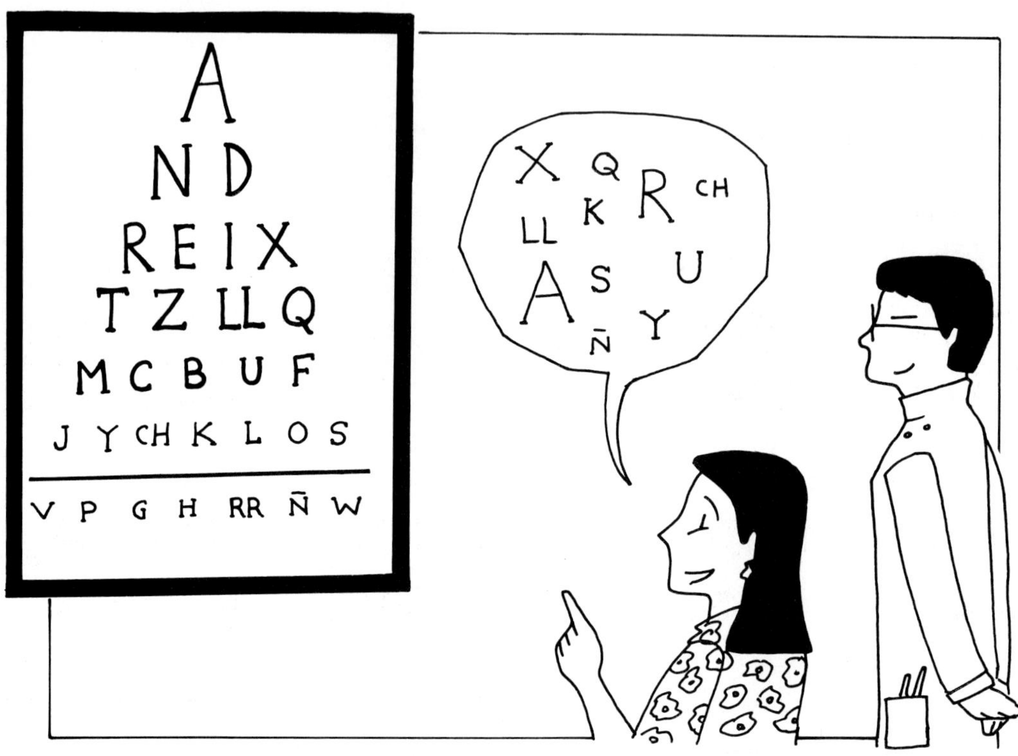

B. Estudiantes bilingües. Help the following students in a bilingual class in Los Angeles spell their names in Spanish.

David
Raquel
Vicente
Guillermo
Cándido
Chavela
Alejandro
Yolanda
Beatriz
Francisca

C. Visado. You are applying for a visa. Spell your first and last name, and the name of the town and the state in which you were born.

D. Autores. A librarian in Spain just acquired works by the following authors. Tell how she would arrange them in alphabetical order.

Alfredo Chavero
Camilo José Cela
Julio Cortázar
Miguel de Cervantes
José Cadalso
Ramón Pacheco
Manuel Puig
Octavio Paz
Heberto Padilla
José María de Pereda
Ignacio de Luzán
Mariano José de Larra
José Alfredo Llerena
Jesús Lara
Luis de León

Los números (1–15)

0	cero	4	cuatro	8	ocho	12	doce
1	uno	5	cinco	9	nueve	13	trece
2	dos	6	seis	10	diez	14	catorce
3	tres	7	siete	11	once	15	quince

Actividades

A. En el aeropuerto. Tell from what gate (**puerta**) the following flights will be leaving.

MODELO **México: la puerta número siete**

B. Pesetas. The **peseta** is the name of the currency used in Spain. How many **pesetas** do you see below?

MODELO **cinco pesetas**

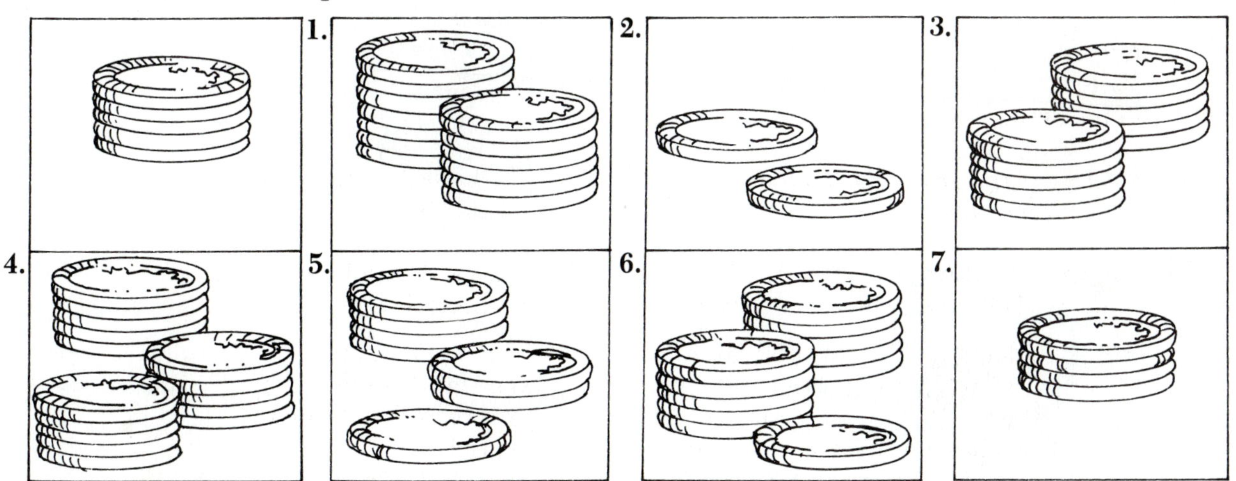

C. Pesos. Imagine you're shopping in one of New York's Spanish neighborhoods where the dollar is referred to as a peso. Read the price tags on the following items.

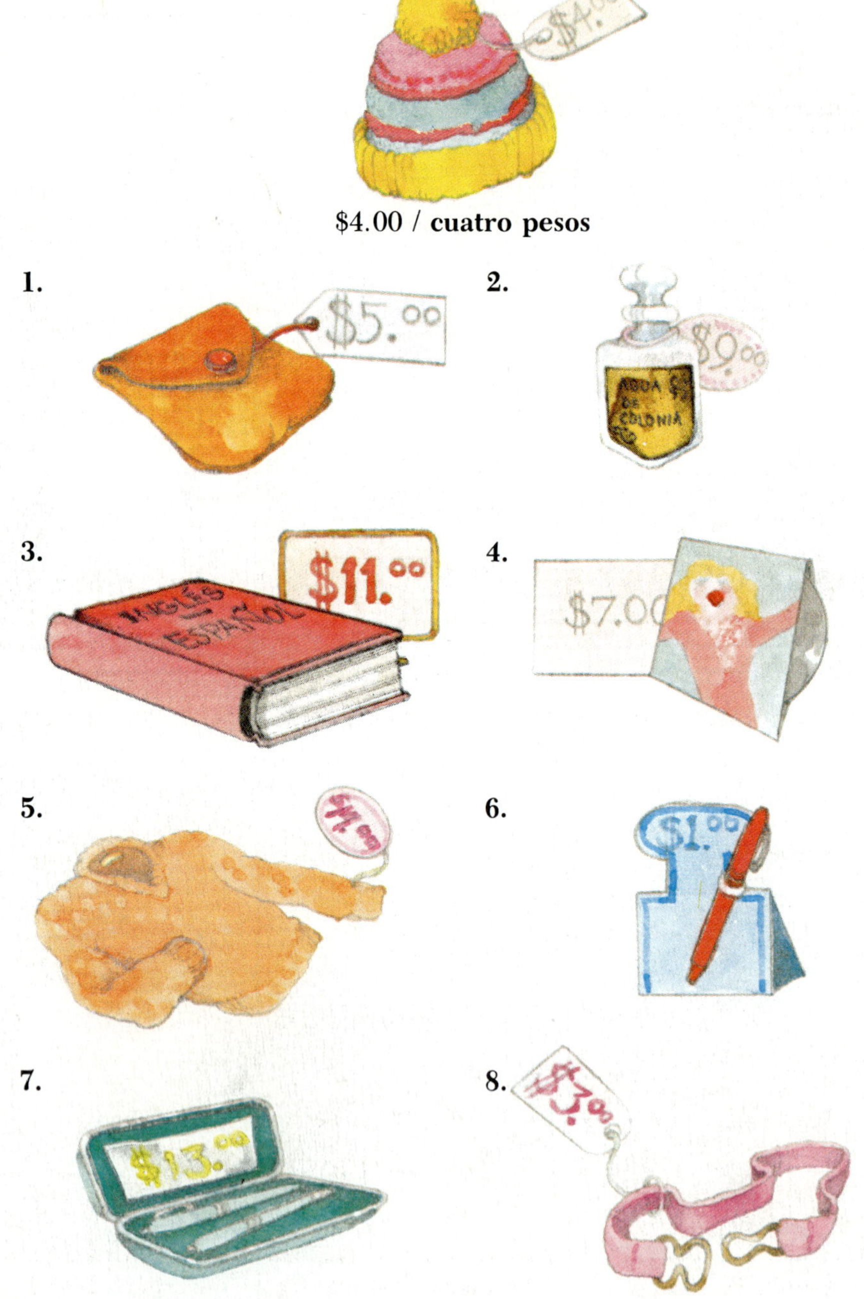

Saying Hello

Get to know other people in your class better and begin speaking Spanish right away. First, listen carefully to your teacher's pronunciation.

To say hello to another student

Hola, Leonor. Hola, Mateo.

To say hello to adults

Buenos días, señor. (*Good morning.*)

Buenas noches, señores. (*Good evening.*)

Buenas tardes, señora. (*Good afternoon.*)

To introduce yourself

Me llamo Marcela.

Mucho gusto.

Actividad

¡Hola! Say hello to other students in your class and tell them your name. If someone else introduces himself or herself, respond politely and give your name.

EJEMPLO Hola. Me llamo Vicente.
Mucho gusto. Me llamo Juan Pablo.

What to say after saying hello

After saying hello, people usually ask each other how they are feeling or how things are going. Here are some expressions you'll want to know.

To ask a friend how he or she is

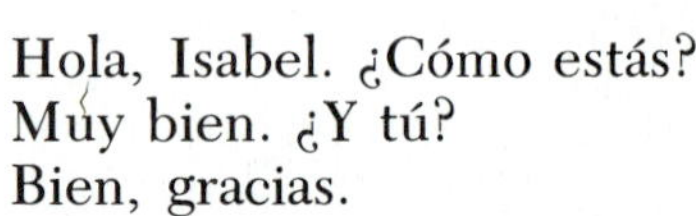

Hola, Isabel. ¿Cómo estás?
Muy bien. ¿Y tú?
Bien, gracias.

Hi, Isabel. How are you?
Fine. And you?
Fine, thanks.

¡Oye, Diego!
Hola. ¿Qué tal?
Así, así.

Hey, Diego.
Hi. How's everything?
Okay.

To ask how someone is in a more formal way

¿Cómo está usted, señor?
Regular, gracias. ¿Y usted?
Pues, bastante bien.

How are you, sir?
So, so, thanks. And you?
Well, pretty well.

To say good-bye to someone

Hasta luego, Julieta.
Hasta mañana, Antonio.

See you later, Julieta.
See you tomorrow, Antonio.

Actividades

A. Saludos. Choose from column B an appropriate response for each question or statement in column A. Then practice with another student. (Remember that more than one response may be appropriate.)

EJEMPLO ¿Cómo estás?
Bien, gracias. ¿Y tú?

A	B
Hola.	Mucho gusto.
Buenos días.	Muy bien. ¿Y tú?
Me llamo Sergio Campos.	Bien, gracias.
¿Cómo estás?	Bastante bien. ¿Y usted?
¿Qué tal?	Hasta luego.
¿Cómo está usted?	Hola.
Hasta mañana.	Buenos días.
¡Oye!	¿Qué tal?

B. ¿Cómo estás? Practice greeting others by asking how they are. First greet other students in your class. Then greet your teacher.

EJEMPLO ¿Cómo estás?
Bastante bien. ¿Y tú?
Bien, gracias.

¿Cómo está usted?
Regular. ¿Y tú?
Bastante bien, gracias.

C. De vacaciones. Imagine you meet some people while on vacation in the Yucatan. What would you say to them in the following situations at the time of day specified?

EJEMPLO	At breakfast in the hotel	After a movie in the evening
	Buenos días.	Hasta mañana.

1. At the beach in the morning
2. Saying good-bye to someone after dinner
3. At a gift shop in the afternoon
4. At dinner in the evening
5. Upon leaving the group after a night tour of the Mayan ruins at Uxmal
6. After lunch when you expect to see the person later that day

D. Una familia cubana. Imagine that a Cuban student in your school has invited you to visit his family. How would you greet each person?

MODELO	his uncle, Mr. Torres	his sister, Rosita
	Buenas tardes, señor Torres.	**Hola, Rosita.**
	¿Cómo está usted?	**¿Cómo estás?**

1. his brother, Paco
2. his mother, Mrs. Silva
3. his cousin, Miss Torres
4. his father, Mr. Silva
5. his sister Teresa
6. his grandmother, Mrs. Ugarte
7. your friend, José

E. Diálogos. Imagine that you are attending summer school in Cuernavaca. Make up two short dialogues. The first dialogue is between you and your Mexican roommate. The second dialogue is between you and your teacher. Practice your dialogues with another student.

Talking about what you like

A. Me gusta . . . People all over the world like to talk about their likes and dislikes. Say whether or not you like the following things.

B. Hola. Introduce yourself to the class and tell the other students something you like.

EJEMPLO Hola. Me llamo Teresa Martín.
Me gusta la música.

C. No me gusta. Introduce yourself to another student and tell that student something you don't like.

EJEMPLO Buenos días. Me llamo Guillermo Walsh.
No me gusta la lucha libre.

Capítulo uno

GETTING TO KNOW OTHERS 1

INTRODUCCIÓN

¡Hola!

Hola. Me llamo Luisa Sánchez y soy de Venezuela. Me gusta el tenis y me gusta el béisbol pero no me gusta esquiar.

I am / from
but / to ski

Soy Felipe Martínez García, de Colombia. Me gusta hablar, escuchar la radio y mirar la televisión. Me gusta la música también pero no me gusta bailar.

to talk / to listen to
to watch / too
to dance

COMPRENSIÓN

Would Luisa or Felipe have made the following statements?

1. Me gusta el béisbol.
2. Me gusta la televisión.
3. No me gusta bailar.
4. Soy de Venezuela.
5. No me gusta esquiar.
6. Soy de Colombia.
7. Me gusta escuchar la radio.

COMUNICACIÓN

A. ¿Te gusta . . . ? Not everyone likes the same things. Ask another student if she or he likes to do the following. Begin your questions with **¿Te gusta . . . ?**

EJEMPLO ¿Te gusta esquiar?
Sí, me gusta esquiar.
No, no me gusta esquiar.

nadar — esquiar — estudiar

trabajar — bailar — cantar

hablar español — escuchar la radio — mirar la televisión

B. Me gusta . . . Tell whether or not you like the following.

EJEMPLO Me gusta la música.
No me gusta la música.

1. la radio	**4.** la tarea
2. la televisión	**5.** la lucha libre
3. el baloncesto	**6.** el béisbol

C. Me gustan . . . Tell whether or not you like the following things. Note that when you talk about one thing, you say **me gusta . . .**, but when you talk about several, you say **me gustan**.

EJEMPLO Me gustan los animales.
No me gustan los exámenes.

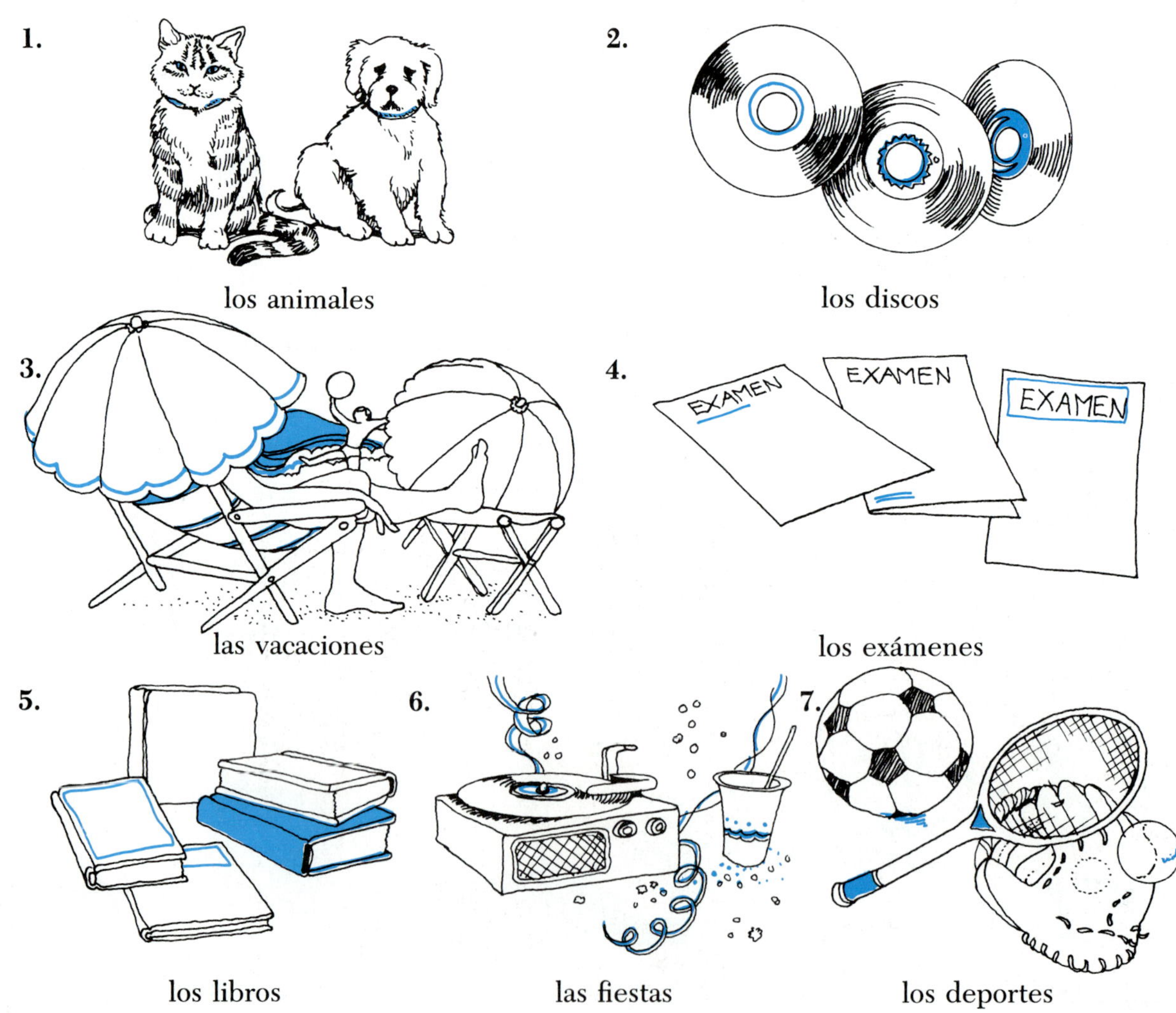

1. los animales
2. los discos
3. las vacaciones
4. los exámenes
5. los libros
6. las fiestas
7. los deportes

D. ¿Te gusta . . . ? Find out the likes and dislikes of other students by asking them questions about some of the things below.

EJEMPLO ¿Te gusta cantar?
¿Te gusta el tenis?
¿Te gustan los libros?

el béisbol	los exámenes	nadar
la música	los deportes	estudiar
el fútbol	las vacaciones	bailar
la televisión (la tele)	los animales	cantar

E. Los gustos de Pedro. Look at the drawing of Pedro's room. Tell how Pedro might identify the things he likes.

EJEMPLO Me gusta el béisbol.

EXPLORACIÓN

Naming things you like or don't like
The definite article

PRESENTACIÓN

When we talk about the things we like, we have to name them. In Spanish the definite article is used with the noun, but in English we don't use an article before the noun.

Me gusta **la** música.	I like music.
Me gustan **los** animales.	I like animals.

A. All nouns—even the names of things—are either masculine or feminine in Spanish: **animal** is masculine and **música** is feminine. The definite article must agree in gender (masculine or feminine) and in number (singular or plural) with the noun.

	SINGULAR	PLURAL
MASCULINE	**el** disco	**los** discos
FEMININE	**la** fiesta	**las** fiestas

B. The definite article is always used when you talk about things in general (such as when you like and dislike something) and when you want to communicate the meaning *the*. Here are some things you may want to say you like or dislike.

la escuela — el dinero — la gimnasia

los coches — los conciertos — los juegos electrónicos

PREPARACIÓN

A. ¡Me gusta! Elena seems to like everything. What does she say about the following things?

MODELO el baloncesto
Me gusta el baloncesto.

1. el español
2. la lucha libre
3. la escuela
4. el béisbol
5. la televisión
6. el volibol
7. el dinero
8. la gimnasia

B. ¡Me gustan! Vicente also likes a number of things. What does he say?

MODELO los libros
Me gustan los libros.

1. los deportes
2. las fiestas
3. los coches
4. los animales
5. los conciertos
6. los discos
7. las vacaciones
8. los juegos electrónicos

C. Gustos. Pilar is talking about some of her favorite things. What does she say?

MODELO el dinero — **Me gusta el dinero.** las fiestas — **Me gustan las fiestas.**

1. el fútbol
2. la escuela
3. los deportes
4. las vacaciones
5. los libros
6. la radio
7. los conciertos
8. la música

D. ¡No! Paco is feeling sad today and does not seem to like anything. What does he say?

MODELO música
No me gusta la música.

1. tenis
2. béisbol
3. gimnasia
4. fútbol
5. escuela
6. volibol
7. radio
8. televisión

E. Amigas. Dolores has met a new friend and is asking about her likes and dislikes. What does she ask?

MODELO tenis
¿Te gusta el tenis?

fiestas
¿Te gustan las fiestas?

1. música
2. libros
3. escuela
4. vacaciones
5. fútbol americano
6. deportes
7. coches
8. español

COMUNICACIÓN

A. Opiniones. Tell whether you like or don't like the following things.

EJEMPLO tele
No me gusta la tele.

fútbol americano
animales
español
tenis
volibol
dinero
radio
escuela
baloncesto
exámenes
deportes
¿ . . . ?

B. Entrevista. Answer the following questions or use them to interview another student.

1. ¿Te gusta el béisbol?
2. ¿Te gustan los deportes?
3. ¿Te gusta mirar la tele?
4. ¿Te gusta la lucha libre?
5. ¿Te gusta escuchar la radio?
6. ¿Te gustan los exámenes?

C. Gustos. Use some of the following words to make up your own questions to ask other students.

EJEMPLO dinero
¿Te gusta el dinero?

fiestas	gimnasia	baloncesto
discos	conciertos	animales
tarea	fútbol	¿ . . . ?
vacaciones	juegos	

RINCÓN CULTURAL

How many of the following famous people of Hispanic background do you recognize? Match the names with the activity that made them famous.

1. José Feliciano
2. Plácido Domingo
3. Geraldo Rivera
4. Nancy López
5. Guillermo Vilas
6. Joan Báez
7. Dave Concepción
8. Erik Estrada

a. el béisbol **b.** el tenis **c.** la música **d.** la televisión **e.** el golf

4.

8.

6.

2.

EXPLORACIÓN

Asking and telling where you are from
The verb **ser**

PRESENTACIÓN

To ask and tell where you are from, you must know the verb **ser**, which means *to be*. Just as we use different verb forms (*am, is, are*) with different subjects in English, we also use different forms of **ser** with different subject pronouns.

ser

SINGULAR			PLURAL		
I am	(yo)	soy	(nosotros) (nosotras)	somos	we are
you are	(tú)	eres			
you are he is she is	usted (él) (ella)	es	ustedes (ellos) (ellas)	son	you are they are

Because the verb forms show what the subject is, the subject pronouns in parentheses in the chart are usually omitted.

Soy de Venezuela.	I'm from Venezuela.
Somos de Nevada.	We're from Nevada.
Vicente y Elena **son** de Chile.	Vicente and Elena are from Chile.

A. The choice of the form of *you* depends on your relationship with the person to whom you are talking.

1. The **tú** form is used when talking to friends, family members, children, and pets. It is called the "familiar" form.
2. **Usted** is used when you talk to someone you aren't so close to. It shows respect and is used, for example, with adults, especially with those you have just met. It is called the "polite" or formal form.
3. **Ustedes** is used for talking to more than one person. It can be either familiar or formal.

B. To ask a yes-no question, raise the pitch of your voice at the end of the sentence.

¿Eres de Arizona? ¿Inés y Tomás son de Cuba?

C. To make a question or a statement negative, put **no** before the verb.

Carmen y Teresa no son de Nueva York.
¿No eres de Buenos Aires?

PREPARACIÓN

A. Somos americanos. Many of our states have Spanish names. Tell where these teens say they're from. Try to pronounce the names of the states in Spanish.

MODELO

B. Hispanos famosos. Yolanda is doing a report on famous Hispanics for social studies class. Where does she say the following people are from?

MODELO Gabriel García Márquez / Colombia
Gabriel García Márquez es de Colombia.

1. Carlos Fuentes / México
2. Alicia Alonso / Cuba
3. Juan Carlos / España
4. Jorge Luis Borges / Argentina
5. Raúl Julia / Puerto Rico
6. Javier Pérez de Cuéllar / Perú

C. Juegos Olímpicos. Members of Olympic teams from Latin America are telling where they are from. What do they say?

MODELO

D. Ciudades. A tour group is signing the register at a **parador** (*inn*) in Granada. Where are the following people from?

MODELO **Pablo y Edita Moreno son de Madrid.**

E. O.E.A. Students in an American school are conducting a model meeting of the **Organización de Estados Americanos (O.E.A.)**. What do they say?

MODELO	Nosotros / Panamá **Somos de Panamá.**	Mariana / Venezuela **Es de Venezuela.**

1. Nosotras / Brasil
2. Yo / Guatemala
3. Adriana / Costa Rica
4. Usted / Argentina
5. Julio / Uruguay
6. Bárbara y Mauro / Chile
7. Nosotros / Colombia
8. Ustedes / Bolivia

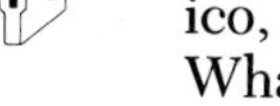

F. En el Yucatán. Pedro is working at the ruins in Chichén Itzá, Mexico, and wants to know where other students and counselors are from. What does he ask?

MODELO Amalia / México
¿Eres de México?

Señor Moreno / Bolivia
Señor Moreno, ¿usted es de Bolivia?

1. Yolanda / Honduras
2. Señor Ramos / Panamá
3. Ángel y Verónica / España
4. Señora Díaz / Paraguay
5. Señor Bonilla y señor Rivera / Costa Rica
6. David / los Estados Unidos

COMUNICACIÓN

A. Soy de . . . Tell where you were born and ask another student where he or she is from.

EJEMPLO Soy de Washington. ¿Y tú?
Soy de Baltimore.

B. ¿Eres de . . . ? Imagine you are an exchange student from a Spanish-speaking country. Other students will try to guess where you are from.

EJEMPLO ¿Eres de Colombia?
No, no soy de Colombia.

¿Eres de Bolivia?
Sí, soy de Bolivia.

C. Personas famosas. Make a list of famous personalities and tell where they are from. Share your list with other students.

EJEMPLO Johnny Carson es de Nebraska.

RINCÓN CULTURAL

Spanish explorers in the New World gave many of our states and cities Spanish names. Since Spain is a Catholic country, the explorers often named the town or region after the saint whose feast was celebrated that day. Other times the names tell us of their impressions of the physical characteristics of the land or its formation. Here are some examples.

San Francisco was named after St. Francis because it was founded on the day on which his feast is celebrated.

Colorado, which means *red*, was given this name because of the reddish color of the earth.

El Paso, which means *the pass*, was named by Juan de Oñete because of its strategic location at a narrow pass on the Río Grande.

Florida was named for Easter Sunday or **Pascua Florida** by Ponce de León, who first arrived there on that day.

Match the cities with the state in which they are found. Note that both city and state have Spanish names.

1. San Agustín	**7.** Albuquerque	**a.** Texas
2. San Francisco	**8.** Santa Fe	**b.** Nuevo México
3. El Paso	**9.** San Antonio	**c.** Florida
4. Los Ángeles	**10.** Amarillo	**d.** California
5. Boca Ratón	**11.** Las Vegas	**e.** Nevada
6. San Diego	**12.** Pueblo	**f.** Colorado

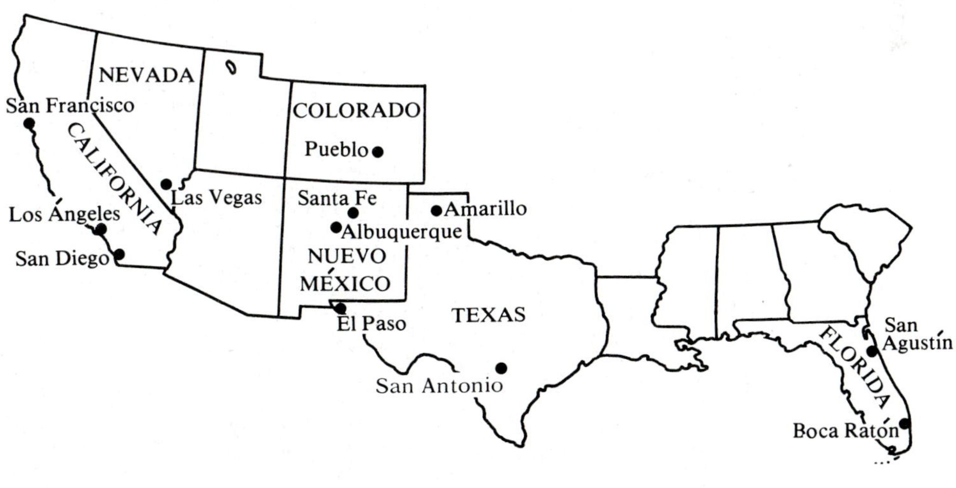

EXPLORACIÓN

Describing people and things
Agreement of nouns and adjectives

PRESENTACIÓN

You have already seen that nouns in Spanish are masculine or feminine, singular or plural. An adjective also agrees in gender (masculine or feminine) and in number (singular or plural) with the noun it modifies.

A. Adjectives ending in **o** form the feminine by changing **o** to **a**.

Juan es alt**o**. María es alt**a**. Juan y María son alt**os**.

bueno good
malo bad
alto tall
bajo short
simpático friendly, nice
antipático unfriendly
bonito pretty, nice
guapo good-looking
divertido fun, amusing
aburrido boring
nuevo new
viejo old

B. Adjectives ending in **e** or a consonant do not change to match the gender of the noun.

El fútbol es popular. La lucha libre es emocionant**e**.

emocionante exciting
excelente excellent
formidable great, wonderful
importante important
independiente independent
inteligente intelligent
interesante interesting
paciente patient
responsable responsible
fácil easy
difícil difficult
popular popular

C. To form the plural of nouns or of adjectives ending in a vowel, add **s**. For nouns or adjectives ending in a consonant, add **es**. Note that the adjective generally follows the noun.

el deporte popular — los deportes populares
el libro nuevo — los libros nuevos
la fiesta divertida — las fiestas divertidas

D. You can also use the adverbs **muy** (*very*) and **bastante** (*fairly*) to qualify what you think about someone or something.

Mario es **bastante** inteligente. Lilia es **muy** inteligente.

PREPARACIÓN

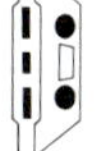

A. ¿Sí? Marisol has met Lourdes while walking down the Ramblas in Barcelona and is asking her about some of her friends. What does she say?

MODELO Angela / paciente
¿Angela es muy paciente?

Mario y Pablo / paciente
¿Mario y Pablo son muy pacientes?

1. Diana / inteligente
2. Esteban y Diego / independiente
3. Javier / popular
4. Miguel y Rafael / interesante
5. María Socorro y Benito / responsable
6. Luisita / paciente

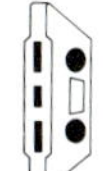

B. ¡Yo también! Paco is bragging about himself, but his sister is not to be outdone. What does she say?

MODELO Soy alto.
Yo también soy alta.

1. Soy simpático.
2. Soy guapo.
3. Soy divertido.
4. Soy bueno.
5. Soy alto.

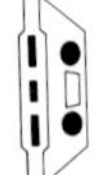

C. Entrevista. Sergio is being interviewed by the school paper for his opinions on school life. What does he say?

MODELO ¿Los exámenes? (difícil)
Los exámenes son difíciles.

1. ¿Las tareas? (fácil)
2. ¿Los libros? (interesante)
3. ¿Los deportes? (aburrido)
4. ¿Las fiestas? (divertido)
5. ¿Las vacaciones? (bueno)
6. ¿Los conciertos? (formidable)

D. Opiniones. Chela is talking to Antonio about some of their mutual friends. How does Antonio respond to her statements?

MODELO Pepe es responsable. (bastante)
Es bastante responsable.

1. Estela es bonita. (muy)
2. Sergio es antipático. (bastante)
3. Beatriz es paciente. (muy)
4. Roberto es guapo. (muy)
5. Eva es independiente. (bastante)
6. Francisco es viejo. (muy)

COMUNICACIÓN

A. Actividades. Not everyone enjoys the same things. Using suggestions below, tell how you feel about various activities.

EJEMPLO La lucha libre no es interesante.

la televisión	es	formidable
el fútbol americano	no es	interesante
el baloncesto	es bastante	popular
el tenis	es muy	emocionante
el volibol	no es muy	importante
la gimnasia		divertido(a)
la lucha libre		aburrido(a)

B. Descripción. How do you rate yourself? Use the adjectives below to describe yourself.

EJEMPLO Soy simpático, inteligente y bastante guapo.

simpático	bueno
independiente	paciente
alto/bajo	responsable
divertido	¿ . . . ?

C. Entrevista. Use the words below to make up questions to ask other students.

EJEMPLO ¿Eres responsable?
Sí, soy bastante responsable.

paciente	independiente	antipático	bueno
inteligente	responsable	aburrido	¿ . . . ?

D. La escuela. Tell whether you agree or disagree with the following statements about school life.

EJEMPLO Los profesores son pacientes.
Sí. Los profesores son pacientes.
No. Los profesores no son pacientes.

1. Los libros son interesantes.
2. Los estudiantes son inteligentes.
3. Los profesores son populares.
4. Las tareas son fáciles.
5. La escuela es buena.
6. Los deportes son emocionantes.

RINCÓN CULTURAL

North Americans often emphasize using time efficiently. In general, Latin Americans aren't as concerned with time as North Americans are. This is especially true in dealing with other people when taking time to enjoy each others' company is important. When invited to dinner, a Spanish-speaker might ask if the time is **hora americana** or **hora latina** to know whether to be punctual. Of course, Spanish-speakers are punctual when they go to work or to school.

Do you think North Americans do or do not take time very seriously?

EXPLORACIÓN

Asking questions
Using **¿verdad?** *and* **¿no?**

PRESENTACIÓN

You already know how to ask questions by raising the pitch of your voice at the end of a sentence. Another way to form questions is to add a tag, an expression similar in meaning to *right?*, *isn't it?*, or *don't you?* at the end of a sentence.

A. One common tag is **¿verdad?**

Los profesores son pacientes, ¿verdad?
Gloria Fuentes es de Paraguay, ¿verdad?

B. Another tag is **¿no?**

La gimnasia es emocionante, ¿no?
Te gustan las vacaciones, ¿no?

C. Answering yes-or-no questions with **sí** and **no** is similar to what we do in English. To answer a question such as **Te gusta el béisbol, ¿verdad?** one could say:

Sí, me gusta el béisbol *or*
No, no me gusta el béisbol.

Or, one could say no and tell what he or she *does* like:

No, me gusta el fútbol.

PREPARACIÓN

A. **Opiniones.** Manuela and her friend Beatriz agree on many things. How does Beatriz answer Manuela's questions?

> **MODELO** La fiesta es aburrida, ¿verdad?
> **Sí, es aburrida.**

1. La música es formidable, ¿verdad?
2. Meche es simpática, ¿verdad?
3. Fernando y Marcos son guapos, ¿verdad?
4. Roberto y Luis son de Guatemala, ¿verdad?
5. El concierto es excelente, ¿verdad?
6. Los exámenes son difíciles, ¿verdad?

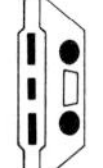

B. **¡No!** José and Sara never agree on anything. Sara always contradicts what he says. What does she say?

> **MODELO** Jorge es inteligente, ¿no?
> **No, no es inteligente.**

1. El fútbol americano es emocionante, ¿verdad?
2. Te gusta nadar, ¿verdad?
3. Bernardo es antipático, ¿no?
4. Te gusta escuchar la radio, ¿no?
5. El dinero es importante, ¿verdad?
6. Los juegos electrónicos son malos, ¿no?

C. **¿Verdad?** Raquel and Eduardo are trying to talk at a basketball game, but Eduardo can't hear her and has to repeat his questions. What does he ask?

> **MODELO** La profesora Iglesias / España
> **La profesora Iglesias es de España, ¿verdad?**
>
> Chela y Claudia / responsables
> **Chela y Claudia son responsables, ¿verdad?**

1. Vicente / guapo
2. Carolina / Argentina
3. Ángel y Jaime / México
4. El libro / bastante interesante
5. La música / buena
6. El baloncesto / emocionante

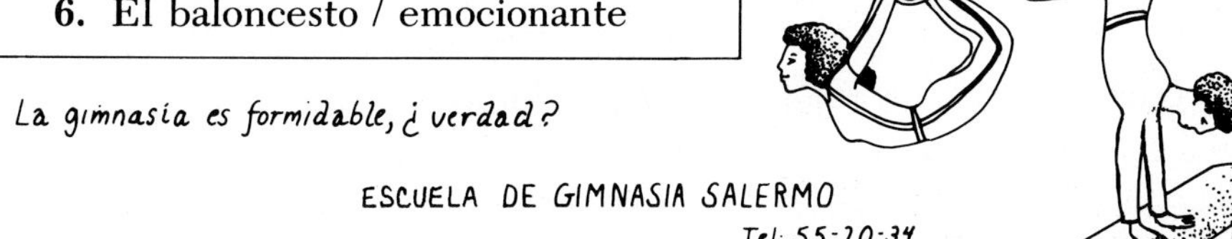

D. La bodega. Miguel is applying for a job in a Hispanic grocery store. What questions would the owner ask him?

MODELO paciente
Eres paciente, ¿no?

1. responsable
2. inteligente
3. independiente
4. simpático
5. paciente

COMUNICACIÓN

A. Entrevista. Interview another student using the following questions.

1. Las fiestas son divertidas, ¿verdad?
2. Te gustan los animales, ¿no?
3. Te gusta bailar, ¿no?
4. Te gusta la televisión, ¿verdad?
5. El fútbol americano es emocionante, ¿verdad?
6. La lucha libre es aburrida, ¿no?
7. Te gustan los conciertos, ¿verdad?
8. Eres de California, ¿no?
9. Te gustan los discos viejos, ¿no?
10. Eres paciente, ¿verdad?

B. Bola de cristal. Try to guess what each person in the class thinks is his or her most outstanding personality trait.

EJEMPLO Tomás, eres paciente, ¿no?
No, soy muy independiente.

PERSPECTIVAS

Querido David

David has received his first letter from a new pen pal who is from Uruguay.

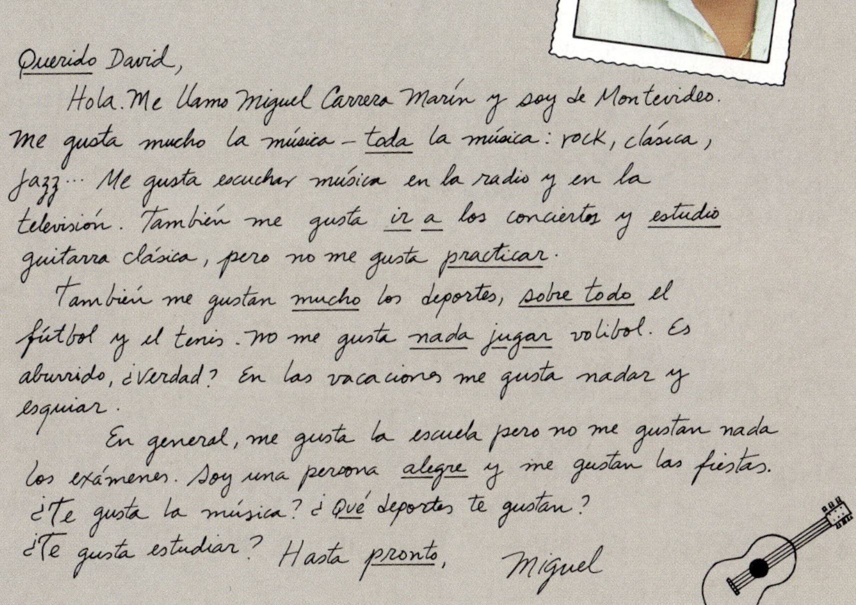

Querido David,

Hola. Me llamo Miguel Carrera Marín y soy de Montevideo. Me gusta mucho la música — toda la música: rock, clásica, jazz... Me gusta escuchar música en la radio y en la televisión. También me gusta ir a los conciertos y estudio guitarra clásica, pero no me gusta practicar.

También me gustan mucho los deportes, sobre todo el fútbol y el tenis. No me gusta nada jugar volibol. Es aburrido, ¿verdad? En las vacaciones me gusta nadar y esquiar.

En general, me gusta la escuela pero no me gustan nada los exámenes. Soy una persona alegre y me gustan las fiestas. ¿Te gusta la música? ¿Qué deportes te gustan? ¿Te gusta estudiar? Hasta pronto,

Miguel

dear
all
to go / to / I study
to practice
a lot / especially
at all / to play
cheerful
what
soon

COMPRENSIÓN

Which of the following statements might Miguel make? If it is something he might say, answer **Sí**, and if it is something he would not say, answer **No**.

1. Me gusta mucho toda la música.
2. Me gustan los conciertos.
3. Me gusta practicar la guitarra.
4. Me gustan el fútbol y el tenis.
5. También me gusta jugar volibol.
6. En las vacaciones no me gusta practicar deportes.
7. En general, me gusta la escuela.
8. No me gustan nada las fiestas.

COMUNICACIÓN

A. Querido David. Using Miguel's letter as a guide, write a letter to David telling him about your likes and dislikes and asking him questions.

B. Actividades favoritas. From the list below, select the four things that you like most. Then see if other students can guess what you chose by asking you questions.

EJEMPLO Te gusta nadar, ¿verdad?
No, me gusta esquiar.

Te gusta la gimnasia, ¿no?
Sí, me gusta mucho la gimnasia.

música	televisión	escuela	cantar
gimnasia	baloncesto	libros	practicar
conciertos	discos	vacaciones	nadar
fiestas	fútbol americano	juegos electrónicos	esquiar

C. Opiniones. Which of the things below do you feel strongly about? Tell how you feel about them.

EJEMPLO Me gusta mucho el jazz. Es formidable.
No me gustan nada los exámenes. Son difíciles.

baloncesto	lucha libre	vacaciones	bailar
béisbol	practicar	nadar	exámenes
escuela	tenis	estudiar	español
discos	televisión	tarea	trabajar

D. Buena memoria. Try to recall what other students in your class have said about themselves. They will tell you whether or not you remember correctly.

EJEMPLO Martín, te gusta el dinero, ¿verdad?
Sí, me gusta mucho el dinero.

Nenita, eres independiente, ¿no?
No, no soy muy independiente.

E. Tele-juego. Take turns pretending you're the mystery guest on a TV quiz show. Others will ask you up to ten questions to find out who you are.

EJEMPLO ¿Te gustan los deportes?
Sí, me gustan los deportes.

¿El fútbol?
Sí.

¿Eres de los Estados Unidos?
No, no soy de los Estados Unidos.

¿Eres de Brasil?
Sí, soy de Brasil.

¿Eres Pelé?
Sí, soy Pelé.

VOCABULARIO DEL CAPÍTULO

NOUNS REFERRING TO SPORTS

el baloncesto basketball **P***
el béisbol baseball **P**
el fútbol soccer **P**
el fútbol americano football **P**
la gimnasia gymnastics **P**
la lucha libre wrestling **P**
el tenis tennis **P**
el volibol volleyball **P**

OTHER NOUNS

el animal animal
el coche car
el concierto concert
el deporte sport
el dinero money
el disco record
la escuela school
el español Spanish
el examen exam
la fiesta party
la guitarra guitar
el jazz jazz (music)
el juego electrónico video game
el libro book
la música music **P**
la persona person
el profesor teacher
la profesora teacher
la radio radio
la tarea homework
la televisión television **P**
las vacaciones vacation

ADJECTIVES

aburrido boring
alegre cheerful, lively
alto tall
antipático unfriendly
bajo short
bonito pretty, lovely, nice
bueno good
clásico classical
difícil difficult
divertido fun, amusing
emocionante exciting
excelente excellent
fácil easy
formidable great, wonderful
guapo good-looking
importante important
independiente independent
inteligente intelligent
interesante interesting
malo bad
nuevo new
paciente patient
popular popular
responsable responsible
rock rock (*music*)
querido dear
simpático nice
todo all
viejo old

VERBS

bailar to dance
cantar to sing
escuchar to listen (to)
esquiar to ski
estudiar to study
hablar to speak, talk
hablar español to speak Spanish
ir to go
jugar to play
mirar to look at, watch
nadar to swim
practicar to practice
ser to be
trabajar to work

ADVERBS

bastante quite, fairly
mucho a lot, much
muy very
pronto soon
sí yes
también also, too

CONJUNCTIONS AND PREPOSITIONS

a to
de from
pero but
y and

OTHER WORDS AND EXPRESSIONS

en general generally
estudio I study
¿no? Isn't that so?, Aren't you?, etc.
Me gusta(n) I like **P**
¿Te gusta(n) Do you like? **P**
¡Hola! Hello!
Me llamo My name is . . .
No me gusta nada. I don't like it at all. **P**
¿qué? what?
sobre todo especially
hasta pronto See you soon
¿verdad? right?, Isn't it true?

*The **P** refers to vocabulary from the **Capítulo preliminar**.

Capítulo dos

GOING PLACES AND DOING THINGS 2

INTRODUCCIÓN

¿Un partido o una película?

game / movie

Joaquín and Diego, who live in Mexico City, are making plans for this evening.

JOAQUÍN	¿Qué vamos a hacer?	What are we going to do?
DIEGO	Pues hay un partido de fútbol en el Estadio Azteca.	there is / a
JOAQUÍN	¡Eres tan fanático de los deportes! Me gustan más los conciertos.	such a fan / more
DIEGO	Un concierto, ¡no! Son tan aburridos. ¿Por qué no vamos al cine? O quizás hay una película en la televisión.	why / to the movies or / perhaps
JOAQUÍN	Bueno, entonces vamos al cine. Oye, ¿qué película vamos a ver?	okay / then to see
DIEGO	Una película buena sobre un jugador de fútbol.	about / player

COMPRENSIÓN

Tell if the following statements based on **¿Un partido o una película?** are true (**sí**) or false (**no**).

1. Joaquín es un fanático del fútbol.
2. Hay un concierto en el estadio.
3. Hay un partido de fútbol en la televisión.
4. Hay una película sobre un jugador de fútbol.

COMUNICACIÓN

A. ¿Qué hacer? Tell which of the following activities you enjoy and which you don't.

EJEMPLO Me gusta tocar el piano.
No me gusta hacer gimnasia.

B. ¿Qué te gusta? Ask another student if he or she likes to do these things.

EJEMPLO bailar
¿Te gusta bailar?

1. llamar por teléfono
2. jugar boliche
3. sacar fotos
4. dar un paseo
5. hacer gimnasia
6. tocar el piano

C. ¿Qué te gusta más? Ask other students which of the following activities they like more.

EJEMPLO ¿Qué te gusta más, trabajar o descansar?
Me gusta más descansar.

1. ¿llamar por teléfono o dar un paseo?
2. ¿tocar discos o escuchar la radio?
3. ¿jugar boliche o jugar fútbol?
4. ¿dar un paseo o montar bicicleta?
5. ¿hacer gimnasia o nadar?
6. ¿bailar o cantar?
7. ¿ir al cine o ver una película en la televisión?
8. ¿practicar el piano o tocar la guitarra?
9. ¿viajar o mirar fotos?
10. ¿ . . . o . . . ?

EXPLORACIÓN

Talking about what you're going to do
The verb **ir**

PRESENTACIÓN

To talk about what you are going to do, you use the verb **ir** (*to go*). Here are its forms.

ir

(yo)	voy	(nosotros) (nosotras)	vamos
(tú)	vas		
(usted) (él/ella)	va	(ustedes) (ellos/ellas)	van

A. In English we can say *you go*, *you are going*, or *do you go . . . ?* In Spanish one verb form alone can have all three meanings.

Vamos al concierto.	We're going to the concert.
José no va a los partidos de fútbol.	José doesn't go to soccer games.
¿Usted va a México?	Are you going to Mexico?
Sí, voy.	Yes, I'm going.

B. When you talk about what you are going to do, use a form of **ir** followed by the preposition **a** and an infinitive.

ir + **a** + infinitive

Voy a descansar.	I'm going to rest.
Ana va a sacar fotos.	Ana's going to take pictures.
¿Vas a esquiar?	Are you going skiing?

C. To make suggestions about things to do, use **Vamos a** (*let's*) plus an infinitive.

Vamos a dar un paseo.	Let's take a walk.
Vamos a jugar boliche.	Let's go bowling.

Here are some useful expressions for telling when you are going to do something.

ahora now	**más tarde** later	**mañana** tomorrow
algún día someday	**hoy** today	**esta noche** tonight

PREPARACIÓN

A. Amigos hispanos. Christopher has many Hispanic pen pals. Where does he say he plans to visit them someday?

MODELO Puerto Rico
Voy a Puerto Rico algún día.

1. México
2. Chile
3. Venezuela
4. Bolivia
5. Honduras
6. Colombia

B. ¿Qué vas a hacer? Señor Álvarez wants to know what his son is going to do this evening. What does he ask?

MODELO jugar boliche
¿Vas a jugar boliche esta noche?

1. practicar fútbol
2. montar bicicleta
3. tocar la guitarra
4. hacer gimnasia
5. llamar por teléfono
6. descansar

C. Sugerencias. Carmen is suggesting some things that she and Marisol can do tomorrow. What does she suggest?

MODELO montar bicicleta
Vamos a montar bicicleta.

1. jugar baloncesto
2. dar un paseo
3. hacer gimnasia
4. tocar el piano
5. sacar fotos
6. hacer la tarea

D. ¡No! María is telling Verónica what several of their friends are going to do this weekend. Verónica disagrees with what María says. What does she say?

MODELO Jorge va a montar bicicleta.
No, él no va a montar bicicleta.

1. Pedro va a nadar.
2. Paco y Elena van a esquiar.
3. Sara y Mariana van a jugar tenis.
4. Anita va a jugar boliche.
5. Roberto va a dar un paseo.

E. Por teléfono. Students in the Spanish class are planning to celebrate **el Día de la Raza** (*Columbus Day*). When do they plan to call the other committee members?

MODELO Camilo / pronto
Camilo va a llamar pronto.

1. Yo / ahora
2. Elsa / más tarde
3. Sarita / hoy
4. Nosotros / esta noche
5. Mónica y Caridad / mañana
6. Pepe y Julio / pronto

COMUNICACIÓN

A. ¿Cuándo? Plan a schedule for doing some of the following activities. Then tell the class when you are going to do them.

EJEMPLO Voy a nadar más tarde.

Voy a	sacar fotos dar un paseo montar bicicleta jugar boliche tocar el piano nadar viajar estudiar ¿ . . . ?	ahora algún día más tarde mañana esta noche hoy

B. Mañana. Get together with a group of students and ask them what they're going to do tomorrow. Then report back to the class.

EJEMPLO Guillermo, ¿qué vas a hacer mañana?
Voy a jugar béisbol.
Guillermo va a jugar béisbol mañana.

C. Algún día. Plan with another student five things you will do someday. Tell the class what both of you plan to do.

EJEMPLO Vamos a ir a Buenos Aires algún día.

RINCÓN CULTURAL

Julio Iglesias was a goalie for the Spanish soccer team *Real Madrid*, but in 1972 an auto accident kept him away from soccer for two years. During that time, while recuperating in the hospital, he taught himself to play the guitar and wrote a few songs to pass the time. From those modest beginnings, Julio Iglesias has gone on to be one of the most popular singers of our time. An idol to many in Latin America, Julio is becoming increasingly popular in the United States. Now Julio sings in English, Italian, German, Portuguese, and, of course, Spanish. He has 350 gold albums and 100 platinum albums and has sold over 70 million records worldwide.

Titles of songs and movies are not always translated literally from one language to another. Here are the titles of some of Julio's ballads. Can you guess their English translations?

1. La Paloma
2. De niña a mujer
3. Candilejas
4. En cualquier parte
5. Amor

EXPLORACIÓN

Talking about going places
The contraction **al**

PRESENTACIÓN

As you already know, to talk about going somewhere, you may use a form of **ir** and the preposition **a**.

México	Van a México.
la escuela	Marta va a la escuela.
las fiestas	Ignacio va a las fiestas.
los partidos de fútbol	Tú vas a los partidos de fútbol.

When the preposition **a** is followed by the definite article **el**, the contraction **al** is formed.

el cine	Vamos **al** cine.
el concierto	Rosa va **al** concierto.

Here is some useful vocabulary for talking about going places.

PREPARACIÓN

A. Muy ocupada. Esperanza has a number of errands to run. Tell where she is going.

MODELO el museo
Esperanza va al museo hoy.

1. el cine
2. la biblioteca
3. el banco
4. el supermercado
5. el correo
6. la tienda

B. En Madrid. While visiting Madrid, Raúl and Vicente are trying to decide where to go. What does Raúl suggest?

MODELO Teatro Calderón
Vamos al Teatro Calderón.

1. el Museo del Prado
2. la Plaza de España
3. el Café Ibiza
4. la Biblioteca Nacional
5. la Iglesia de San Francisco
6. el Restaurante Goya

C. Distrito Federal. Pablo is asking Dolores about the places she is going to visit in Mexico City tomorrow. What does he ask her?

MODELO Parque de Chapultepec
¿Vas al Parque de Chapultepec mañana?

1. Hotel El Presidente
2. Plaza Garibaldi
3. Estadio Azteca
4. Cine Ariel
5. Parque Alameda
6. Café Sanborns

COMUNICACIÓN

A. ¿Vas o no? Tell whether or not you plan to go to some of the following places this week.

EJEMPLO Voy al teatro.
No voy a las tiendas.

1. escuela	**4.** museos	**7.** supermercado
2. parques	**5.** correo	**8.** biblioteca
3. cine	**6.** piscina	**9.** ¿ . . . ?

B. Reportero. Use these suggestions to interview others about their plans. Report their answers to the rest of the class.

EJEMPLO ¿Vas al correo hoy?
Sí, voy al correo más tarde.
No, no voy al correo hoy.

¿Vas	al a la	tienda biblioteca museo cine teatro supermercado escuela café parque clase de español banco estadio piscina ¿ . . . ?	mañana? más tarde? hoy? algún día? pronto? ahora? esta noche?

C. Turistas. Tell where you enjoy going when you are in another city. Then ask other students if they share your interests.

EJEMPLO Me gusta ir a los museos.
¿Te gusta ir a los museos también?

RINCÓN CULTURAL

If you go to Puerto Rico on vacation some day, you will probably visit these sights. Try to match each photo with its description.

a. **El Viejo San Juan**, the oldest part of the city, was once enclosed by the city wall. The area has been restored to the way it was in colonial times.

b. **Luquillo** is a famous beach about 30 miles east of San Juan.

c. **Bahía Fosforescente,** a phosphorescent bay, is near the fishing village of La Parguera. At night the water sparkles whenever the marine life is disturbed. Even just trailing your hand in the water is enough to set off the chemical display of lights.

d. **El Morro**, a castle at the entrance to San Juan Bay, was built in 1591 to protect against attacks by raiders such as Sir Francis Drake.

e. **La Plaza de Cristóbal Colón** in Mayagüez honors the man who discovered the island on November 19, 1493, on his second voyage to America. Ponce de León, who accompanied Columbus, started the first settlement.

f. **El Yunque** is a tropical forest with a rainfall of 100 billion gallons a year. It has over 240 different species of trees and is home to many rare birds and to a type of tiny tree frog called the **coquí**, a symbol of Puerto Rico.

g. **La Universidad de Puerto Rico** was founded in 1903 and enrolls 52,000 students at several campuses. One of the prettiest is at Río Piedras, where the annual Casals Festival and many other concerts are held.

EXPLORACIÓN

Asking and telling what you want
The verb **querer**

PRESENTACIÓN

To talk about what you want or what you want to do, you need to use the verb **querer**. You already know that the endings of a Spanish verb tell you what the subject is. Here are the forms of **querer**.

querer

(yo)	quiero	(nosotros) (nosotras)	queremos
(tú)	quieres		
(usted) (él/ella)	quiere	(ustedes) (ellos/ellas)	quieren

Quiero ir al partido de volibol hoy.
Pablo y Luis quieren montar bicicleta.
El señor López quiere descansar.

In English when we ask questions we often use helping verbs such as *do* or *does*: "Do you want to . . . ?" "Does she want to . . . ?" In Spanish we use only the verb form.

¿Quieres ir al aeropuerto?	Do you want to go to the airport?
¿Qué quiere hacer ahora?	What does he (she) want to do now?

Here are some things we sometimes want or don't want to do.

lavar los platos — ayudar en casa — cocinar

arreglar el cuarto — ir de compras — lavar el coche — ganar dinero

PREPARACIÓN

A. Planes. José is making plans for the weekend. What does he say he wants to do?

MODELO jugar fútbol
Quiero jugar fútbol.

1. ir a la piscina
2. tocar la guitarra
3. cocinar
4. ganar dinero
5. ir al parque
6. lavar el coche
7. ir de compras
8. arreglar el cuarto

B. ¿Y ustedes? Alberto is asking some friends what they want to do this weekend. What do his friends say?

MODELO ¿Ustedes quieren ir a la piscina? (Sí)
Sí, queremos ir a la piscina.

1. ¿Ustedes quieren ir al cine? (Sí)
2. ¿Ustedes quieren ir al concierto? (No)
3. ¿Ustedes quieren ir a la plaza? (No)
4. ¿Ustedes quieren ir a la fiesta? (Sí)
5. ¿Ustedes quieren ir al café? (No)

C. ¿Qué vamos a hacer? Bárbara is telling Laura what some students and teachers want to do after school. What does she say?

MODELO La señora Velázquez / ir de compras
La señora Velázquez quiere ir de compras.

Lola y Alicia / ayudar en casa
Lola y Alicia quieren ayudar en casa.

1. Claudio y Jesús / ir de compras
2. yo / cocinar
3. la señora Estrada / hacer gimnasia
4. Nicolás y Luis / ayudar en casa
5. ustedes / descansar
6. nosotros / arreglar el cuarto
7. Jaime y Adán / ganar dinero
8. la señora Álvarez / ir al correo

D. De vacaciones. The following people are dreaming about their vacation plans. Ask them what they want to do.

MODELO

Jorge
¿Quieres viajar?

Los señores Peña
¿Ustedes quieren jugar tenis?

1. el señor López
2. Juan y Pablo
3. la señora Chávez
4. Luisa
5. yo
6. nosotros

COMUNICACIÓN

A. Esta noche. What do your friends want to do this evening? Use the suggestions below to interview another student or students. Then report back to the class.

EJEMPLO ir a bailar
Juan, ¿quieres ir a bailar?

mirar la tele
Rosa y Marta, ¿ustedes quieren mirar la tele?

escuchar la radio	llamar por teléfono	ir de compras
mirar la tele	hacer gimnasia	jugar baloncesto
ir a la piscina	montar bicicleta	¿ . . . ?
trabajar	dar un paseo	

B. Gustos. Whom do you know who might want to do the following?

EJEMPLO escuchar discos
David quiere escuchar discos.

viajar
La señorita Díaz y la señora Ríos quieren viajar.

jugar boliche	ayudar en casa	ir al museo
mirar la tele	bailar	estudiar español
cocinar	tocar el piano	ganar dinero
esquiar	lavar el coche	¿ . . . ?

C. ¿Qué vamos a hacer? Your friends and you are discussing weekend plans. Tell what you want to do and don't want to do.

EJEMPLO Queremos escuchar discos.
No queremos ayudar en casa.

RINCÓN CULTURAL

Dating customs in Spanish-speaking countries are considerably different from those in the United States. The first difference is that boys and girls usually attend different schools, although some co-ed schools do exist. Most of the opportunities to socialize take place within the context of the family. Parties are usually family gatherings that include friends and family members of all ages.

When Hispanic teens date, they tend to go out in groups. The idea of dating several different people or of dating just one person without being "serious" is more American than Latin. When a Hispanic person says **Tengo novio** (**novia**) (*I have a boyfriend / girlfriend*), she or he implies a much more formal relationship than an American counterpart. In Hispanic countries, when one dates another exclusively, it is usually a sign that the couple plans to marry.

In the past, when a couple dated seriously, it was the custom for a **dueña** (*chaperone*) or an older brother to accompany them. Although the custom still exists, it is less common in large cities in Spain and Latin America.

EXPLORACIÓN

Asking for information
Interrogatives and inversion

PRESENTACIÓN

You already know how to ask a yes-no question by raising your voice at the end of a sentence or by adding a tag question.

¿José Luis quiere ir al concierto?
Quieres ir también, ¿verdad?

A. Another common way to ask a question in Spanish is to place the subject either after the verb or at the end of the sentence.

¿Quiere **Ramón** hacer gimnasia?
¿Van a dar un paseo **Vicente y Esteban**?

B. To ask a question when you want additional information, use interrogative words such as **¿Qué?** (What? Which?), **¿Quién?** (Who?), **¿Cuándo?** (When?), **¿Dónde?** (Where?), **¿Adónde?** (To where?), and **¿De dónde?** (From where?).

¿Qué discos tocas?	Which records do you play?
¿Qué deportes te gustan?	What sports do you like?
¿Quién es?	Who is it?
¿Cuándo vas a estudiar?	When are you going to study?
¿Adónde van ustedes?	Where are you going?
¿De dónde eres?	Where are you from?

The subject follows the verb when interrogative words are used.

¿Adónde va Ricardo?	¿Cuándo va al café el señor Puig?
¿De dónde es usted?	¿Cuándo van al cine Pepe y Daniel?

PREPARACIÓN

A. ¡Imposible! Paco cannot believe what his friends are telling him. How does he respond to what they say?

MODELO Alicia escucha discos ahora.
¿Escucha Alicia discos ahora?

1. Los exámenes son difíciles.
2. Ángela y Luis son de Chile.
3. María Elena es inteligente.
4. Marcela va a estudiar mucho.
5. La película es interesante.
6. Vicente y Pablo quieren arreglar el cuarto.

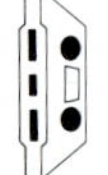

B. ¿Qué quieres hacer? Two friends are trying to decide what to do this evening. What does one ask the other?

MODELO mirar
¿Qué quieres mirar?

1. jugar
2. cocinar
3. escuchar
4. tocar
5. hacer
6. ver

C. ¿Quién? Marinela is trying to find out what her friends want to do tonight. What does she ask?

MODELO ir al concierto
¿Quién quiere ir al concierto esta noche?

1. ir al teatro
2. jugar volibol
3. ir a la biblioteca
4. ir a la piscina
5. montar bicicleta
6. dar un paseo

D. ¿Qué te gusta? Eduardo is an exchange student from Chile, and Lucía wants to learn more about him. What does she ask about the things Eduardo says he likes?

MODELO Me gustan los libros.
¿Qué libros te gustan?

1. Me gustan las películas.
2. Me gustan los animales.
3. Me gustan los restaurantes.
4. Me gustan los discos.
5. Me gustan los coches.
6. Me gustan los deportes.

COMUNICACIÓN

A. Actividades. Ask your fellow students whether anyone wants to do the following things and report back to the class.

EJEMPLO jugar tenis
¿Quién quiere jugar tenis?
Alejandro quiere jugar tenis.

1. jugar boliche
2. montar bicicleta
3. ir de compras
4. ir a la biblioteca
5. bailar
6. dar un paseo
7. cocinar
8. practicar
9. tocar el piano
10. ir al teatro

B. Preferencias. Make up questions to ask another student about the following things.

EJEMPLO deporte
¿Qué deporte te gusta más?

1. película
2. coche
3. tienda
4. juego electrónico
5. música
6. restaurante

C. Una conversación. Imagine you are talking with some Spanish-speaking friends who say the following. Make up questions to continue the conversation.

EJEMPLO Me gusta jugar volibol.
¿Qué te gusta más, el volibol o el tenis?

Quiero escuchar discos.
¿Cuándo quieres escuchar discos?

1. Me gusta escuchar la radio.
2. Me gusta viajar.
3. Quiero esquiar.
4. Quiero jugar baloncesto.
5. Me gusta jugar volibol.
6. Me gustan los discos.
7. Quiero trabajar.
8. Me gusta ir de compras.
9. Me gusta mirar la tele.
10. Quiero descansar.

PERSPECTIVAS

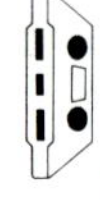

Un amigo de Puerto Rico

friend

Hola, me llamo Ángel Luis Rivera. Soy de Ponce, Puerto Rico. Soy fotógrafo aficionado y para ganar unos pesos me gusta sacar fotos de los turistas que visitan Puerto Rico.

amateur / to earn
visit

También me gustan mucho los deportes, especialmente el béisbol. Soy un jugador bastante bueno. Estoy en el equipo "los Toros." Los fines de semana siempre hay un partido contra otros equipos de aquí.

I'm on / team / on the weekends / always against / other / here

También, me gusta la música, especialmente la salsa y el rock. Me gusta tocar la guitarra y trabajo en una tienda de discos. Soy una persona de muchos talentos, ¿verdad?

I work

Bueno, ahora tengo que trabajar.

well / I have to

COMPRENSIÓN

Select the best way to complete each sentence.

1. ¿De dónde es Ángel Luis?
   a. de San Juan **b.** de Ponce **c.** de Santurce
2. Para ganar unos pesos le gusta . . .
   a. visitar Puerto Rico **b.** sacar fotos de los turistas **c.** tocar el piano

3. ¿Qué son "los Toros"?
   a. unos animales **b.** un café **c.** un equipo
4. ¿Qué tipo de música es de Puerto Rico?
   a. la salsa **b.** el jazz **c.** el tango
5. ¿Dónde va a trabajar Ángel Luis?
   a. en un equipo **b.** en un concierto **c.** en una tienda de discos

COMUNICACIÓN

A. ¿Qué quieres hacer? If you had a choice of one activity in each of the five groups below, tell which one you would choose.

EJEMPLO ¿Quieres ir al parque, a la plaza o al restaurante?
Quiero ir al parque.

1. ¿Quieres . . . escuchar discos, llamar por teléfono o ir de compras?
2. ¿Quieres ir . . . a la piscina, al concierto o al cine?
3. ¿Quieres . . . jugar boliche, tocar la guitarra o jugar béisbol?
4. ¿Quieres ir . . . a una fiesta, al teatro o al museo?
5. ¿Quieres . . . montar bicicleta, hacer gimnasia o dar un paseo?
6. ¿Quieres . . . . . . ?

B. Preferencias. Using the following suggestions, ask other students what they want to do and don't want to do this weekend.

EJEMPLO Paco, ¿quieres jugar volibol?
No, tengo que arreglar el cuarto.

ir de compras	ir a bailar
ayudar en casa	arreglar el cuarto
lavar el coche	hacer la tarea
trabajar	ir al cine
ir a la fiesta	montar bicicleta
jugar tenis	tocar la guitarra

C. Problemas. How would you handle the following problems? Tell what you would or would not do in these situations.

EJEMPLO You are on a desert island.
Voy a descansar.
No voy a esquiar.

1. You have no money.
2. You are alone in the house.
3. You are sick and have to stay in bed.
4. You want to get better grades.
5. You just got your paycheck or allowance.
6. You want to get some exercise.

VOCABULARIO DEL CAPÍTULO

NOUNS REFERRING TO PLACES

el aeropuerto airport
el banco bank
la biblioteca library
el café café
el cine movies, movie theater
el correo post office
el estadio stadium
el hotel hotel
la iglesia church
el museo museum
el parque park
la piscina swimming pool
la plaza plaza, square
el restaurante restaurant
el supermercado supermarket
el teatro theater
la tienda store

OTHER NOUNS

el amigo, la amiga friend
el equipo team
el fin de semana weekend
la foto photo
el fotógrafo photographer
el jugador player
el partido game, match
la película movie
el piano piano
el plato dish, plate
el talento talent
el teléfono telephone
el (la) turista tourist

ADJECTIVES

aficionado amateur
otros other
un, una a, an, one

VERBS

cocinar to cook
descansar to rest
ganar to earn
hacer to do, make
ir to go
lavar to wash
querer to want, wish
tocar to play (an instrument, a record)
ver to see
viajar to travel
visitar to visit

QUESTION WORDS

¿adónde? to where?
¿cuándo? when?
¿de dónde? from where?
¿dónde? where?
¿por qué? why?
¿qué? what, which?
¿quién? who?

VERB PHRASES

arreglar el cuarto to straighten up one's room
ayudar en casa to help at home
dar un paseo to take a walk
hacer gimnasia to do gymnastics
ir de compras to go shopping
jugar boliche to bowl, go bowling
llamar por teléfono to phone, to call
montar bicicleta to ride a bike
sacar fotos to take pictures
ser fanático de to be a fan of

ADVERBS EXPRESSING TIME

ahora now
algún día some day
esta noche tonight
hoy today
mañana tomorrow
más tarde later
siempre always

OTHER ADVERBS

aquí here
contra against
entonces then
especialmente especially
más more
quizás maybe, perhaps
tan such a, so

PREPOSITIONS AND CONJUNCTIONS

o or
para to, in order to
sobre about, on

OTHER WORDS AND EXPRESSIONS

bueno okay, well
hay there is, there are
oye hey, listen
¿Qué vamos a hacer? What are we going to do?
Tengo que . . . I have to . . .

Capítulo tres

FEELINGS 3

INTRODUCCIÓN

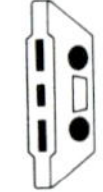

Una visita al hospital

Ana and Marta meet in the lobby of the Hospital Eugenio Espejo in Quito.

ANA	¡Hola, Marta! ¿Qué tal?	
MARTA	Bien, gracias. ¿Por qué estás aquí?	are you
ANA	Para visitar a Carlos. Está enfermo.	sick
MARTA	¡Qué pena! ¿Qué tiene?	Too bad! / What's wrong with him?
ANA	No sé, pero no es nada serio.	I don't know / nothing
MARTA	¿No es serio? ¿Por qué está Carlos en el hospital?	
ANA	Es un chico muy exagerado. Pero me gusta Carlos y voy a comprar una tarjeta para él.	boy / theatrical to buy / card
MARTA	Buena idea. Yo también quiero comprar algo para él.	something

COMPRENSIÓN

Answer the following questions based on **Una visita al hospital**.

1. ¿Dónde está Ana? ¿Por qué?
2. ¿Quién está enfermo?
3. ¿Qué tiene?
4. ¿Para Marta, Carlos es muy exagerado?
5. ¿Qué va a comprar Ana para Carlos?

COMUNICACIÓN

If you're happy about something, you might say:

¡Qué bueno!	Good!
¡Cuánto me alegro!	I'm so glad!
¡Fantástico!	Great!

If you're sad or sorry, you might say:

¡Qué pena!	What a shame!
¡Cuánto lo siento!	I'm so sorry!

If you have negative feelings, you might say:

¡Qué tontería!	What nonsense!
¡Qué importa!	Who cares!
¡Qué pesado!	How boring! What a nuisance!

To express surprise or disbelief, you might say:

¡No me digas!	Don't tell me!
¡No puede ser!	It can't be!

A. ¿Qué vas a hacer? Your classmates are telling you what they plan to do Friday night. What is your reaction to what each one says?

EJEMPLO Voy a escuchar discos.
¡Qué bueno!

1. Voy al partido
2. Voy a una fiesta.
3. Voy a practicar el piano.
4. Voy a estudiar en la biblioteca.
5. Voy a mirar la televisión.
6. Voy a visitar a un amigo en el hospital.

B. Reacciones. How would you react if friends were to tell you the following things?

EJEMPLO No hay tarea hoy.
¡Cuánto me alegro!

1. Un amigo está enfermo.
2. No hay dinero en el banco.
3. Vamos a esquiar en Colorado.
4. Hay examen mañana.
5. Hay una fiesta mañana.
6. Vamos a ir a un restaurante hoy.
7. Vamos a ver lucha libre en la tele.
8. Los animales van a hablar algún día.
9. No hay tarea.
10. No vas al cine. Vas a arreglar el cuarto.

EXPLORACIÓN

Identifying people and things
Indefinite articles

PRESENTACIÓN

To identify people and things, we use indefinite articles. Here are the indefinite articles.

	SINGULAR	PLURAL
MASCULINE	un	unos
FEMININE	una	unas

A. **Un** and **una** are the equivalents of *a* or *an* in English.

Es **un** coche. — It's *a* car.
Quiere **una** bicicleta. — He wants *a* bicycle.

B. **Unos** and **unas** may mean *some*, *any*, or *a few*. These plurals, however, are often omitted in Spanish as they are in English.

Quiere **unas** tarjetas. — He wants *a few* cards.
Hay **unos** profesores aquí. — There are *some* teachers here.
¿Hay tarjetas en español aquí? — Are there cards in Spanish here?

C. To ask what something is, say:

¿Qué es esto? — What's this? ¿Qué es eso? — What's that?

D. Here are some things you will want to be able to identify as you speak Spanish.

una cámara

un reloj

un radio

un televisor

un tocadiscos

una grabadora

una moto
una máquina de escribir
un bote
un perro
un gato

PREPARACIÓN

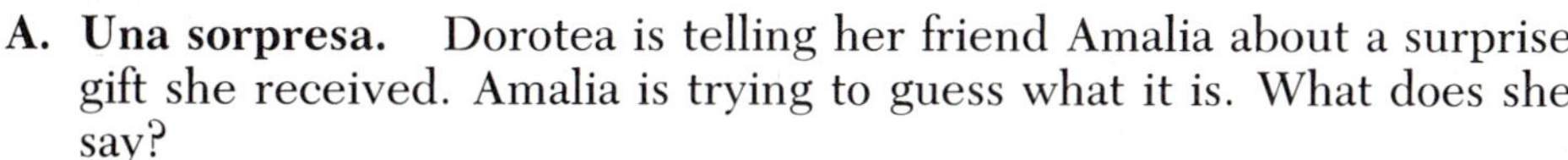

A. Una sorpresa. Dorotea is telling her friend Amalia about a surprise gift she received. Amalia is trying to guess what it is. What does she say?

MODELO ¿una cámara?
¿Es una cámara?

1. ¿un perro?
2. ¿una grabadora?
3. ¿un tocadiscos?
4. ¿un televisor?
5. ¿un reloj?
6. ¿una máquina de escribir?
7. ¿un radio?
8. ¿una moto?

B. La rifa. Pablo wants to know what items are going to be in his school's raffle. What does he ask?

MODELO moto
¿Hay una moto?

1. bote
2. tocadiscos
3. televisor
4. cámara
5. coche
6. grabadora

C. ¿Qué es eso? Mark is visiting a Spanish family and is asking how to say things in Spanish. What does he say?

MODELO

¿Qué es eso?
Es una cámara.

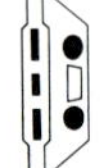

D. Un regalo. Teri's friends want to buy her a birthday gift. What do they suggest?

MODELO fotos
¿Quieres unas fotos?

1. tarjetas
2. libros
3. fotos
4. discos
5. juegos electrónicos
6. cámaras

COMUNICACIÓN

A. ¿Qué quieren ustedes? Using the following suggestions, ask other students about things they would like as gifts.

EJEMPLO ¿Quieres un coche?
Sí, quiero un coche.
No, no quiero un coche.

reloj	teléfono	bicicleta	piano
televisor	bote	perro	cámara
guitarra	grabadora	tocadiscos	¿ . . . ?

B. Jardín de la infancia. A kindergarten class is showing its artwork. Describe each child's drawing.

EJEMPLO

Es un coche.

1.

2.

3.

4.

5.

RINCÓN CULTURAL

If you were going to visit a good friend at his or her home, how would you greet the other members of the family—a hello, a smile, a handshake, or a kiss? Latin Americans tend to think of Americans as cold and distant. Latins are generally more effusive in their emotions and have more physical contact. For example, in social situations it is common for women to kiss each other on the cheek upon saying hello and again at parting. Members of the opposite sex may behave likewise. Men greet each other with a handshake or a warm pat on the back, and there is nothing unusual about a friendly embrace.

EXPLORACIÓN

Expressing feelings
estar *with adjectives*

PRESENTACIÓN

A. To talk about how you or others feel, the verb **estar** (*to be*) is often used with an adjective. Although **estar** has the same meaning as **ser** (*to be*), the two verbs are not interchangeable. **Ser** is used with identifying characteristics.

Laura es alta.
El profesor es paciente.

Estar is used with conditions that can change, such as feelings. Here are the present-tense forms of the verb **estar**.

estar

estoy	estamos
estás	
está	están

B. You learned in Chapter 1 that an adjective must agree in number and in gender with the noun it modifies. Study the forms of the adjective **enfermo** that are given below.

	SINGULAR	PLURAL
MASCULINE	enferm**o**	enferm**os**
FEMININE	enferm**a**	enferm**as**

La chica está enferma.
Luis está enfermo.

Jaime y Rafael no están enfermos.
Elena y Pilar están enfermas.

C. When the same adjective modifies both a masculine and a feminine noun, the adjective is in the masculine plural form.

La señora Castillo y el señor Sánchez están **enfermos**.
Marcela, Rosa y Tomás están **nerviosos**.

D. Here are adjectives to describe yourself and others.

aburrido, aburrida bored
contento, contenta happy
encantado, encantada delighted
cansado, cansada tired
emocionado, emocionada excited
celoso, celosa jealous
sorprendido, sorprendida surprised
enojado, enojada angry
nervioso, nerviosa nervous
deprimido, deprimida depressed
preocupado, preocupada worried
desilusionado, desilusionada disappointed

PREPARACIÓN

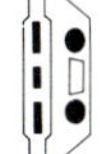

A. Yo también. Eduardo and Elsa are twins and usually share the same feelings. Whenever Eduardo tells how he feels, Elsa says the same thing about herself. What does she say?

MODELO Estoy cansado.
Yo también estoy cansada.

1. Estoy nervioso.
2. Estoy aburrido.
3. Estoy preocupado.
4. Estoy emocionado.
5. Estoy enfermo.
6. Estoy deprimido.

B. Actores y actrices. The cast list for the drama club's new production has just been posted. Tell how the following people feel.

MODELO Elisa / encantado
Elisa está encantada.

Vicente / nervioso
Vicente está nervioso.

1. Felisa / contento
2. Esteban / emocionado
3. Nicolás / desilusionado
4. Diana / celoso
5. Juanita / sorprendido
6. Rodolfo / enojado

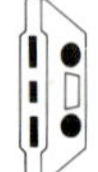

C. ¿Cómo están? Teresa's parents notice that her little brothers react to everything the same way she does. What do they say?

MODELO Teresa está nerviosa.
Juanito y Carlitos están nerviosos también.

1. Teresa está enojada.
2. Teresa está nerviosa.
3. Teresa está cansada.
4. Teresa está celosa.
5. Teresa está preocupada.
6. Teresa está contenta.

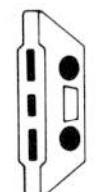

D. El partido. The soccer game has just ended. Tell how the fans of the losing team feel.

MODELO Tomás y Julián / celoso
Tomás y Julián están celosos.

Dolores / desilusionado
Dolores está desilusionada.

1. Silvia y Gustavo / enojado
2. Caridad y Pilar / preocupado
3. Victoria / bastante sorprendido
4. Gabriela y David / cansado
5. Inés y Ángel / desilusionado
6. Ángel / muy deprimido

E. Consejeros. Two counselors are discussing how some of their students feel. What do they say?

MODELO Nicolás está contento. (Graciela)
Graciela está contenta también.

1. Felipe y Arturo están aburridos. (Rosa y Luisa)
2. Eduardo está nervioso. (Mercedes)
3. Lilia está deprimida. (Francisco)
4. Joaquín y Antonio están emocionados. (Marisol y Celia)
5. Evita y Rosa están desilusionadas. (Diego y Alicia)
6. Diana está preocupada. (Víctor y Miguel)

COMUNICACIÓN

A. Barómetro de los sentimientos. Check your mood barometer for each situation in the four categories below.

EJEMPLO ¿Cómo estás hoy?
Estoy cansada.

1. emocionado encantado contento	**a.** No hay escuela mañana. **b.** Vas a viajar. **c.** Vas a ganar mucho dinero.
2. bien cansado desilusionado	**a.** ¿Cómo estás hoy? **b.** Es tarde y hay mucha tarea. **c.** El restaurante adonde vas es malo.
3. preocupado nervioso enojado	**a.** Hay un examen difícil mañana. **b.** Estás enfermo y vas al hospital. **c.** Estás en el aeropuerto y no te gusta viajar.
4. sorprendido celoso deprimido	**a.** Otros van a México para las vacaciones. **b.** Mamá va a escuchar música rock. **c.** Hay algo bueno en la televisión pero hay tarea.

B. La Copa Mundial. Teams from Spanish-speaking countries compete with teams from all over the world in the World Cup Soccer play-offs, and millions of fans follow these games. Look at the photos and describe the emotions of the players and spectators.

EJEMPLO Están emocionados.

RINCÓN CULTURAL

Gestures are an important part of communication, and each culture has its own particular gestures with their own meanings. Can you guess the meanings of these gestures?

1.

2.

3.

4.

5.

EXPLORACIÓN

Talking about what you have, have to do, or feel like doing
tener *and expressions with* **tener**

PRESENTACIÓN

A. To talk about what you have, the verb **tener** (*to have*) is used. Here are the present-tense forms of **tener**.

tener

tengo	tenemos
tienes	
tiene	tienen

Tengo una tarjeta.	I have a card.
¿Tiene Pablo un coche nuevo?	Does Pablo have a new car?
Tienen unos discos fantásticos.	They have some fantastic records.

B. **Tener** is used to tell what is wrong when you are feeling sick.

tener gripe (*f*)	to have the flu
tener catarro	to have a cold
tener fiebre (*f*)	to have a fever
tener tos (*f*)	to have a cough
tener dolor de cabeza	to have a headache
tener dolor de estómago	to have a stomachache
tener dolor de garganta	to have a sore throat
tener dolor de muelas	to have a toothache
tener dolor de espalda	to have a backache

¿Tienes dolor de cabeza?	Do you have a headache?
No tenemos catarro.	We don't have colds.

C. To say that you *have to* do something, use the correct form of **tener que** plus an infinitive.

Tengo que practicar ahora.	I have to practice now.
Tienen que ir al supermercado.	They have to go to the supermarket.

D. To say that you *feel like* doing something, use a form of **tener ganas de** plus an infinitive.

Tenemos ganas de dar un paseo.	We feel like going for a walk.
Esteban no tiene ganas de cantar.	Esteban doesn't feel like singing.

PREPARACIÓN

A. Posesiones. Pablo is talking about the things his friends and he don't have but would like to own. What does he say?

MODELO Consuelo / grabadora
Consuelo no tiene grabadora.

1. yo / radio
2. Juan / gato
3. Celia y Eva / bote
4. nosotros / perro
5. tú / tocadiscos
6. ustedes / reloj

B. ¡Yo también! It seems that every time one of Estela's friends is feeling bad, Estela also feels bad. What does she say?

MODELO Victoria tiene dolor de cabeza.
Yo también tengo dolor de cabeza.

1. Rafael tiene tos.
2. Ramón tiene gripe.
3. Consuelo tiene fiebre.
4. Jesús tiene dolor de estómago.
5. Carmela tiene dolor de garganta.
6. Enrique tiene catarro.

C. Obligaciones. Verónica's parents are reminding her about what she has to do. What do they tell her?

MODELO lavar los platos
Tienes que lavar los platos.

1. ir al correo
2. hacer la tarea
3. practicar más el piano
4. ir de compras
5. ayudar en casa
6. cocinar

D. Enfermos. Some students need to go home early. What does the school nurse say they have?

MODELO Arturo / fiebre
Arturo tiene fiebre.

Miguel y Juan / dolor de cabeza
Miguel y Juan tienen dolor de cabeza.

1. Andrés y Silvia / tos
2. Raúl y Antonio / dolor de estómago
3. Caridad / dolor de garganta
4. Alejandro / dolor de muelas
5. Pablo y Luis / catarro
6. Virginia / dolor de espalda

E. Un día libre. Today's a school holiday. What does everyone feel like doing?

MODELO Geraldo / jugar fútbol
Geraldo tiene ganas de jugar fútbol.

1. Julia / ir a las tiendas
2. yo / ir a la piscina
3. Pilar y Luisa / sacar fotos
4. usted / ir al cine
5. Tomás y Carlos / montar bicicleta
6. nosotros / hacer gimnasia

F. ¿Qué tenemos que hacer? Alonso is telling where he and his friends have to go. What does he say?

MODELO Juan / al correo
Juan tiene que ir al correo.

1. tú / banco
2. María / iglesia
3. ustedes / teatro
4. nosotros / aeropuerto
5. yo / plaza
6. Dorotea / café

COMUNICACIÓN

A. Síntomas. Tell whether or not you have the following symptoms today. Then add a comment about how you feel.

EJEMPLO Tengo dolor de cabeza. Estoy cansado.

catarro / fiebre / tos / dolor de cabeza / gripe / dolor de estómago / dolor de espalda / dolor de muelas

B. ¿Tienes ganas? Tell whether or not you feel like doing the following and ask other students if they want to do the same thing.

EJEMPLO ir al cine
Tengo ganas de ir al cine. ¿Y ustedes?

1. hacer gimnasia
2. montar bicicleta
3. mirar fotos
4. lavar el coche
5. escuchar jazz
6. cocinar algo bueno
7. descansar
8. ver una película
9. jugar un partido de fútbol
10. ir a una fiesta

C. Tareas domésticas. Use the suggestions below to find out what your friends' chores are at home.

EJEMPLO ayudar en casa
¿Tienes que ayudar en casa hoy?

1. lavar los platos
2. ir al supermercado
3. ir de compras
4. arreglar el cuarto
5. cocinar
6. practicar el piano

D. ¡Qué dolor! Describe the problems of these people.

EJEMPLO Tiene dolor de cabeza.

RINCÓN CULTURAL

Cognates are words from two different languages that look or sound alike and have the same meaning. They often make it easier to understand another language. For example, which doctors would you call for each of the following?

1. stomach pain
2. a toothache
3. a broken arm
4. sleeplessness
5. plastic surgery
6. chest pain
7. a rash
8. an eye injury

CIRUGIA PLASTICA
Reconstructiva - Estética
Dr. Sergio Herrera Soler
Dra. Angela Escobar Ruiz
San Ignacio, 83 230 58 00

DR. ANTONIO BRETON VIVES
DERMATOLOGIA - ALERGIAS
Consulta previa cita
Plaza Colón 17 455 88 54

CLINICA DE ORTODONCIA
Trabajos dentales exclusivamente finos
Anestesia General
Rehabilitación Oral - Tratamientos anticaries
Dra. Lourdes Aguilar R.
Dr. Alejandro Aguilar R.
Consulta Previa Cita 547 12 62
Independencia 54 547 40 43

CLINICA DE ORTOPEDIA Y TRAUMATOLOGIA
Dr. Ricardo Calderón R.
- Enfermedades de los Huesos
- Reumatismo
- Rayos X
- Cirugía de Columna
- Fracturas en niños y adultos

Visitas a Domicilio
Servicio las 24 horas
Cervantes 42, 5° piso 5-24-91-11

EMERGENCIA
24 HORAS
MEDICO OCULISTA
328 54 17 328 54 21

C. Vargas Cardenal L. Durán Otero
INSTITUTO DE ANGIOLOGIA
Cardiología y cirugía cardiovascular
Avda. San Francisco 131-4
6-74-24-44

MEDICINA INTERNA
GASTRITIS - COLITIS
APARATO DIGESTIVO
Dr. Tomás Muñoz Yglesias
Sanatorio Juárez
299-22-06

INSTITUTO AMERICANO DE HIPNOSIS MEDICA Y MEDICINA PSICOSOMATICA
Director Dr. Alfonso Ortega Fuentes
Enfermedades Nerviosas
(Neurosis, Insomnia, etc.)
Alternativa a la Psiquiatría
Virgen de Guadalupe 200 497 20 15

EXPLORACIÓN

Talking about the weather
Weather expressions

PRESENTACIÓN

The weather often affects how we feel. Here are some expressions you will find useful in talking about the weather.

¿Qué tiempo hace?

Hace buen tiempo. Hace mal tiempo. Hace fresco.

Hace frío. Hace calor. Hace sol.

Hace viento. Está nevando. Está lloviendo.

Notice how you tell what the weather is going to be like.

¿Qué tiempo hace hoy? ⟶ ¿Qué tiempo va a hacer mañana?

Hace sol. ⟶ Va a hacer sol.
Está lloviendo. ⟶ Va a llover.

PREPARACIÓN

A. En la tele. A Spanish-language cable TV network is reporting the weather for the Americas. What is the forecast?

MODELO

En Lima está lloviendo.

1. En Santo Domingo . . .

2. En Nueva York . . .

3. En Caracas . . .

4. En Acapulco . . .

5. En Bariloche . . .

B. Boletín meteorológico. A weather reporter for a Miami radio station is giving tomorrow's forecast for Latin America. What does she say?

MODELO En Bogotá / buen tiempo
En Bogotá va a hacer buen tiempo mañana.

1. En Santiago / sol
2. En La Paz / viento
3. En Quito / frío
4. En San Juan / calor
5. En Montevideo / lloviendo
6. En Lima / fresco

COMUNICACIÓN

A. El tiempo de hoy. Describe the weather in each of the following drawings.

EJEMPLO

Hace fresco.

1.

2.

3.

4.

5.

6.

B. ¿Te afecta el tiempo? Tell how the weather affects your mood by completing the following sentences with an appropriate weather expression.

EJEMPLO No me gusta viajar cuando . . .
No me gusta viajar cuando hace mal tiempo.

1. Me gusta jugar tenis cuando . . .
2. No tengo ganas de nadar cuando . . .
3. Estoy contento/contenta cuando . . .
4. Me gusta sacar fotos cuando . . .
5. Me gusta mirar la tele cuando . . .
6. No voy a lavar el coche cuando . . .
7. No tengo ganas de estudiar cuando . . .
8. Estoy deprimido/deprimida cuando . . .
9. Me gusta esquiar cuando . . .
10. Me gusta estar en casa cuando . . .

C. ¿Qué tiempo hace? Discuss the weather with another student. You can talk about today's weather, tomorrow's weather, and the weather in other places.

EJEMPLO ¿Qué tiempo hace?
Hace calor aquí pero hace frío en Chicago.

D. Pronóstico del tiempo. Imagine you are giving the weather forecast on the morning news. Tell what the weather is like today and what it will be like tomorrow.

EJEMPLO Hace calor hoy pero va a llover mañana.

PERSPECTIVAS

Radio Hidalgo

A student who works at the Hidalgo High School radio station is announcing the school news.

Buenos días, amigos. Aquí estamos otra vez con las noticias de nuestra escuela. La clase de español está emocionada porque esta noche todos van al baile en el Centro Hispano. ¡Qué fantástico!	again / with / news dance
Mañana la familia de Roberto Herrera va de vacaciones a Puerto Rico, pero él no va. Tiene tres exámenes esta semana y si no estudia, va a tener problemas. ¡Buena suerte, Roberto!	week / if good luck
Y ahora el tiempo para hoy. Hace viento y está lloviendo. ¡Qué pena!, porque hoy Marta León quiere montar bicicleta, Pablo García tiene ganas de ir a nadar y Francisca Fuentes quiere sacar fotos.	because
Una mala noticia: el profesor de matemáticas todavía está enfermo y no va a estar en la escuela por una semana. ¡Qué pena!, ¿no?	still for
Bueno, ahora vamos a escuchar el nuevo disco de Julio Iglesias y después, regresamos con más noticias.	afterward we return

COMPRENSIÓN

Decide if the following sentences are correct (**sí**) or not (**no**).

1. La clase está deprimida porque hay noticias hoy.
2. Roberto va a Puerto Rico con la familia.
3. Francisca quiere sacar fotos.
4. El profesor de matemáticas no está en la escuela.
5. Van a escuchar las noticias con Julio Iglesias.

COMUNICACIÓN

A. ¡No me digas! How would you react in the following situations?

1. Un amigo está enfermo y tiene que estar en el hospital unos días.
   a. ¡Qué bueno!
   b. ¡Qué pena!
   c. ¡Qué importa!
2. Vas a estar en la televisión.
   a. ¡Qué pesado!
   b. ¡Cuánto lo siento!
   c. ¿Yo? ¡No puede ser!
3. Una persona no va de vacaciones porque no tiene cámara.
   a. ¡Qué tontería!
   b. ¡No me digas!
   c. ¡Qué importa!
4. Un fanático de la música va a comprar un piano pero no tiene talento.
   a. ¡Increíble!
   b. ¡Qué horror!
   c. ¡Cuánto me alegro!
5. Quieres viajar pero no hay dinero en el banco.
   a. ¡Qué pena!
   b. ¡No puede ser!
   c. ¡Fantástico!

B. Intereses. Make a list of the things you have to do and a list of things you feel like doing.

EJEMPLO Tengo que practicar el piano.
Tengo ganas de ir de vacaciones.

1. tocar el piano
2. trabajar
3. jugar baloncesto
4. ir de compras
5. ayudar en casa
6. ir de vacaciones
7. comprar un televisor
8. sacar fotos
9. ir a un baile
10. comprar una grabadora
11. jugar boliche
12. estudiar
13. comprar un coche
14. regresar a casa
15. arreglar el cuarto
16. ¿ . . . ?

C. Sentimientos. Tell how you feel in the following situations.

EJEMPLO Hace buen tiempo.
Cuando hace buen tiempo, estoy contento.

1. Hace mal tiempo.
2. Estoy de vacaciones.
3. Tengo que trabajar.
4. Hace calor.
5. Tengo catarro.
6. Tengo que estudiar.
7. Voy al cine.
8. Tengo gripe.
9. Está nevando.
10. Estoy en la escuela.

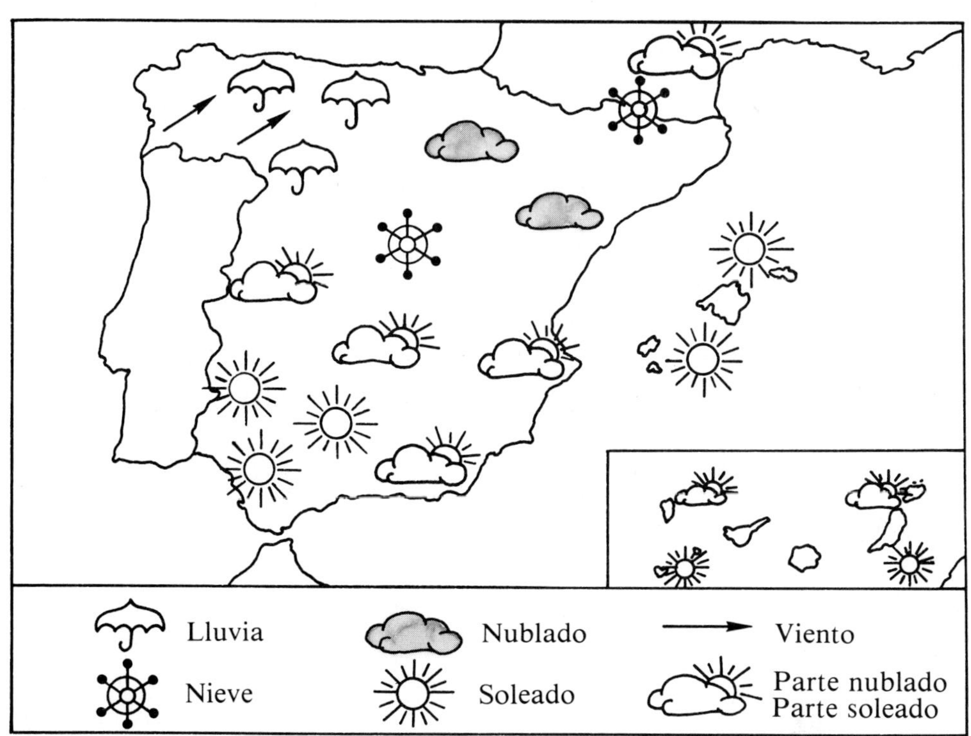

VOCABULARIO DEL CAPÍTULO

NOUNS

el baile dance
el bote boat
la cámara camera
el centro center
la chica girl
el chico boy
el dolor ache, pain
la familia family
el gato cat
la grabadora tape recorder
el hospital hospital
la idea idea
la máquina de escribir typewriter
las matemáticas math
la moto motorbike
las noticias news
el perro dog
el problema problem
el radio radio (set)
el reloj watch, clock
la semana week
la tarjeta card
el televisor television set
el tocadiscos record player
la visita visit

ADJECTIVES DESCRIBING FEELINGS

aburrido bored
cansado tired
celoso jealous
contento happy
deprimido depressed
desilusionado disappointed
emocionado excited
encantado delighted
enfermo sick, ill
enojado angry
nervioso nervous
preocupado worried
sorprendido surprised

OTHER ADJECTIVES

hispánico Hispanic
serio serious

VERBS

comprar to buy
estar to be
¡Mira! Look!
regresar to return
tener to have

ADVERBS

algo something
después afterward
nada nothing
todavía still, yet

PREPOSITIONS AND CONJUNCTIONS

con with
por for
porque because

EXPRESSIONS OF FEELING

¡Buena suerte! Good luck!
¡Cuánto lo siento! I'm so sorry!
¡Cuánto me alegro! I'm so glad!
¡Fantástico! Fantastic!, Great!
¡No me digas! Don't tell me!
¡No puede ser! It can't be!
¡Qué bueno! Good!
¿Qué importa? Who cares?
¡Qué pena! What a shame!
¡Qué pesado! What a bore!, What a nuisance!
¡Qué tontería! What nonsense!

EXPRESSIONS WITH *TENER*

tener . . . to have . . .
  catarro a cold
  dolor de cabeza a headache
  dolor de espalda a backache
  dolor de estómago a stomachache
  dolor de garganta a sore throat
  dolor de muelas a toothache
  fiebre (*f*) a fever
  gripe (*f*) the flu
  tos (*f*) a cough
tener ganas de to feel like (doing something)
tener que to have to (do something)

WEATHER EXPRESSIONS

¿Qué tiempo hace? How's the weather?
Hace buen tiempo. It's nice.
Hace mal tiempo. It's nasty.
Hace calor. It's warm.
Hace fresco. It's cool.
Hace frío. It's cold.
Hace sol. It's sunny.
Hace viento. It's windy.
Está lloviendo. It's raining.
Está nevando. It's snowing.

OTHER WORDS AND EXPRESSIONS

de vacaciones on vacation
Es muy exagerado. He's overly theatrical.
le gustaría she/he/you would like
No sé. I don't know.
¿Qué es eso? What's that?
¿Qué es esto? What's this?
otra vez again
si if
todos everyone, all

Capítulo cuatro

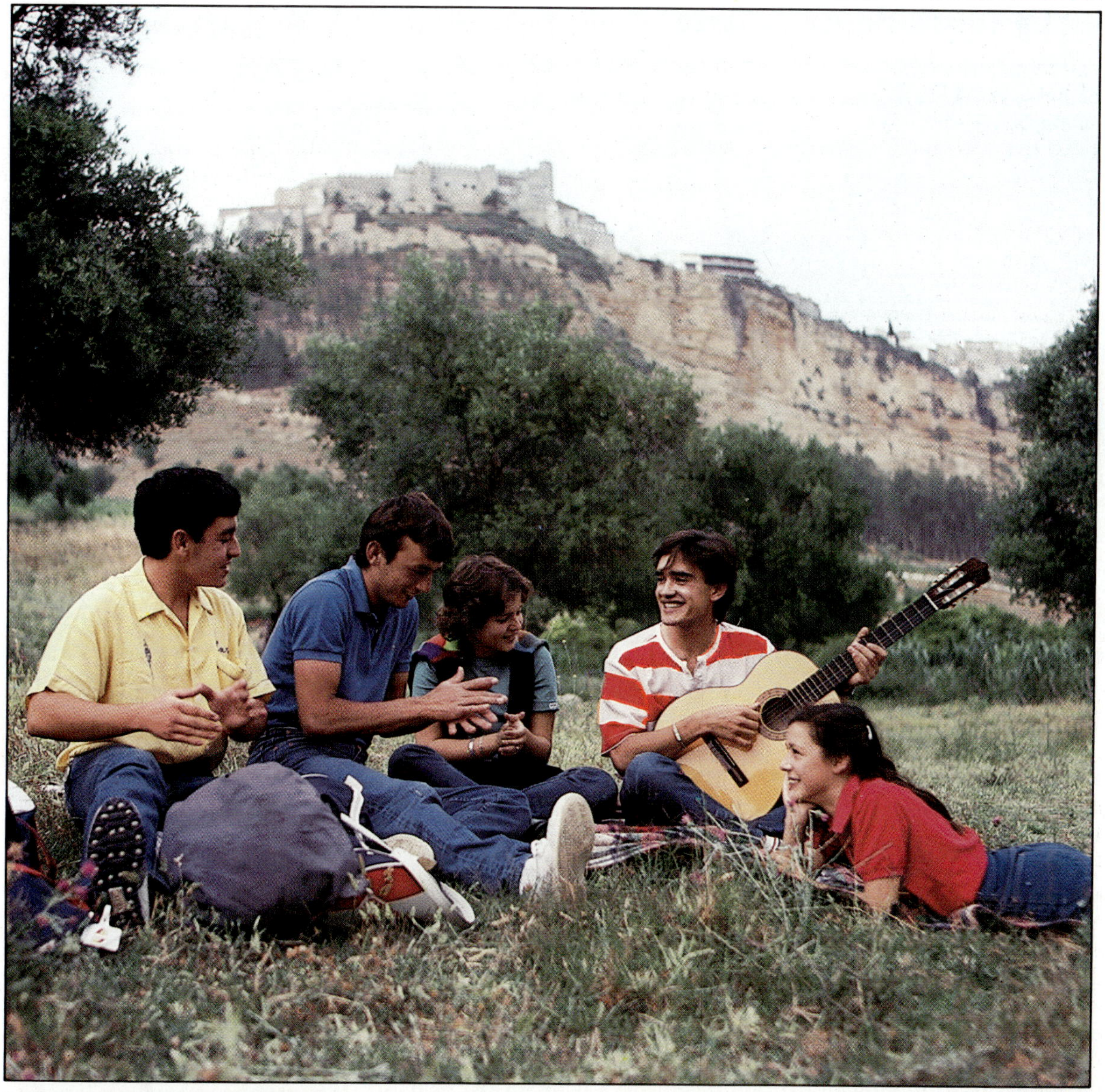

HAVING AND SHARING 4

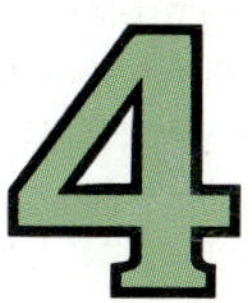

INTRODUCCIÓN

La fiesta de Ana María

Miguel and David have been invited to a party to celebrate Ana María's fifteenth birthday.

MIGUEL	¿Cuándo es el cumpleaños de Ana María? ¿Mañana?	birthday
DAVID	No, pasado mañana. ¿Vas a la fiesta?	day after tomorrow
MIGUEL	Sí, pero no tengo regalo todavía.	present, gift
DAVID	¿Por qué no compras un osito de felpa?	teddy bear
MIGUEL	¡Qué tontería! ¡Ana María va a cumplir quince años!	to be ___ years old
DAVID	Entonces, ¿qué te parece una pulsera?	what do you think about / bracelet /
MIGUEL	No, son muy caras.	expensive / cheap
DAVID	Bueno, ¿y un disco? Son más baratos.	
MIGUEL	Perfecto, porque ya tengo un álbum nuevo de Menudo en casa. Soy un genio, ¿verdad?	already genius
DAVID	¡Genio, nada! ¡Eres tacaño!	stingy

COMPRENSIÓN

Answer the following questions based on **La fiesta de Ana María**.

1. ¿Cuándo es el cumpleaños de Ana María?
2. ¿Ya tiene Miguel regalo?
3. ¿Por qué no va a comprar Miguel un osito de felpa?
4. ¿Por qué no va a comprar una pulsera?
5. ¿Por qué no va a comprar un álbum?
6. ¿Es tacaño Miguel?

COMUNICACIÓN

A. Catálogo. Tell which of the following items in a mail order catalogue you want or don't want to order for yourself.

EJEMPLO

un anillo
Quiero un anillo.

una pulsera
No quiero una pulsera.

un cartel — un suéter — una cinta

un rompecabezas — una camiseta — un perfume

una cartera — una camisa — una calculadora

B. Regalos. Imagine you are buying birthday presents for friends. For whom are you going to buy the following gifts?

EJEMPLO un álbum
Voy a comprar un álbum para Alicia.

1. una camiseta
2. una cámara
3. un cartel
4. un álbum
5. un suéter
6. una pulsera
7. una cinta
8. un rompecabezas
9. un perfume
10. una cartera
11. un anillo
12. una calculadora

C. ¿Qué quieres? Ask other students if they want these things for their birthday.

EJEMPLO

¿Quieres una bicicleta?
Sí, quiero una bicicleta.
No, no quiero una bicicleta.
No, pero quiero una moto.

1. **2.** 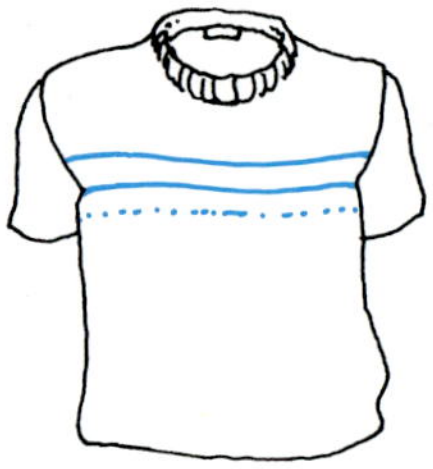 **3.**

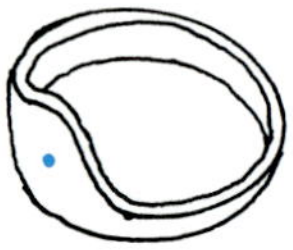

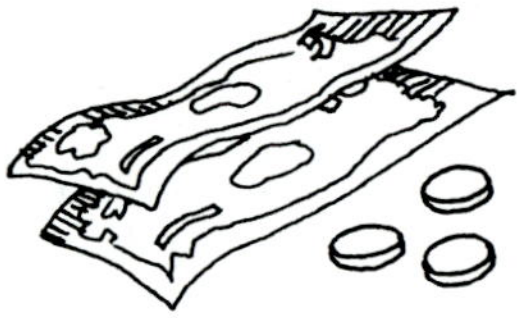

4. 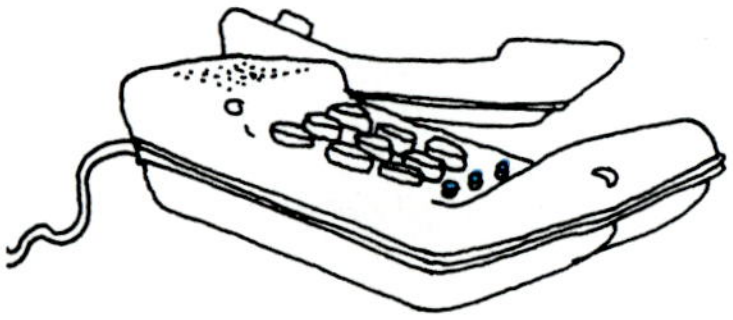 **5.**  **6.**

7. 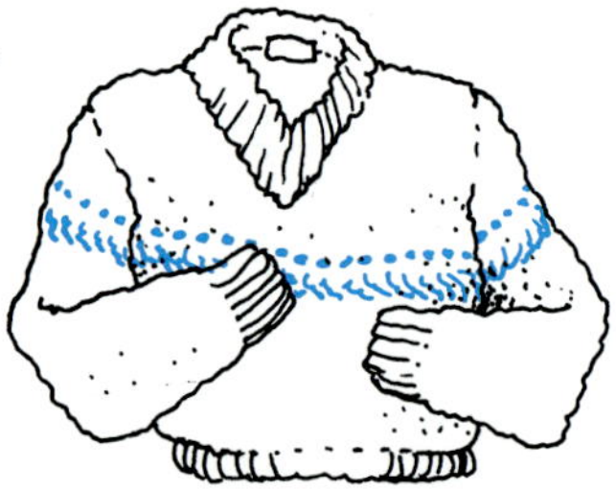 **8.**  **9.**

D. ¿Qué tienes en casa? Tell whether or not you already own the following things.

EJEMPLO Ya tengo máquina de escribir.
No tengo coche.

1. televisor	**5.** guitarra	**9.** máquina de escribir
2. tocadiscos	**6.** teléfono	**10.** calculadora
3. bicicleta	**7.** coche	**11.** cámara
4. reloj	**8.** grabadora	**12.** radio

EXPLORACIÓN

Indicating possession
*Using **de** phrases*

PRESENTACIÓN

To indicate possession, the preposition **de** is used, followed by a noun telling who the owner is. **De** has the same meaning here as the English *of*.

La pulsera de Diana es cara.	Diana's bracelet is expensive.
Me gusta la casa de la señorita García.*	I like Miss García's house.
Las camisetas de los chicos son nuevas.	The boys' tee-shirts are new.

A. When the preposition **de** is followed by the definite article **el**, the contraction **del** is formed.

Es el perro **del** señor León.*	It's Mr. León's dog.

B. To ask to whom something belongs, use the question **¿De quién?** (*Whose?*). Use **¿De quiénes?** if you think the object may belong to more than one person.

¿De quién son las pulseras?	Son de Anita.
¿De quiénes son las fotos?	Son de Pablo y Ricardo.
¿De quién es la moto?	Es la moto de Carlos.

C. You may have already noticed that a **de** phrase may also function as an adjective.

la clase de música	the music class
un partido de fútbol	a soccer match

Here are some additional things you may own:

*Note that the definite article is used before titles such as **señor**, **señora**, and **señorita**.

PREPARACIÓN

A. ¿De quiénes son? Some Spanish students have gone to visit **la Catedral de Sevilla** and have left many of their things on the bus. Víctor recognizes to whom various things belong. What does he say?

MODELO el papel / Gregorio
Es el papel de Gregorio.
las cintas / Blanca
Son las cintas de Blanca.

1. el diccionario / la profesora Pérez
2. las historietas / Julio
3. el bolígrafo / Marcos
4. los lentes / el señor Miranda
5. la calculadora / Mela
6. la cámara / Jorge
7. las llaves / Juanita
8. la mochila / Pablo

B. En la oficina. Alonso and Luisa are straightening up an office at school. Luisa tells Alonso whose things they find. What does she say?

MODELO

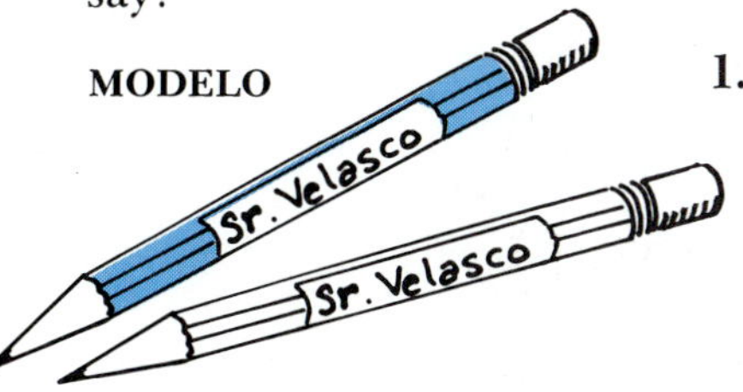

¿De quién son los lápices?
Son los lápices del señor Velasco.

1.

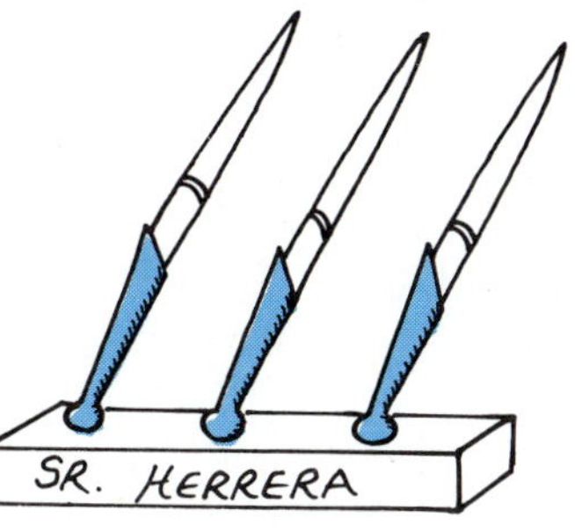

2.

3.

4.

5.

6.

7.

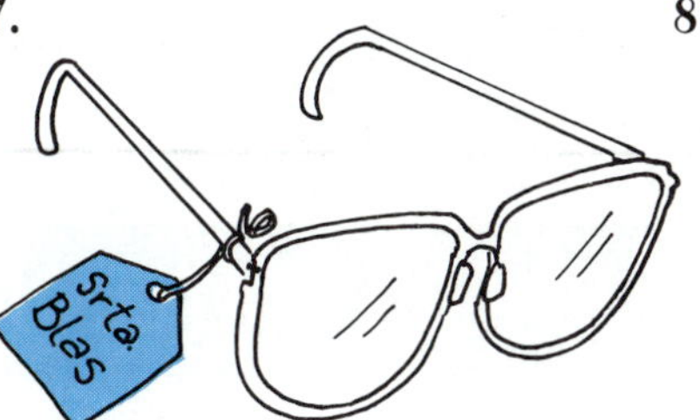

8.

C. ¿De quién es? Julio is always asking questions because he's usually uncertain about things. Give the answers to his questions.

MODELO Es la cámara de Marisa, ¿no? (No, . . . el turista)
No, es la cámara del turista.

1. Es el coche de Ricardo, ¿no? (No, . . . señor Sánchez)
2. Son los suéteres de Mónica, ¿no? (No, . . . señora García)
3. Es la amiga de Victoria, ¿no? (No, . . . Emilia)
4. Son las camisas del equipo, ¿no? (No, . . . señor González)
5. Son las fotos de la biblioteca, ¿no? (No, . . . el museo)
6. Es el álbum de la señorita Jiménez, ¿no? (No, . . . el fotógrafo)
7. Es la mochila de Carmencita, ¿no? (No, . . . María)

D. La gaceta. Verónica and Javier, who are on the staff of the newspaper at Roberto Clemente High School in New York City, are arranging photos. What do they say about each one?

MODELO equipo / fútbol americano
Es el equipo de fútbol americano.

1. concierto / jazz
2. fiesta / cumpleaños
3. equipo / baloncesto
4. jugadores / béisbol
5. clase / español
6. museo / deportes

COMUNICACIÓN

A. ¿De quién es? Think of something that someone in your class has. Other students can guess who you're thinking of.

EJEMPLO pulsera

¿Es la pulsera de Marta?
No, no es la pulsera de Marta.

¿Es la pulsera de Laura?
Sí, es la pulsera de Laura.

Sugerencias: reloj, cuaderno, lentes, suéter, lápiz, anillo, libros, bolígrafo, mochila

B. Posesiones. Look around the class and describe other people's possessions.

EJEMPLO Las historietas de María son divertidas.
No me gustan los lentes del profesor.

RINCÓN CULTURAL

People in Spanish-speaking countries don't just celebrate their own birthday but also **el día del santo,** the feast day of the saint after whom they were named. There is a saint's day for each day of the year. If you were named for the saint sharing your birthday, you would have a doubly important celebration. If you were named for a saint honored on a different day, you would celebrate the saint's day as an extra birthday. Look at the calendar on p. 201. On what day might you celebrate your **santo?**

EXPLORACIÓN

Indicating possession
Using possessive adjectives

PRESENTACIÓN

You have already learned one way to indicate possession: **el reloj de Roberto**, for example, means *Roberto's watch*.

Another way to show possession is to use possessive adjectives (*my*, *your*, *his*, *her*, etc.). Like other adjectives, a possessive adjective must agree in number with the noun it modifies. Notice that **nuestro** must also agree in gender.

my	mi, mis	nuestro, nuestros nuestra, nuestras	our
your (familiar)	tu, tus		
your (polite) his, her, its	su, sus	su, sus	your, their

¿Quieres mi tarea?	Do you want my homework?
Tengo tus cintas viejas.	I have your old tapes.
¿No tienen nuestras llaves?	Don't they have our keys?
Sus juegos electrónicos son caros.	Their electronic games are expensive.
¿Dónde está su coche?	Where is your car?

Note that **su** and **sus** can mean *his*, *her*, *its*, *their*, and *your*, depending on whom you are talking about. In conversation it's always easy to tell the meaning.

El bote **de Juanito y Pablo** es caro. ⟶ **Su** bote es caro. (*their* boat)
¿Dónde está la casa **de ustedes**? ⟶ ¿Dónde está **su** casa? (*your* house)

PREPARACIÓN

A. Posesiones. Paula is showing Ana some of the things in her room. What does she say?

MODELO gato — **Es mi gato.** cintas — **Son mis cintas.**

1. grabadora
2. mochila
3. calculadora
4. carteles
5. revistas
6. historietas

B. En casa de una amiga. A friend is coming to study, and Diana asks her if she has what she needs. What does she ask?

MODELO bolígrafo — **¿Tienes tu bolígrafo?** libros — **¿Tienes tus libros?**

1. llaves
2. reloj
3. lentes
4. diccionario
5. tarea
6. dinero
7. calculadora
8. cintas
9. cuadernos

C. Mi santo. Inés' mother is showing a friend the gifts Inés received for her **santo**. What does she ask?

MODELO

¿Te gusta su cámara?

¿Te gustan sus carteles?

1\.

2\.

3\.

4\.

5\.

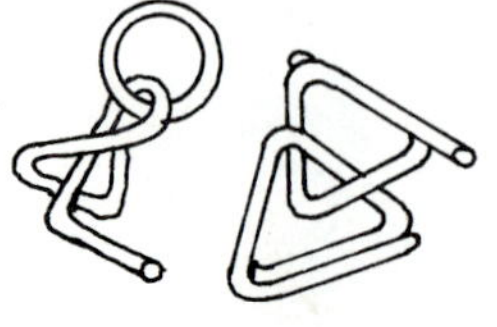

6\.

7\.

8\.

D. Ay, ¡qué fiesta! Miguel is cleaning up after the party and trying to figure out to whom things belong. Use the cues to help him.

MODELO ¿Las fotos son de Vicente? (Sí)
Sí, son sus fotos.

1. ¿Los discos son de Silvia? (No)
2. ¿La guitarra es de Mario? (No)
3. ¿Las cintas son de tu profesor? (No)
4. ¿El tocadiscos es de tus amigos? (Sí)
5. ¿La cartera es de tu amiga Inés? (No)

E. Casa nueva. Lucía's family has just moved. As she unpacks, what does she say to her twin sister?

MODELO diccionario
Tengo nuestro diccionario.

1. grabadora
2. cámara
3. camisetas
4. discos
5. calculadora
6. historietas
7. cintas
8. papeles

F. En una tienda. Carlos is working in the pick-up department of a large store. What does he ask each customer?

MODELO cartera
¿Es su cartera?

1. anillo
2. pulseras
3. suéter
4. calculadora
5. camisas
6. perfume

COMUNICACIÓN

A. Preguntas. Make up questions to ask other students about some of the people they know or things they have.

EJEMPLO amigos / simpáticos
¿Son simpáticos tus amigos?

1. equipo / bueno
2. exámenes / fáciles
3. fiestas / divertidas
4. televisor / viejo
5. cámara / mala
6. tareas / aburridas

B. Descripción. Using words from the right-hand column, create sentences describing the persons and things listed in the left-hand column. Be sure your adjectives agree. Use different possessive adjectives in your sentences.

EJEMPLO Mi perro es inteligente.

fin de semana	bonito
cuarto	alegre
coche	interesante
clases	formidable
perro / gato	simpático / antipático
perros / gatos	inteligente
amigo / amiga	fantástico
amigos / amigas	guapo
escuela	pesado
casa	bueno / malo
reloj	nuevo / viejo
tocadiscos	divertido / aburrido

RINCÓN CULTURAL

A girl's fifteenth birthday (**la fiesta de los quince**) is a special occasion in Latin American countries because it is usually at this age that dating begins. Traditionally the 15-year-old (**la quinceañera**) dresses in white and is accompanied by 14 girls dressed in a color selected for the party. After being escorted to the party, she changes from low-heeled to high-heeled shoes to show that she is a young woman. According to custom, the **quinceañera** dances first with her father and then with the young man she has chosen as her date. The 14 girls join in, followed by the other guests. Even when the family does not have a large party, the fifteenth birthday is still a very special event.

How do Americans celebrate a girl's sixteenth birthday?
How is it similar to and different from the **quinceañera** party?

EXPLORACIÓN

Talking about things we do
Using **ar** *verbs*

PRESENTACIÓN

Verbs make it possible to talk about things we do. Most Spanish verbs fall into one of three groups.

One group of verbs has infinitives ending in **ar** (**cantar**, **hablar**, **comprar**). Note in the chart below that different endings are added to the stem of the verb to show who is doing the action. The stem is found by dropping the **ar** from the infinitive (**hablar—habl**, **cantar—cant**, **comprar—compr**).

bailar

bail**o**	bail**amos**
bail**as**	
bail**a**	bail**an**

A. Some of the **ar** verbs that you have already learned are: **arreglar**, **ayudar**, **cantar**, **cocinar**, **comprar**, **descansar**, **escuchar**, **esquiar**, **estudiar**, **ganar**, **hablar**, **lavar**, **llamar**, **mirar**, **nadar**, **practicar**, **regresar**, **sacar**, **tocar**, **trabajar**, **viajar**, and **visitar**.

B. Here are some ways to tell how often you do things.

todos los días	every day	**muchas veces**	often
a veces	sometimes	**pocas veces**	rarely
todavía	yet, still	**nunca**	never

PREPARACIÓN

A. Rutina. Some friends are talking about what they do every day. What do they say?

MODELO ayudar en casa
Ayudamos en casa todos los días.

1. arreglar el cuarto	**3.** trabajar	**5.** montar bicicleta
2. escuchar música	**4.** estudiar español	**6.** mirar la tele

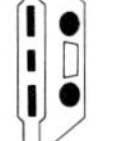

B. A larga distancia. A friend who's moved away has called Juan. How does Juan answer his friend's questions?

MODELO ¿Estudias español todavía?
Sí, todavía estudio español.

1. ¿Montas bicicleta los fines de semana?
2. ¿Todavía trabajas en el cine?
3. ¿Todavía tocas la guitarra?
4. ¿Practicas fútbol todos los días?
5. ¿Estudias más ahora?
6. ¿A veces regresas tarde a casa?

C. ¿Qué pasa? Vicente wants to know what everyone is doing. What does he ask?

MODELO

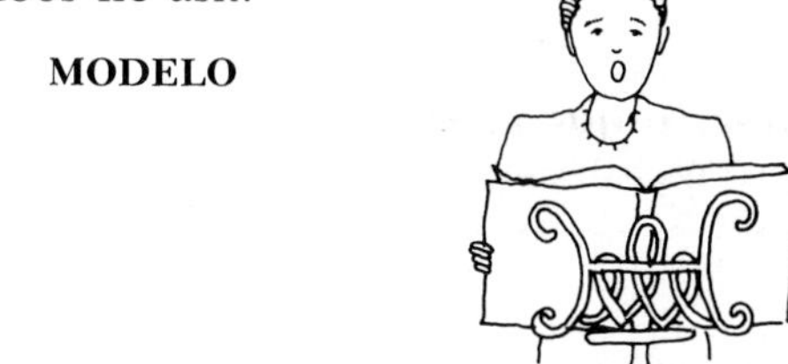

¿Qué cantas?

1.

2.

3.

4.

5.

6.

D. Siempre lo mismo. Some students have found that they often do the same thing every weekend. What do they do?

MODELO Marta y Ana / sacar fotos
Marta y Ana muchas veces sacan fotos.

1. Ángel y Ramón / visitar el museo
2. Celia y Bárbara / comprar algo
3. Luis, David y Tomás / cantar en la iglesia
4. Simón y Francisco / cocinar algo
5. Alicia y Carmen / estudiar en casa
6. José y Susana / escuchar música
7. Ángela y Vicente / trabajar en la biblioteca

E. Compañeros. Felipe is popular, and people are glad to be with him. Tell who sometimes joins Felipe in his activities.

MODELO Felipe nada en la piscina. (Ernesto)
Felipe y Ernesto a veces nadan en la piscina.

1. Felipe compra discos. (Pepe)
2. Felipe baila. (María)
3. Felipe practica tenis. (Teodoro)
4. Felipe mira televisión. (Susana)
5. Felipe monta bicicleta. (Luis)

F. También. Rosa is asking her teacher about her interests. What does she ask?

MODELO viajar en las vacaciones
¿Viaja usted en las vacaciones?

1. estudiar piano
2. esquiar
3. sacar fotos
4. escuchar jazz
5. cocinar
6. mirar películas viejas

G. Responsabilidades. A foreign teacher is asking American students about their responsibilities. What does he ask?

MODELO ayudar en casa
¿Ayudan ustedes en casa?

1. arreglar el cuarto
2. lavar los platos
3. trabajar para ganar dinero
4. cocinar
5. lavar el coche
6. ayudar en la escuela

H. Nuestras fiestas. When Francisca and her friends get together for a party, Francisca always knows what to expect. What does she say?

MODELO Angelina / nunca / lavar los platos
Angelina nunca lava los platos.

1. Miguel y Natalia / nunca / hablar
2. Tú / siempre / ayudar
3. Mis amigos / siempre / tocar la guitarra
4. Yo / nunca / cantar
5. Paco / siempre / tocar los discos
6. Luis y Olga / siempre / cocinar
7. Andrés y yo / nunca / bailar
8. Alberto / siempre / mirar la televisión

COMUNICACIÓN

A. ¿Con qué frecuencia? Tell how often you do the following activities.

EJEMPLO bailar
Nunca bailo.

nunca — pocas veces — a veces — muchas veces — todos los días

1. estudiar
2. cocinar
3. visitar el museo
4. nadar
5. arreglar el cuarto
6. hablar por teléfono
7. esquiar
8. montar bicicleta

B. ¿Quién? Find out who does the following activities and report back to the class.

EJEMPLO ¿Quién monta bicicleta?
Gloria y David montan bicicleta.

1. ¿Quién esquía?
2. ¿Quién cocina en casa?
3. ¿Quién canta en la iglesia?
4. ¿Quién estudia música?
5. ¿Quién habla mucho por teléfono?
6. ¿Quién trabaja los fines de semana?
7. ¿Quién mira deportes en la tele?
8. ¿Quién habla español en casa?

C. A veces. There are many things you sometimes like to do. Use the suggestions below to make up sentences describing things you and your friends do.

EJEMPLO A veces yo practico el piano.

A veces	yo ustedes mis amigos nosotros	arreglar . . . ? practicar español con . . . ? escuchar discos . . . ? viajar . . . ? ganar dinero en . . . ? practicar . . . ? mirar . . . ? tocar . . . ? sacar fotos de . . . ?

RINCÓN CULTURAL

Do you consider yourself a good friend to others? Are you **generoso** (**generosa**) with your friends, or are you **tacaño** (**tacaña**)? Friendship and generosity go hand in hand in Latin America. As an expression of your regard for a good friend, would you give him or her a tee-shirt he or she liked? How about a favorite sweater or even a ring your friend admired? This sort of gift is not an unusual display of generosity in Latin America, where it is common to offer a personal item to a friend who admires it.

EXPLORACIÓN

Asking how much and how many Numbers to 100

PRESENTACIÓN

To talk about quantity—how much or how many—you need numbers. Use the tables below to learn to count to 100.

A. Here is how you count by 10's. Learn the tens digits.

10	diez	60	sesenta
20	veinte	70	setenta
30	treinta	80	ochenta
40	cuarenta	90	noventa
50	cincuenta	100	ciento (cien) **Ciento** becomes **cien** before a noun.

B. To form numbers to 100 combine a tens digit with a ones digit.

16	dieciséis	18	dieciocho
17	diecisiete	19	diecinueve
21	veintiuno	26	veintiséis
22	veintidós	27	veintisiete
23	veintitrés	28	veintiocho
24	veinticuatro	29	veintinueve
25	veinticinco		
38	treinta y ocho	85	ochenta y cinco
43	cuarenta y tres	99	noventa y nueve

C. When numbers ending in **uno** (21, 51, etc.) are followed by a noun, they must agree in gender. **Uno** becomes **un** before a masculine noun and **una** before a feminine noun.

¿Hay veintiún chicos aquí hoy? — Sí, hay veintiuno.
Ella tiene cuarenta y una historietas. — Tiene cuarenta y una.

D. To ask *how much*, **¿Cuánto?** and **¿Cuánta?** are used.

¿Cuánto talento tienes en música? ¿Cuánta tarea tienen ustedes?

To ask *how many*, the questions **¿Cuántos?** and **¿Cuántas?** are used.

¿Cuántos carteles hay? ¿Cuántas llaves tienes?

Note that they agree with the noun that follows.

PREPARACIÓN

A. En Madrid. Students in a summer program in Madrid are exchanging their addresses. What do they say?

MODELO Goya 55
Goya cincuenta y cinco

1. Fernando el Católico 38
2. Trafalgar 16
3. Ronda de Toledo 22
4. Paseo del Prado 75
5. Alcalá 97
6. José Antonio 44

B. El bazar sábado. John is learning the art of bargaining (**regateo**) in Mexico City's Saturday market. In response to the vendor's price, what does he offer?

MODELO veintidós pesos (17)
¡Diecisiete!

1. treinta y cuatro pesos (25)
2. ochenta y ocho (73)
3. cincuenta y nueve (42)
4. cien (89)
5. setenta y uno (64)
6. noventa y nueve (80)
7. cuarenta y cinco (36)
8. sesenta (57)

C. Baloncesto. Basketball scores are being given by a Spanish radio station in San Antonio. What are the scores?

MODELO Indiana 83, Wisconsin 80
Indiana ochenta y tres, Wisconsin ochenta

1. Ohio State 96, Michigan 84
2. Kentucky 100, Tennessee 89
3. Stanford 76, Washington 75
4. Alabama 63, Georgia 52
5. Brown 67, Yale 65
6. Texas 81, North Carolina 78

D. Precios especiales. Some friends are reading sale ads. How much does each item cost?

MODELO un albúm de tres discos ($21)
veintiún dólares

1. un televisor ($99)
2. una grabadora ($85)
3. un anillo ($33)
4. un osito de felpa ($18)
5. una calculadora ($47)
6. una cartera ($23)

COMUNICACIÓN

A. Números de teléfono. Ask your fellow students for their telephone numbers.

EJEMPLO Tu número de teléfono, por favor.
(254-6193) Es el dos, cincuenta y cuatro, sesenta y uno, noventa y tres.

B. Concurso matemático. Conduct a math contest to see who's quickest with a calculator in doing problems in Spanish. Use numbers up to 100 only.

EJEMPLO ¿Cuántos son veintiocho y treinta y dos?
Son sesenta.

C. ¿Cuántas millas? Give the mileage between towns in your area.

EJEMPLO Helena está a 90 millas de Great Falls, Montana.

PERSPECTIVAS

El álbum de fotos de Ana Gabriela

¿Quieres ver unas fotos de mi familia? Aquí estamos todos: mi padre, mi madre, mi hermano José, mi hermana Rosa María y yo. Papá es alto pero ahora está un poco gordo porque tiene que comer con sus clientes en muchos restaurantes. Mamá trabaja en una tienda. Es joven y muy bonita, ¿no te parece?

brother / sister
overweight / to eat
young
Don't you think so?

Aquí están mis hermanos. Rosa María tiene dieciocho años y va a la universidad. Yo voy a cumplir quince. José, el pequeño, solamente tiene once años. Es muy pesado.

is eighteen years old

Mira. Aquí están mis abuelos. Son muy simpáticos. Siempre pasamos las vacaciones con ellos en la Florida. Me gusta estar con ellos porque siempre hablamos español—pues casi no hablan inglés.

grandparents
we spend
almost / English

Aquí están mis tíos. Mi tía trabaja mucho porque tiene una casa grande y muchos hijos que cuidar.

aunt and uncle

large / children / to take care of

Mi prima favorita es María Cristina. Es muy delgada porque es profesora de gimnasia. Me gustaría ser profesora como ella.

cousin
slim
like

COMPRENSIÓN

Answer the following questions on **El álbum de fotos**.

1. ¿Cuántas personas hay en la familia de Ana Gabriela?
2. ¿Quiénes son?
3. ¿Por qué está un poco gordo su papá?
4. ¿Cuántos años tienen sus hermanos?
5. ¿Dónde pasa Ana Gabriela las vacaciones?
6. ¿Por qué trabaja mucho en casa su tía?
7. ¿Quién es su prima favorita? ¿Por qué?

COMUNICACIÓN

A. Mi familia. Describe your own family.

EJEMPLO Mi tío Ricardo es muy simpático.
Mis abuelos son bastante pacientes.

B. ¿Cuántos años? Tell how old some of your family and friends are or are going to be.

EJEMPLO Mi hermana tiene cinco años.
Mi abuelo va a cumplir sesenta y cinco años.

VOCABULARIO DEL CAPÍTULO

NOUNS RELATING TO THE FAMILY

el abuelo grandfather
la abuela grandmother
los abuelos grandparents
la familia family
el hermano brother
la hermana sister
los hermanos brothers and sisters
el hijo son
la hija daughter
los hijos children
la madre (mamá) mother
el padre (papá) father
los padres parents
el primo, la prima cousin
el tío uncle
la tía aunt
los tíos aunt and uncle

NOUNS RELATING TO BIRTHDAYS AND PRESENTS

el álbum album
el anillo ring
la calculadora calculator
la camisa shirt
la camiseta tee-shirt
el cartel poster
la cartera wallet
la cinta tape
el cumpleaños birthday
el osito de felpa teddy bear
el perfume perfume
la pulsera bracelet
el regalo gift, present
el rompecabezas puzzle
el suéter sweater

OTHER NOUNS

el bolígrafo ball-point pen
el (la) cliente customer
el cuaderno notebook
el diccionario dictionary
el genio genius
la historieta comic book
el inglés English
el lápiz (lápices) pencil(s)
los lentes (eye)glasses
la llave key
la mochila backpack, knapsack
el papel paper
la revista magazine
la universidad university

ADJECTIVES

barato cheap
caro expensive
delgado slim
favorito favorite
gordo overweight
grande large
joven young
pequeño small
perfecto perfect
tacaño stingy

VERBS

comer to eat
cuidar to take care of
pasar to spend (time)

ADVERBS

a veces sometimes
casi almost
como like
muchas veces often
nunca never
pocas veces rarely
poco a little
solamente only
todos los días every day
ya already, yet

EXPRESSIONS

¿Cuánto/a . . . ? how much?
¿Cuántos/as . . . ? how many?
cumplir . . . años to turn ___ years old
¿De quién, de quiénes . . . ? Whose?
¿No te parece? Don't you think so?
pasado mañana day after tomorrow
¿Qué te parece? What do you think?

Capítulo cinco

SCHOOL LIFE 5

INTRODUCCIÓN

Un día pesadísimo*

very heavy

Pepe meets Alonso during their break (**recreo**) at the Colegio San Ignacio in Río Piedras, Puerto Rico.

ALONSO	Pepe, ¿tienes planes para esta tarde? Hoy hay un partido de baloncesto y después vamos en grupo a comer.	this
PEPE	¿Estás loco? ¡Imposible! Hoy estoy muy ocupado.	crazy / busy
ALONSO	¿Por qué?	
PEPE	Porque después del colegio todavía tengo tanto que hacer. A las tres tengo mi clase de inglés en el instituto y a las cinco tengo una clase de guitarra.	school / so much to do / at three
ALONSO	¡Pobrecito!	poor thing
PEPE	¡Sí! Y mañana tenemos examen.	
ALONSO	¿Tenemos examen? ¿Qué examen?	
PEPE	De biología. A las nueve de la mañana en punto.	sharp
ALONSO	¡Dios mío! ¡Adiós!	
PEPE	Oye, ¿adónde vas?	
ALONSO	A la biblioteca . . . a estudiar.	
PEPE	¿Y el partido?	
ALONSO	¡Qué partido! Primero la biología.	first

*Note that **ísimo/ísima** when added to an adjective or an adverb means *very* or *extremely*: **pesado** + **ísimo** = **pesadísimo**; **fácil** + **ísimo** = **facilísimo**.

COMPRENSIÓN

Answer the following questions based on **Un día pesadísimo**.

1. ¿Qué planes tiene Alonso para esta tarde?
2. ¿Por qué no quiere ir Pepe?
3. ¿Qué tiene Pepe a las tres?
4. ¿Cuándo es su clase de guitarra?
5. ¿Qué hay mañana a las nueve en punto?
6. ¿Adónde va Alonso?

COMUNICACIÓN

Here are some school subjects that both you and students in Spanish-speaking countries might take.

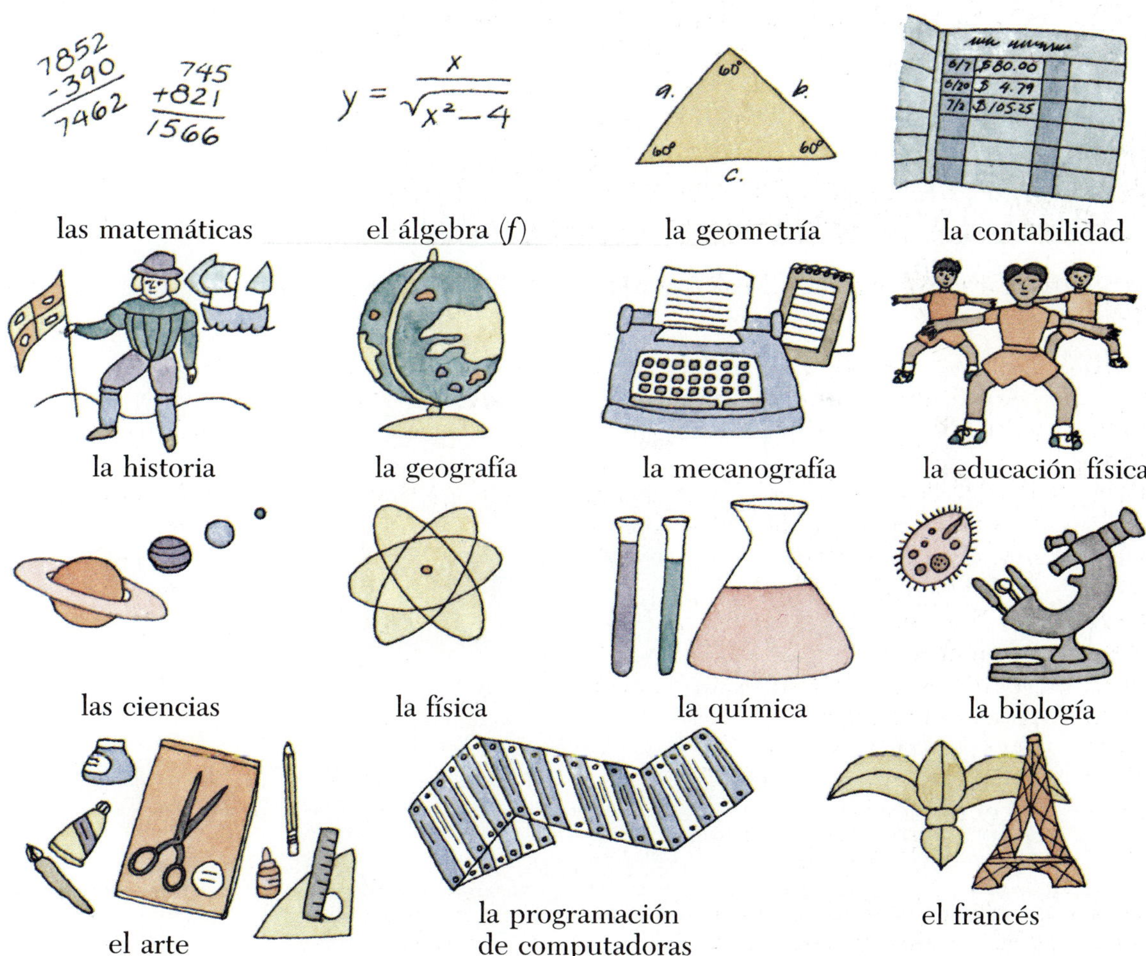

A. **Mis clases favoritas.** Tell which subjects you like and which you do not like.

EJEMPLO Me gusta el arte.
No me gusta la programación de computadoras.

B. **Ahora.** Tell which subjects you are studying this year and which ones you are not studying.

EJEMPLO Estudio matemáticas.
No estudio biología.

C. **En mi opinión.** Use the adjectives below to describe classes you've taken.

EJEMPLO La clase de álgebra es fantástica.

importante	excelente	fantástico
interesante	popular	fácil/difícil
pesado	aburrido	divertido

D. **¿Cuándo?** Use **antes de** (*before*) or **después de** (*after*) to tell when you have a particular class.

EJEMPLO Tengo la clase de álgebra antes del recreo.
Voy a la clase de arte después de la clase de historia.

EXPLORACIÓN

Telling time
Expressions of time

PRESENTACIÓN

To ask what time it is, you say: **¿Qué hora es?**

This question can be answered in the following ways:

A. On the hour

Son las dos.

Son las ocho.

Es la una.

Es mediodía.

Es medianoche.

B. On the quarter or half-hour

Son las tres y cuarto.

Es la una menos cuarto.

Son las diez y media.

C. Minutes before or after the hour

Son las cinco **y** diez.

Son las siete **menos** cinco.

Es la una **menos** veinte.

D. To ask or tell when an event occurs **a** is used.

¿A qué hora vas al cine?	Voy a las ocho.
¿A qué hora tienes la clase de inglés?	A la una.

E. A.M. and P.M. are not used in Spanish. The expressions **de la mañana**, **de la tarde**, and **de la noche** indicate the time of day.

La clase de inglés es a las ocho de la mañana.
Vamos a dar un paseo a las seis de la tarde.
Voy a hacer la tarea a las ocho de la noche.

F. However, when no specific hour is given use **por**: **por la mañana** (*in the morning*), **por la tarde** (*in the afternoon/evening*), **por la noche** (*at night*).

Estudio por la noche.
Hoy no tenemos clases por la tarde.

PREPARACIÓN

A. Relojes. Look at the clocks and tell what time it is.

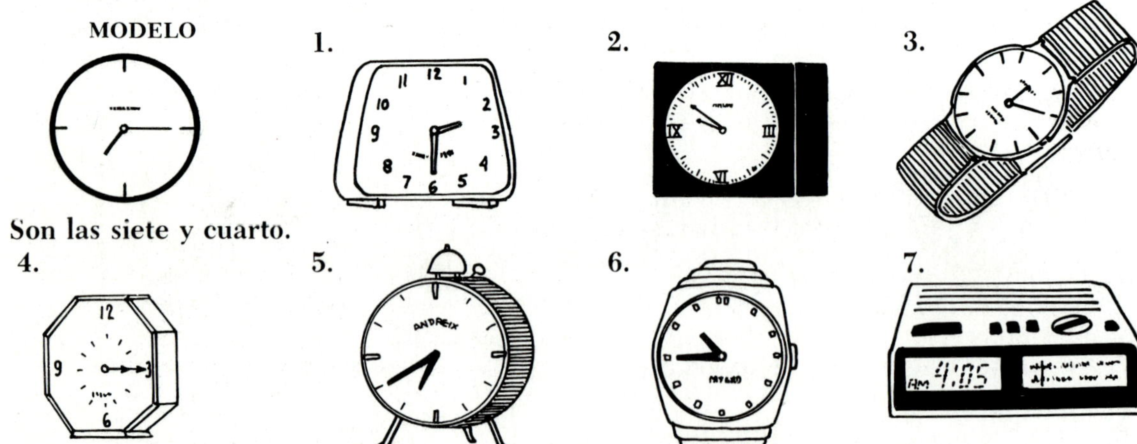

Son las siete y cuarto.

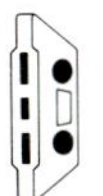

B. **¿Qué hora es?** Irene Salazar, a Panamanian disc jockey, works a long shift from ten in the morning to eight in the evening. At various intervals, she gives the time. What does she say?

MODELO 8:15 A.M.
Son las ocho y cuarto de la mañana.

1. 10:25 A.M.
2. 11:15 A.M.
3. 11:50 A.M.
4. 12:30 P.M.
5. 1:20 P.M.
6. 6:45 P.M.
7. 7:55 P.M.
8. 8:00 P.M.

C. **Horario de clases.** Use the schedule below to tell where Alejandro will be at the times listed.

8:30 - 9:15	geometría
9:20 - 10:05	español
10:10 - 10:55	geografía
11:00 - 11:45	ciencias
11:50 - 12:30	recreo
12:35 - 1:20	programación de computadoras
1:25 - 2:10	educación física
2:15 - 3:00	inglés

MODELO 9:55
A las diez menos cinco va a estar en la clase de español.

1. 1:05
2. 10:35
3. 2:30
4. 1:55
5. 10:10
6. 11:20
7. 8:40
8. 12:25

D. **El domingo en la tele.** Ricardo is deciding what to watch on TV this Sunday. When are the following programs scheduled?

MODELO el tiempo para mañana (6:00)
El tiempo para mañana es a las seis.

1. el show de Roberto Carlos (8:00)
2. la gimnasia (4:45)
3. el fútbol (2:30)
4. la película *Anita la huerfanita* (9:00)
5. la lucha libre (8:15)
6. *Supermán III* (5:30)

COMUNICACIÓN

A. Los programas de esta noche. Imagine you are looking at a schedule of a Spanish television channel. Read the schedule below and answer the questions that follow.

Hoy

4:00 La programacion de esta noche

4:10 Yogi y sus amigos (caricaturas)

5:00 El gran show (variedades)

6:15 24 Horas (informaciones)

6:50 Boletín meterologico: el tiempo para mañana

7:05 Fútbol: Barcelona-Valencia

7:20 Un amor imposible (melodrama)

8:30 Concierto de Julio Iglesias

9:45 Panorama de Africa (documental)

10:00 Tele-Cine: E.T. (película de ciencia-ficción)

1. ¿A qué hora hablan de la programación de esta noche?
2. ¿A qué hora es el boletín meteorológico?
3. ¿A qué hora hay un programa interesante para los chicos?
4. ¿Qué hay en la tele a las 6:15?
5. ¿La película es a las 7:05?
6. ¿A qué hora es el concierto de Julio Iglesias?
7. ¿Qué programa te gusta más? ¿A qué hora es?

B. Tu horario. Use the following suggestions to ask other students questions about their schedules.

EJEMPLO ¿A qué hora tienes la clase de física?
A las ocho y media.

¿A qué hora tienes la clase de . . . ?
- inglés
- álgebra
- historia
- español
- educación física
- arte
- biología
- música
- ?

C. ¿A qué hora? Answer the following questions or use them to interview another student.

1. ¿A qué hora vas al colegio por la mañana?
2. ¿A qué hora es tu clase de español?
3. ¿A qué hora es el recreo?
4. ¿A qué hora vas a casa?
5. ¿A qué hora escuchas la radio?
6. ¿A qué hora estudias?
7. ¿A qué hora descansas por la noche?

RINCÓN CULTURAL

Would you be surprised if you took a trip to Spain and found out that the bullfight you had tickets for began **a las 17:00**? Would you be on time for a lunch **a las 14:50**? When would you show up for a party given **a las 21:00**?

Spanish-speaking people, in Spain and in Latin America, do use our system of telling time but to avoid the confusion of a.m. or p.m. (**las diez de la mañana o de la noche**), times are often given on a 24-hour basis.

Look at your first day's schedule in Spain. Can you tell when you do what?

Madrid ~ Primer día

8,50 h. Desayuno
9,50 h. Excursión a Toledo
14,00 h. Almuerzo
16,00 h. Visita al museo del Prado
18,00 h. De compras
21,00 h. Cena

A. G. T. - 168

PUENTE - BUS: BARCELONA - MADRID

Enlaces a: Extremadura, La Mancha, Castilla

Con autocares de lujo -:- Servicio regular y diario

SALIDAS DE BARCELONA

Laborables (excepto Viernes)	7,00 horas
Viernes	15,00 y 22,00 horas
Domingos y Festivos	7,00 y 22,00 horas

SALIDAS DE MADRID

Laborables (excepto Viernes)	15,00 horas
Viernes	15,00 y 22,00 horas
Domingos y Festivos	15,00 y 22,00 horas

HORARIOS

Desayuno - Petit déjeuner - Breakfast

Habitación / Chambre / Room	de 8 a 11
Bar	de 11 a 13

Almuerzo - Déjeuner - Lunch

Hotel	de 13 a 15
Beach - Club	de 13 a 16

Cena - Diner - Dinner

Hotel	de 20'30 a 22'30
Beach - Club	de 21 a 24

Bares

Hotel	de 11 a 24
Beach - Club	de 11 a 01

EXPLORACIÓN

Talking about people
The personal **a**

PRESENTACIÓN

You have already used sentences with direct objects. Up to now, these direct objects have been things rather than people.

Escucho el tocadiscos.
Pedro visita Miami.

A. When the direct object is a person (or a pet), the preposition **a** is used before the direct object. Note that the personal **a** cannot be translated into English.

Visitan a su tío mañana.

B. The personal **a** is used with **¿quién?** and **¿quiénes?** when they are direct objects, meaning *whom*.

¿A quién miras?	Whom are you looking at?
¿A quiénes vas a visitar?	Whom are you going to visit?

C. The personal **a** is not generally used with **tener**.

Tengo veinte primos.

D. Here are verbs that often use the personal **a**: **buscar** (*to look for*), **esperar** (*to wait for*), **mirar** (*to look at*). You also know **ayudar**, **cuidar**, **llamar**, and **visitar**.

¿Siempre espera a Luisa?	Does he always wait for Luisa?
Busco a mi perro.	I'm looking for my dog.

PREPARACIÓN

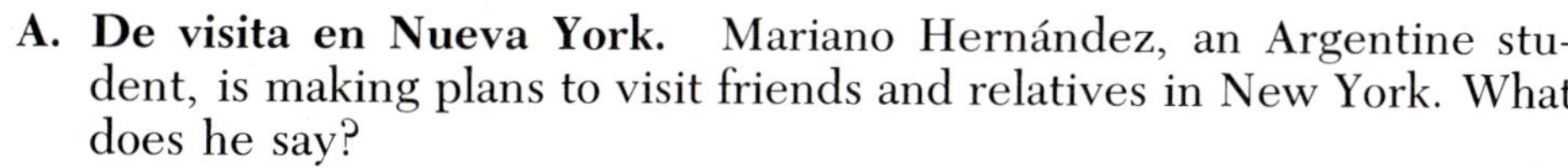

A. De visita en Nueva York. Mariano Hernández, an Argentine student, is making plans to visit friends and relatives in New York. What does he say?

MODELO José María
Voy a visitar a José María.

1. Alicia
2. mis primos
3. Rafael
4. Pablo y Jesús
5. la señora Suárez
6. el señor González
7. mi tía
8. el señor Jiménez

B. Una familia ocupada. A Mexican-American family is visiting relatives in Guadalajara, and señora Sánchez is having difficulty keeping track of what everyone is doing. What does she ask?

MODELO ¿A quién ayuda Sarita? (su padre)
Sarita ayuda a su padre.

1. ¿A quién mira Marta en la tele? (Rita Moreno)
2. ¿A quiénes llama José por teléfono? (sus amigos)
3. ¿A quién espera Pablo? (el tío Jesús)
4. ¿A quiénes cuidan Antonia y Elena? (sus hermanos)
5. ¿A quién busca Anita? (su gato)

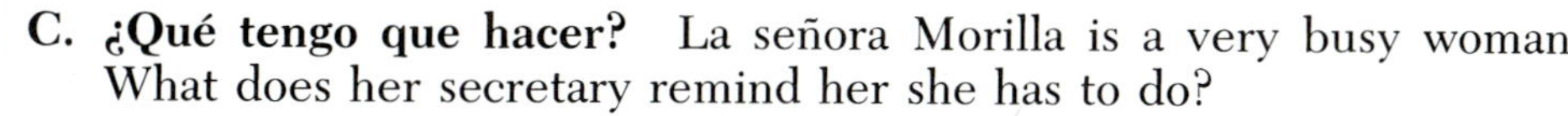

C. ¿Qué tengo que hacer? La señora Morilla is a very busy woman. What does her secretary remind her she has to do?

MODELO llamar / el señor Sánchez
Usted tiene que llamar al señor Sánchez.

1. comprar / un regalo para su hija
2. visitar / el señor López en el hospital
3. llamar / Teresita antes de las tres
4. visitar / el colegio de sus hijos
5. invitar / la señorita Torres a comer

COMUNICACIÓN

A. ¿Qué miras? Using vocabulary you know, make a list of five things or people you are looking at in the classroom.

EJEMPLO Miro los libros.
Miro al profesor.

B. Curiosidad. Make up questions to ask others about their lives. Then, have them answer your questions.

EJEMPLO ¿Escuchas a tu hermana?
Sí, escucho a mi hermana.
No, no escucho a mi hermana.

llamar	tus amigos
mirar	la radio
escuchar	los discos de los Beatles
ayudar	la profesora / el profesor
esperar	la música clásica
invitar	tus padres
buscar	los partidos de fútbol
cuidar	¿ . . . ?

RINCÓN CULTURAL

Each year high school students from the United States participate in exchange programs with schools in Spanish-speaking countries. One of the surprises in store for them in the new culture comes the day they receive report cards. How would you react if you got a "7" in algebra? or a "5" in geography? Instead of using letter grades, these schools use a 10-point grading system.

Look at Olivia Sánchez's report card. Would you say her parents are going to be happy or upset about her grades?

EVALUACION FINAL

Materias	Notas
Lengua Española Literatura	5
Lengua Extranjera(. . inglés . .)	7.5
Historia-Geografía	9
Matemáticas	7
Ciencias Naturales	5.7
Educación Física	6.5
Latín-Griego	4
Dibujo	7
Música	6.5

Notas

8.5 Sobresaliente	5 Suficiente
7 Notable	2.5 Insuficiente
5.6 Bueno	0 Muy Deficiente

EXPLORACIÓN

Talking about things you do
Regular **er** *verbs and* **ver**

PRESENTACIÓN

Just as there is a group of verbs with infinitives ending in **ar**, there is another group with infinitives ending in **er**. Study the endings of the verb **comprender** (*to understand*).

comprender

comprend**o**	comprend**emos**
comprend**es**	
comprend**e**	comprend**en**

Here are some other verbs like **comprender**.

aprender (a) to learn (to)
comer to eat
leer to read
deber should, to have to
prometer to promise

¿Aprendes francés en el colegio? — Are you learning French in school?
Mi padre lee muchas revistas. — My father reads a lot of magazines.
¿A qué hora comen ustedes? — At what time do you eat?
Prometo llamar más tarde. — I promise to call later.

Ver is regular except for its **yo** form. Learn its forms.

ver

veo	vemos
ves	
ve	ven

Veo bien con lentes. — I see well with glasses.
Vemos al señor Peña todos los días. — We see Mr. Peña every day.

Here are some vocabulary words often used with **leer**.

la novela (*novel*)
el periódico (*newspaper*)
la lección (*lesson*)
la poesía (*poetry*)

PREPARACIÓN

A. Salón de estudios. Yolanda is noticing the variety of materials her friends are reading in study hall. What does she say?

MODELO Tomás / un libro de poesía
Tomás lee un libro de poesía.

1. Jesús y yo / un libro de geografía
2. Ángela / una novela
3. Adán y Alfonso / unas revistas
4. Marina / un periódico
5. Yo / un libro de contabilidad
6. Tú / unas historietas

B. ¿Qué aprenden? The Marín family keeps active. Tell what they say they are learning to do.

MODELO

La señora Marín aprende a jugar tenis.

1. El señor Marín

2. Luis y Víctor

3. Yo

4. Nosotros

5. Tú

6. Evita

C. Deberes. Señora García is telling her family what everyone ought to do today. What does she say?

MODELO Mauricio / estudiar matemáticas
Mauricio debe estudiar matemáticas.

1. Mario y Lorenzo / ayudar en casa
2. Tú / hacer la tarea
3. Nosotros / cocinar ahora
4. Ustedes / lavar el coche
5. Yo / ir de compras más tarde
6. Verónica / estudiar su lección de álgebra

D. Una fiesta. Señor Romero is planning a party and wants to make sure it's a success. How do his students promise to help?

MODELO Pablo / cocinar
Pablo promete cocinar.

1. Nosotros / invitar a todos
2. Los chicos / bailar
3. Yo / lavar los platos
4. Alonso / tocar la guitarra
5. Ustedes / cantar
6. Tú / sacar muchas fotos

E. ¿Ves bien? Señora Gutiérrez is checking students for eye problems. What does she say?

MODELO Rosa
¿Ve Rosa bien el cartel?

1. Josefa y María
2. Manuel
3. Usted
4. Ustedes
5. Tú
6. Los chicos

F. ¡Qué mañana! The Suárez family is having a hectic morning, and no one can find anything. What do they say?

MODELO Yo / mis llaves
Yo no veo mis llaves.

1. Antonio / su calculadora
2. Lidia / su mochila
3. Los abuelos / su cámara
4. Tú / tus lentes
5. Nosotros / nuestros cuadernos

COLEGIO SAN IGNACIO
Río Piedras, Puerto Rico 00927
TARJETA DE IDENTIFICACION DE ESTUDIANTES
Expira el 15 de junio
Sr. Antonio Suárez
Clase '88 Tel. 781-6980

G. El reportero. Pablo Quintero, a reporter for New York's *El diario*, has questions for students who have won scholarships to the university. What does he ask?

MODELO leer / mucha poesía
¿Leen ustedes mucha poesía?

1. aprender / programación
2. comprender / matemáticas
3. leer / muchos periódicos
4. ver / muchas películas
5. aprender / español aquí
6. deber / estudiar mucho

COMUNICACIÓN

A. Tareas difíciles. Tell which homework assignments you understand and which you don't.

EJEMPLO Comprendo la tarea de matemáticas.
No comprendo la tarea de contabilidad.

matemáticas	programación de computadoras
francés	ciencias
economía	química
biología	historia
mecanografía	?

B. Obligaciones. Use the suggestions below to tell what you ought to do.

EJEMPLO estudiar
Debo estudiar historia.

estudiar	leer	mirar	comprar
ir	practicar	aprender (a)	arreglar

C. Promesas. You've decided to turn over a new leaf. What do you promise?

EJEMPLO Prometo escuchar a los profesores.
Prometo no mirar la tele cuando debo estudiar.

RINCÓN CULTURAL

Teen-agers in the United States go to high school. But Spanish-speaking teen-agers have other options, such as attending an ***escuela normal***, which prepares the student to be a teacher, or an ***escuela técnica***, which prepares the student for an office career. The equivalent of the American high school is the ***colegio***, which prepares students in the liberal arts and for further study in the universities.

There are many similarities between high school and ***colegio***, but there are some differences, too. For example, how would you feel about going to school for five hours a day instead of six? How would you react to not having weekly tests and quizzes but rather having your entire grade depend on your final exam—part of which is oral?

Finally, not all secondary schools in Latin America are ***mixtos*** (*co-ed*). Do you think you'd be able to concentrate better in class if you were in an all boys' or all girls' school?

Would you rather go to a ***colegio*** than to a high school?

EXPLORACIÓN

Telling when
Days of the week

PRESENTACIÓN

To talk about when things happen, you need to know the days (**los días**) of the week.

lunes Monday	**martes** Tuesday	**miércoles** Wednesday	**jueves** Thursday	**viernes** Friday	**sábado** Saturday	**domingo** Sunday
	1	2	3	4	5	6
7	8	9	10	11	12	13
14	15	16	17	18	19	20
21	22	23	24	25	26	27
28	29	30	31			

A. Usually the definite article is used with the days of the week.

El lunes es mi cumpleaños. Monday is my birthday.

B. To indicate that the action happens *on* a particular day, the definite article **el** is used. If something happens repeatedly on a certain day, **los** is used with the day of the week in the plural.

Tenemos examen **el** viernes.
We have a test *on* Friday.

Visito a mis abuelos **los** domingos.
I visit my grandparents *on* Sundays.

C. To ask what day of the week it is, say:

¿Qué día es hoy? Hoy es miércoles.

Notice that the definite article is not used after **es** with words like **hoy** or **mañana**.

PREPARACIÓN

A. Una semana de exámenes. Margarita's friend Sergio has lost his schedule and needs to know when the exams are. How does Margarita answer his questions?

	L	M	M	J	V
Mañana	*educación física*	*historia*	*inglés*	*francés*	*arte*
Tarde	*matemáticas*		*biología*		

MODELO ¿Cuándo es el examen de inglés?
Es el miércoles por la mañana.

1. ¿Cuándo es el examen de arte?
2. ¿Cuándo es el examen de matemáticas?
3. ¿Cuándo es el examen de francés?
4. ¿Cuándo es el examen de historia?
5. ¿Cuándo es el examen de biología?
6. ¿Cuándo es el examen de educación física?

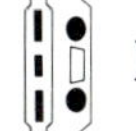

B. Siempre ocupada. Susana wants to set a date with Marisela, but her friend has commitments for every day of the week for months. What does Marisela say?

MODELO domingo / cantar en la iglesia
Los domingos canto en la iglesia.

1. lunes / ayudar a mi abuela en casa
2. martes / deber arreglar mi cuarto
3. miércoles / trabajar en la biblioteca
4. jueves / practicar tenis
5. viernes / tener una clase de francés
6. sábado / ir de compras
7. domingo / comer en casa de mis abuelos

COMUNICACIÓN

A. Visita de un amigo español. Imagine that a Spanish exchange student is spending a week with you. Plan different activities for each day of the week.

EJEMPLO El lunes visitamos el museo.

lunes	
martes	
miércoles	
jueves	
viernes	
sábado	
domingo	

B. Esta semana. Using vocabulary you know, plan your activities for the coming week.

EJEMPLO El sábado por la tarde voy a ver una película.
El martes tengo una clase de baile después de la escuela.

PERSPECTIVAS

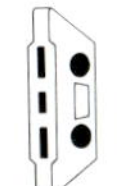

La hora de la verdad

truth

get up

glove, mitt

Es el lunes por la mañana y los estudiantes del Colegio Simón Bolívar siempre están contentos de ir a la escuela. Por ejemplo, aquí vemos a Vanesa que pronto debe salir para la escuela.

students

who / to leave

what

Por la tarde cuando entra el profesor de química en el laboratorio todos están listos para escuchar las explicaciones del profesor. ¡Tienen tanto que aprender!

ready

Al día siguiente, durante el examen de química, los futuros científicos finalmente aprenden su lección. next / during / scientists

I don't believe it.

COMPRENSIÓN

Answer the following questions based on **La hora de la verdad**.

1. ¿Cómo están los estudiantes el lunes por la mañana?
2. ¿A qué hora llama a Vanesa su madre?
3. ¿Qué busca Vanesa?
4. ¿Qué deben hacer los estudiantes en la clase de química?
5. ¿Qué planes tiene el chico para esta noche?
6. ¿Qué leen las chicas?
7. Al día siguiente, ¿qué aprenden los estudiantes?

COMUNICACIÓN

A. Un día en la vida de un(a) estudiante. Answer the questions below or use them to interview another student about a typical day in his or her life.

1. ¿Cuándo vas al colegio por la mañana?
2. ¿Qué clases tienes por la mañana? ¿ Y por la tarde?
3. ¿Vas a la biblioteca todos los días?
4. ¿Con quién comes al mediodía?
5. ¿A quién esperas después del colegio?
6. ¿A qué hora regresas a casa?
7. ¿Trabajas después de la escuela? ¿Dónde trabajas?
8. ¿Cuándo debes hacer la tarea?
9. ¿Qué ves en la tele por la noche?
10. ¿Lees por la noche? ¿Qué lees?

B. **Intercambio estudiantil.** Imagine you are an exchange student at the Colegio Luis Vives in Valencia, Spain. What would you ask in order to find out as much as possible about your new school?

EJEMPLO ¿Son difíciles los exámenes?
¿Tienen recreo aquí?

C. **¿Qué debes hacer?** Using the cues or other words you know, tell what you should do in the following situations.

EJEMPLO Tienes un examen muy difícil mañana. (estudiar)
Debo estudiar mucho esta noche.
Debo escuchar muy bien la explicación del profesor hoy.

1. Hay examen mañana y tu libro está en el colegio. (buscar)
2. Tienes que buscar un libro sobre la historia de España. (biblioteca)
3. Tu hermano nunca está listo para ir al colegio por la mañana. (mirar/reloj)
4. No te gusta la comida de la cafetería. (comer/casa)
5. Quieres aprender programación de computadoras pero no hay clases en tu escuela. (leer/comprar)
6. Hay una fiesta y quieres invitar a tus amigos. (llamar)

VOCABULARIO DEL CAPÍTULO

NOUNS RELATING TO SCHOOL SUBJECTS

el álgebra (*f*) algebra
el arte art
la biología biology
las ciencias science
la contabilidad bookkeeping, accounting
la educación física physical education
la física physics
el francés French
la geografía geography
la geometría geometry
la historia history
las matemáticas math
la mecanografía typing
la programación de computadoras computer programming
la química chemistry

OTHER NOUNS

el científico scientist
el colegio school
el (la) estudiante student
la explicación explanation
el grupo group
el guante glove, mitt
la hora time, hour
el instituto institute
el laboratorio laboratory
la lección lesson
la novela novel
el periódico newspaper
la poesía poetry
los planes plan
el programa program
el recreo recess
la verdad truth

ADJECTIVES

esta this
futuro future
listo ready
loco crazy
ocupado busy
pesadísimo very heavy
siguiente next, following

VERBS

aprender (a) to learn (to)
buscar to look for
comer to eat
comprender to understand
deber to have to, should
entrar (en) to enter
esperar to wait for
invitar to invite
leer to read
prometer to promise
salir to leave
ver to see

ADVERBS AND PREPOSITIONS

después de after, afterwards
durante during
finalmente finally
para for, headed for
primero first

EXPRESSIONS OF TIME

cuarto quarter (hour)
en punto sharp, on the dot
la medianoche midnight
el mediodía noon
menos before the hour
por la mañana in the morning
por la noche at night
por la tarde in the afternoon, evening
¿Qué hora es? What time is it?

OTHER EXPRESSIONS

al día siguiente the next day
¡Arriba! Get up!
¡Ay, no! Oh, no!
¿cuál? what, which one?
¡Dios mío! My goodness!
¡No lo creo! I don't believe it!
pobrecito poor little thing
por supuesto of course
tanto que hacer so much to do

Capítulo seis

FAVORITE FOODS

6

INTRODUCCIÓN

¿Cuál es tu problema?

Cecilia Martín has decided to improve her health and has found some good advice in a magazine article. What does the article suggest for various problems its readers have?

Tu problema	Nuestra solución	
Quiero bajar de peso, pero me gusta la comida, y sobre todo me gustan los dulces.	¿Por qué no comes menos carne y más vegetales y frutas? También debes tomar más agua.	lose weight / meat food sweets / drink / water
Tengo problemas para dormir por la noche.	Durante el día, tienes que evitar el café y el té. Antes de dormir, debes tomar un poco de leche.	sleeping / avoid a little / milk
Durante el día siempre estoy cansada. No tengo ni energía ni ganas de trabajar.	Necesitas más ejercicio. ¿Qué te parece hacer gimnasia, o quizás practicar un deporte?	neither / nor
Por la mañana, no tengo tiempo para preparar el desayuno.	No hay problema. ¡Es fácil! ¿Porqué no comes pan con mantequilla y mermelada?	time breakfast / bread butter
Quiero aumentar de peso.	¡Fantástico! Tienes que comer más postres y helado.	to gain weight desserts / ice cream

COMPRENSIÓN

Fill in the blanks based on **¿Cuál es tu problema?**

1. Si quieres bajar de peso, debes comer más ________ y ________.
2. Para dormir bien tienes que tomar ________.
3. Si siempre estás cansado durante el día, necesitas más ________.
4. Un desayuno fácil es pan con ________ y ________.
5. Para aumentar de peso, debes comer más ________ y ________.

COMUNICACIÓN

What kinds of food do you like? Using the scale below, indicate how much you like or dislike each item.

no me gusta nada	no me gusta	me gusta bastante	me gusta mucho

1. ¿Qué comida te gusta más?

el desayuno

el almuerzo

la cena

2. ¿Qué clase de carne te gusta más?

la carne asada

el pollo

el pescado

las chuletas de cerdo (*pork chops*)

el bistec

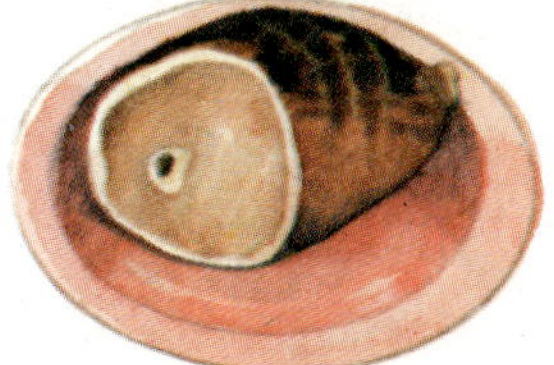

el jamón

3. ¿Qué vegetales te gustan más?

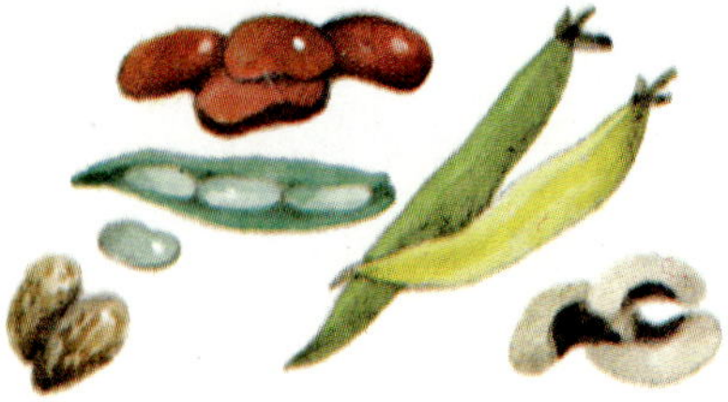

las habichuelas (*beans*)  | las papas  | los plátanos

el arroz  | los tomates  | la ensalada

4. ¿Qué clase de postres te gustan más?

el queso  | los pasteles  | las frutas  | el helado

5. ¿Qué clase de frutas te gustan más?

las manzanas  | las uvas  | las peras

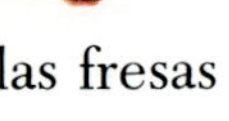

las fresas

las naranjas

el melón

6. ¿Qué te gusta tomar con las comidas?

el chocolate | el agua mineral | el té

los refrescos | el café con leche | el jugo de naranja

7. ¿Qué clase de desayuno te gusta más?

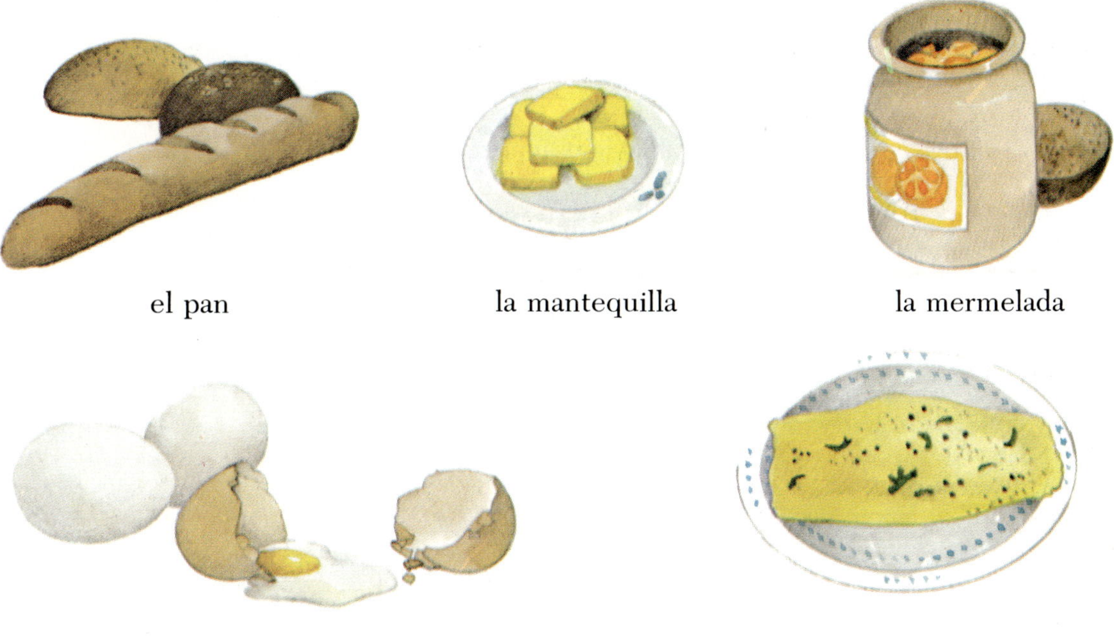

el pan | la mantequilla | la mermelada

los huevos | la tortilla

EXPLORACIÓN

Talking about things you do
ir *verbs and irregular* **er** *and* **ir** *verbs*

PRESENTACIÓN

There are three classes of verbs in Spanish. You have already learned the endings for **ar** verbs and **er** verbs. The third class ends in **ir**.

A. Regular **ir** verbs differ from the **er** verbs only in the **nosotros** form. Study the forms of **vivir** (*to live*).

vivir

viv**o**	viv**imos**
viv**es**	
viv**e**	viv**en**

Here are some other regular **ir** verbs.

abrir to open
permitir to permit, allow
asistir a to attend
insistir (en) to insist on
recibir to receive
escribir to write

Carlos abre sus regalos de cumpleaños.
Siempre insisten en hablar español.
Mi mamá nunca permite perros en la casa.
Recibimos tarjetas de nuestros amigos.
Su hermano asiste a clases todos los días.

B. Some **er** or **ir** verbs are irregular because the **yo** form does not follow the pattern. The other forms are like those of regular **er** or **ir** verbs. Study the forms of **hacer** (*to do, to make*).

hacer

hago	hacemos
haces	
hace	hacen

Here are other verbs that are irregular in the **yo** form.

verbo		yo	nosotros
traer	to bring	**traigo**	traemos
poner	to put, place, set	**pongo**	ponemos
salir (se)	to leave, go out	**salgo**	salimos

PREPARACIÓN

A. ¿Qué traes? The Spanish class at Balboa High School is having a **comilona** (*feast*). Tell what the following people say they are bringing.

MODELO el profesor / pan
El profesor trae pan.

1. Celia y Lola / arroz con pollo
2. Carolina / jugo de manzana
3. Yo / ensalada
4. Miguel y Geraldo / unos pasteles
5. Tú / helado
6. Nosotros / queso

B. ¿Dónde . . . ? Miguelina's party guests are arriving and want to know where to put things. What do they ask?

MODELO Nosotros / ensalada
¿Dónde ponemos la ensalada?

1. Yo / los discos
2. Tú / la comida
3. César y yo / la cámara
4. David y Enrique / las cintas
5. Rita / los juegos electrónicos
6. Nosotros / los refrescos

C. ¡Viva la cocina! Some students are interested in cooking. What are they preparing?

MODELO Tito / un pastel
Tito hace un pastel.

1. Tú / una chuleta
2. Nosotros / un bistec
3. Mónica y Francisca / una ensalada
4. Rafael / un jamón
5. Yo / un pastel
6. Los chicos / un pollo

D. ¡Qué barbaridad! A television program has given surprise gifts to the winners of a contest. As the winners read their gift certificates, they realize they all receive the same thing. What do they say?

MODELO ¿Y Margarita?
Margarita también recibe una cena.

1. ¿Y la señora Ramírez?
2. ¿Y ustedes?
3. ¿Y Emilio y Verónica?
4. ¿Y nosotros?
5. ¿Y yo?
6. ¿Y tú?

E. ¡Qué decisión! Pablo's friends have strong opinions and are making it difficult for him to plan his weekend. Where do his friends insist on going?

MODELO Jaime / cine
Jaime insiste en ir al cine.

1. Salvador y Tomás / café
2. Yo / parque
3. Lucía y Felicia / estadio
4. Ustedes / restaurante
5. Tú / partido de béisbol
6. Manuel / concierto

F. Una familia estricta. Manolo's family is very strict. He is telling his friends what he is not allowed to have or do.

MODELO Mi padre / los refrescos
Mi padre no permite los refrescos.

1. Mi abuelo / la lucha libre
2. Mi tía / los dulces
3. Mi abuela / el café
4. Mis tíos / las novelas
5. Mi padre / la música rock
6. Mi familia / los juegos electrónicos

G. ¡Qué vida! The following people spend so much time in these places that they seem to live there. What do they say?

MODELO Yo . . . escuela
Yo vivo en la escuela.

1. Usted . . . el bote
2. Juan Miguel . . . la biblioteca
3. Tú . . . la plaza
4. Nosotros . . . el museo
5. Ellos . . . el parque
6. Yo . . . el cine

H. ¿A qué hora? Throughout the day, students have appointments with the guidance counselor. When is each interview over?

MODELO José Luis / 2:15
José Luis sale a las dos y cuarto.

1. Marilú / 8:45
2. Yo / 9:00
3. Los hermanos Díaz / 10:15
4. Nosotros / 11:30
5. Tú / 12:20
6. Ustedes / 1:50

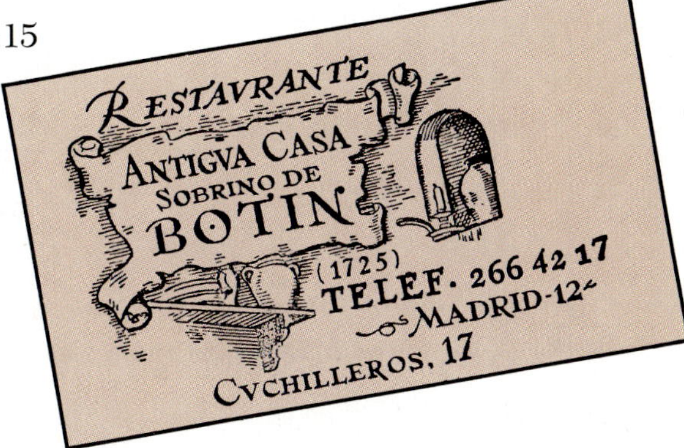

COMUNICACIÓN

A. Entrevista. Answer the following questions or use them to interview other students.

EJEMPLO En general, ¿traes fruta a la escuela?
Sí, traigo fruta a la escuela.

1. ¿Siempre traes tu almuerzo al colegio?
2. ¿Qué traes para comer al mediodía?
3. ¿Quién hace el desayuno en tu casa?
4. ¿Pones queso o jamón en la tortilla?
5. ¿Quién hace la cena en tu casa?
6. ¿Quieres aumentar o bajar de peso?
7. ¿Insiste tu mamá en salir a comer para su cumpleaños?
8. ¿Permite la profesora de español comer dulces en su clase?
9. Y tú, ¿insistes en comer dulces en clase?
10. ¿Cuántas horas necesitas dormir?
11. ¿Escribes tarjetas?

B. Una cena perfecta. Imagine you're serving a perfect dinner. What dishes are you setting on the table for your friends?

EJEMPLO Pongo arroz con pollo, una ensalada y queso.

C. Nueva imagen. Imagine you've decided to take better care of yourself. However, your friends aren't as health conscious, and so you have to insist on following your diet.

EJEMPLO Insisto en no tomar refrescos.

Insisto en
Insisto en no

dormir ocho horas
tomar leche
comer dulces
hacer gimnasia
tomar agua
tomar el desayuno
comer postres
descansar
tomar helado
comer más vegetales
¿ . . . ?

RINCÓN CULTURAL

¿Comen hamburguesas en Latinoamérica y España? Sí, pero pocas veces. La hamburguesa hispana es diferente a la hamburguesa norteamericana. Tiene muchos condimentos y siempre tiene cebollas (*onions*).

En España y en Latinoamérica hoy día existen varios restaurantes de comida al paso (*fast food*). Pero la mayoría de los hispanos prefieren el almuerzo tradicional. En general, las tiendas y las oficinas cierran (*close*) entre las doce y las dos de la tarde. Todos van a casa para comer. Y después de un almuerzo grande toman una siesta antes de regresar al trabajo. ¡Qué bueno!, ¿verdad?

EXPLORACIÓN

Talking about how you feel
Expressions with **tener**

PRESENTACIÓN

To talk about how you feel at certain times, such as being hungry or sleepy, you need to use **tener**.

A. To talk about being cold or afraid, the verb **tener** is used with the nouns **frío** (*cold*) and **miedo** (*fear*). This is different from English, which uses the verb *to be* with adjectives. Compare:

Tengo frío.	I'm cold.
¿Tienes miedo?	Are you afraid?

B. Here are expressions with **tener** that will help you express how you feel.

tener calor (*m*)	to be hot
tener frío	to be cold
tener hambre (*f*)	to be hungry
tener sed (*f*)	to be thirsty
tener sueño	to be sleepy
tener razón (*f*)	to be right
tener miedo	to be afraid
tener prisa	to be in a hurry

C. Note that when you say that you are very hungry or very sleepy, you use **mucho** or **mucha**.

Vicente no tiene mucha hambre ahora.
Felisa siempre tiene mucho sueño por la mañana.

PREPARACIÓN

A. En el café. The Cordero family is ordering things to eat and drink. Based on what they say, complete their statements with the appropriate form of **tener hambre** or **tener sed**.

MODELO

B. ¡Típico! Liliana's friends can be described by how they always feel. What does she say about herself and her friends?

MODELO Diana / frío
Diana siempre tiene frío.

1. Pilar / sueño
2. Nosotras / prisa
3. Miguel y Pepe / hambre
4. Ustedes / calor
5. Tú / miedo
6. Yo / razón

C. ¡Atención! La señora Martínez is always concerned that her children be well taken care of. Give their answers to her questions.

MODELO ¿Tienen ustedes sueño? (no)
No, no tenemos sueño.

1. ¿Tienes mucha hambre, Mónica? (sí)
2. Y tu hermana, ¿tiene sueño? (no)
3. Y tus hermanos, ¿tienen sed? (sí)
4. ¿Tienen Roberto y Santiago calor? (no)
5. ¿Tienen ustedes mucho frío? (no)

COMUNICACIÓN

A. Reacciones. How would you feel if you were in each of the following situations?

EJEMPLO Son las nueve menos diez y tienes que estar en clase a las nueve.
Tengo mucha prisa.

1. Nunca tomas el desayuno y ahora es mediodía.
2. Hace mucho frío en la casa y no tienes suéter.
3. Después de hacer gimnasia, no tienes dinero para un refresco.
4. Siempre estudias de noche. ¿Cómo estás por la mañana?
5. Tu hermanita insiste en que dos y dos son cinco. Tú insistes que no.
6. Estás en un parque. Es muy tarde por la noche y tú no ves nada.

B. Entrevista. Answer the following questions or use them to interview another student.

1. ¿Tienes mucha sed o mucha hambre ahora?
2. ¿Tienes calor o frío ahora?
3. ¿Siempre tienes razón?
4. ¿A veces tienes miedo de noche?
5. Cuando tienes hambre, ¿qué comes?
6. Cuando tienes sed, ¿qué tomas?
7. ¿Muchas veces tienes sueño en el colegio?

RINCÓN CULTURAL

Las ilustraciones siguientes representan comidas bastante típicas de una familia hispana.

El desayuno
Por la mañana hay . . .
café con leche o chocolate
pan
mantequilla
mermelada

El almuerzo
Al mediodía hay . . .
arroz con pollo
ensalada
queso y guayaba
café

La cena
Por la noche hay . . .
sopa de vegetales
una tortilla y papas fritas
fresas con crema

Y tú, ¿qué comes para el desayuno, el almuerzo y la cena?

EXPLORACIÓN

Talking about what you know
The verbs **saber** *and* **conocer**

PRESENTACIÓN

The verbs **saber** and **conocer** both mean *to know.* Except for the **yo** form, all forms of these two verbs are regular.

saber

sé	sabemos
sabes	
sabe	saben

conocer

conozco	conocemos
conoces	
conoce	conocen

A. **Saber** means *to know a fact, to have information,* or *to know how to do something.* It can, therefore, be followed by a noun, a clause, or an infinitive.

José sabe francés.	José knows French.
Sé dónde está.	I know where he is.
No saben cocinar.	They don't know how to cook.

B. **Conocer** means *to be acquainted with* or *to be familiar with.* It is usually followed by names of people, places, or things.

¿Conocen a mi hermana?	Do you know my sister?
No conocemos Madrid.	We don't know Madrid.
¿Conoces la revista *Tú*?	Are you familiar with the magazine *Tú*?

C. Here are some expressions for talking about the restaurants you know.

saber conocer

el menú el precio la camarera el camarero el cocinero la cocinera

PREPARACIÓN

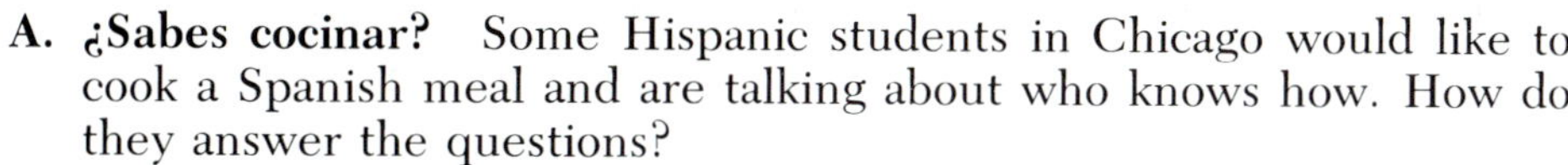

A. ¿Sabes cocinar? Some Hispanic students in Chicago would like to cook a Spanish meal and are talking about who knows how. How do they answer the questions?

MODELO ¿Mariano? (sí)
Sí, Mariano sabe cocinar.

1. ¿Y Jesús? (sí)
2. ¿Y tú? (no)
3. ¿Y ustedes? (sí)
4. ¿Y Olga? (sí)
5. ¿Y Dolores y Ricardo? (no)
6. ¿Y Marisela? (sí)

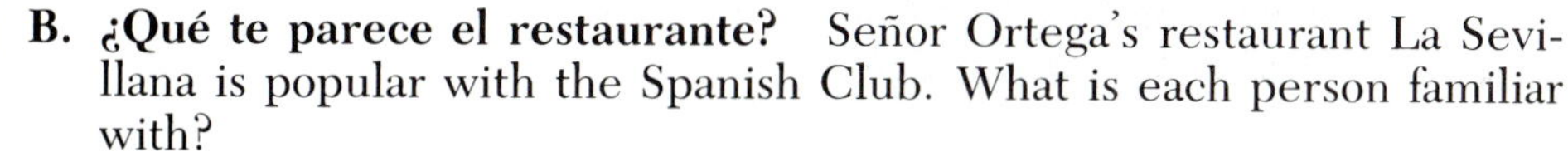

B. ¿Qué te parece el restaurante? Señor Ortega's restaurant La Sevillana is popular with the Spanish Club. What is each person familiar with?

MODELO Marisol / el restaurante
Marisol conoce el restaurante.

1. Tú / el menú
2. Nosotros / al señor Ortega
3. Alicia y Patricia / al cocinero
4. Ustedes / a los camareros
5. Yo / la comida
6. Usted / el restaurante

C. Hamburguesas al minuto. Paco is applying for a job in La Hamburguesa Real. Using **saber** or **conocer**, tell what the owner asks him.

MODELO hacer hamburguesas — **¿Sabes hacer hamburguesas?**
mi restaurante — **¿Conoces mi restaurante?**

1. los clientes
2. el menú
3. cocinar
4. los precios
5. el cocinero
6. hacer una tortilla

COMUNICACIÓN

A. ¿Qué sabes hacer? Using the words below, make up questions to find out what your classmates know how to do.

EJEMPLO hacer hamburguesas
¿Sabes hacer hamburguesas?

1. hacer pan
2. preparar un bistec
3. cocinar arroz
4. hacer café
5. cocinar plátanos
6. preparar una tortilla
7. hacer un pastel de manzana
8. qué hacer para bajar de peso

B. Conocer es comprender. Get to know the people in your class by asking them questions using **saber** or **conocer**.

EJEMPLO hacer arroz con pollo
¿Sabes hacer arroz con pollo?

jugar volibol
la música de Kenny Rogers
nadar
preparar un plato español
el museo de arte
si hay una fiesta hoy
el número de teléfono de tus amigos
hacer arroz
si va a hacer frío mañana
programar computadoras
un restaurante español
el precio de tu bicicleta
francés
¿ . . . ?

RINCÓN CULTURAL

Cuando los norteamericanos necesitan pan, leche o frutas, generalmente van al supermercado. También los hispanos muchas veces van al supermercado. Pero muchos de ellos prefieren ir a las tiendas pequeñas. ¿A qué tiendas van? Cuando necesitan leche, yogur, mantequilla o queso, van a la lechería. Para comprar fruta van a la frutería y si quieren dulces buscan una dulcería. Para comprar café, agua mineral, frutas, y vegetales, los hispanos van a la bodega.

Para comprar pan, van a la panadería.

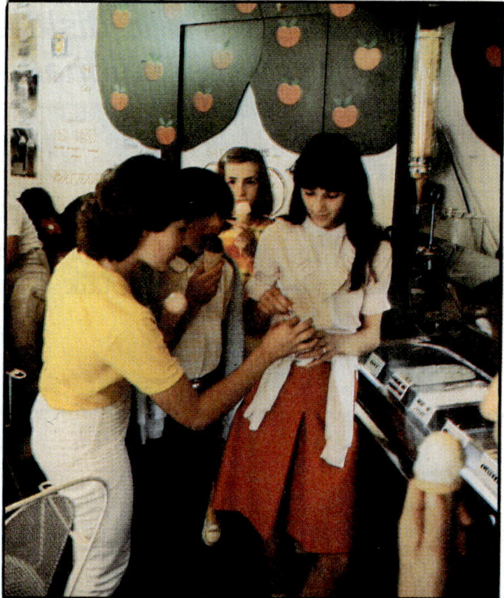

Compran helados en la heladería.

Cuando necesitan carne, van a la carnicería.

Y bueno, para comprar tartas y pasteles, van a la pastelería.

VOCABULARIO DEL CAPÍTULO

NOUNS REFERRING TO FOOD

el agua (*f*) water
el arroz rice
el bistec steak
el café coffee
el camarón shrimp
la carne meat
la carne asada roast beef
el cliente customer
la comida food
el chocolate chocolate, hot chocolate
la chuleta de cerdo pork chop
los dulces sweets
la ensalada salad
la fresa strawberry
la fruta fruit
las habichuelas beans
el helado ice cream
el huevo egg
el jamón ham
el jugo juice
la leche milk
la mantequilla butter
la manzana apple
el melón melon
la mermelada jam
la naranja orange
el pan bread
la papa potato
el pastel pastry, cookie, cake
la pera pear
el pescado fish
el plátano banana
el pollo chicken
el postre dessert
el queso cheese
el refresco soft drink
la salsa sauce
la sopa soup
la tarta tart, pie
el té tea
el tomate tomato
la tortilla omelet
la uva grape
el vegetal vegetable

OTHER NOUNS

el almuerzo lunch
el camarero waiter
la cena supper, dinner
el cocinero cook
el desayuno breakfast
la dificultad difficulty
el ejercicio exercise
la energía energy
la entrada appetizer
el menú menu
el minuto minute
el precio price
la selección selection
la solución solution
el tiempo time

VERBS

abrir to open
asistir a to attend
conocer to know
desear to want, wish
dormir to sleep
escribir to write
evitar to avoid
hacer to do, make
insistir en to insist on
necesitar to need
permitir (de) to permit
poner to put, place, set
preparar to prepare
recibir to receive
saber to know
salir (de) to leave, go out
tomar to take, have (eat, drink)
traer to bring
vivir to live

EXPRESSIONS WITH *TENER*

tener calor (*m*) to be hot
tener frío to be cold
tener hambre (*f*) to be hungry
tener miedo to be afraid
tener prisa to be in a hurry
tener razón (*f*) to be right
tener sed (*f*) to be thirsty
tener sueño to be sleepy

OTHER WORDS AND EXPRESSIONS

aumentar de peso to gain weight
bajar de peso to lose weight
con mucho gusto with pleasure
de noche at night
lo mismo the same
ni . . . ni neither . . . nor
un poco de a little of

Capítulo siete

ENTERTAINMENT 7

INTRODUCCIÓN

Un juego electrónico en la familia

CARLOS	Emilio, ¿qué haces aquí todavía?	
EMILIO	¡Caramba! Carlos, ¿no ves que tengo un minuto extra? Mi total es de 2.365* puntos.	Wow!
CARLOS	¡No es para tanto! Pero debes bajar la voz. Mamá quiere oír su programa.	Big deal! / voice / to hear
EMILIO	Está bien. Mira 3.000 . . . 3.500* ¡No lo creo!	
MAMÁ	Niños, ¿qué hacen aquí todavía? Ya son las nueve de la noche y tienen tarea.	children
LOS NIÑOS	Pero mamá, por favor, unos minutos más.	
MAMÁ	¡No! Porque mañana van a estar cansados.	
ABUELA	Silvia, no debes ser así. Un rato más, ¿no? En mi opinión, este juego enseña mucho.	while / teaches
LOS NIÑOS	Gracias, abuelita.	
MAMÁ	Bueno, está bien. Pero sólo unos minutos más.	only
ABUELA	Sí, además, yo también quiero jugar.	

COMPRENSIÓN

Tell which members of the family would probably make the following statements.

1. No queremos hacer la tarea.
2. Éste es mi mejor juego.
3. ¡Caramba! ¡Tú y tu minuto extra!
4. Yo también voy a jugar.
5. Van a estar cansados mañana.

*Dos mil trescientos sesenta y cinco; tres mil . . . tres mil quinientos.

COMUNICACIÓN

¿Cuáles son tus programas favoritos? Using the scale below, tell how well you like each type of program.

No me gusta nada. No me gusta mucho.  Me gusta.  Me gusta mucho.  Me encanta.

los reportajes deportivos

los partidos

los concursos

los anuncios

los documentales

las novelas

las películas policíacas

las películas de ciencia-ficción

las noticias

los dibujos animados

las comedias

las variedades

el pronóstico del tiempo

EXPLORACIÓN

Referring to something or someone already mentioned
Direct object pronouns **lo, la, los, las**

PRESENTACIÓN

Just as we use subject pronouns to avoid repetition of names, we can use direct object pronouns to refer to someone or something already mentioned. The direct object tells who or what receives the action of the verb.

Singular	
him, it, you	lo
her, it, you	la

Plural	
los	them, you
las	them, you

A. The pronoun agrees in gender and in number with the noun replaced and comes right before the verb (even if there is a negative word or verb phrase).

Raúl escucha **el disco**.	Raúl **lo** escucha.
Ella comprende **la lección**.	Ella **la** comprende.
¿Quieres **los libros**?	¿**Los** quieres?
No miro **las noticias**.	No **las** miro.

Note that it may also be attached to the infinitive.

¿Vas a buscar **las llaves**?	¿**Las** vas a buscar? ¿Vas a buscar**las**?

B. When the pronoun replaces a person as direct object, the personal **a** is no longer needed.

Manuel escucha **a Carlos**.	Manuel **lo** escucha.
¿Conoces **a las niñas**?	¿**Las** conoces?

C. **Lo**, **la**, **los**, and **las** are also used in place of **usted** and **ustedes** as direct objects.

La ayudo.	I'm helping *you*. (*fem. sing.*)
Lo vamos a invitar.	We're going to invite *you*. (*masc. sing.*)
Las llama.	He calls *you*. (*fem. pl.*)
Los necesitamos.	We need *you*. (*masc. and fem. pl.*)

D. Los is used when referring to both masculine and feminine nouns.

¿Conoces **a Luis y a Elena**? — Sí, **los** conozco.
¿Quieren ver **la revista y el periódico**? — Sí, quieren ver**los**.

PREPARACIÓN

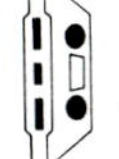

A. El fin de semana. Carmen is going away for the weekend and is checking to see if she has everything she needs. What does she ask herself?

MODELO ¿el libro?
Sí, lo tengo.

1. ¿el disco de Julio Iglesias?
2. ¿el juego electrónico?
3. ¿el suéter?
4. ¿el diccionario?
5. ¿el reloj?
6. ¿el gato?

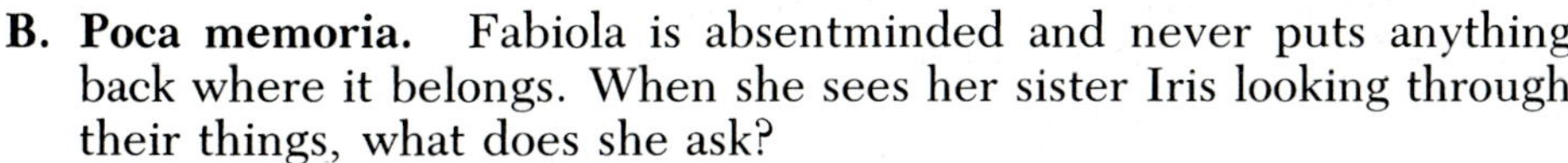

B. Poca memoria. Fabiola is absentminded and never puts anything back where it belongs. When she sees her sister Iris looking through their things, what does she ask?

MODELO ¿Buscas mi grabadora?
Sí, la busco.

1. ¿Buscas mi máquina de escribir?
2. ¿Buscas mi novela?
3. ¿Buscas mi pulsera?
4. ¿Buscas mi revista?
5. ¿Buscas mi calculadora?
6. ¿Buscas mi radio?

C. Julio, el fanático. An avid TV fan, Julio is taking part in a survey of teenagers' viewing habits. How does he answer?

MODELO ¿Miras los anuncios?
Sí, los miro siempre.

1. ¿Miras los documentales?
2. ¿Miras los concursos?
3. ¿Miras los programas en español?
4. ¿Miras los reportajes deportivos?
5. ¿Miras los partidos?
6. ¿Miras los dibujos animados?

D. ¡Nunca! Lola, on the contrary, finds TV programs very boring. What does she say?

MODELO ¿Miras las novelas?
¡Ay no! Nunca las miro.

1. ¿Miras las noticias?
2. ¿Miras las comedias?
3. ¿Miras las películas de ciencia-ficción?
4. ¿Miras las variedades?
5. ¿Miras las películas policíacas?

E. En el cine. Ramona is at the movies with friends. Before the film begins, she wants to know who's there. What do her friends answer?

MODELO ¿Ves a José? **Sí, lo veo.** ¿Ves a María? **Sí, la veo.**

1. ¿Ves a Pedro?
2. ¿Ves a la señora Jiménez?
3. ¿Ves a tu prima?
4. ¿Ves a Juana y a Rosa?
5. ¿Ves a Ricardo y a José?
6. ¿Ves al señor Fernández?

F. Excursión. Before a Spanish Club trip, students are reassuring parents and teachers that they will be fine. What do they say?

MODELO señor Silva / ayudar
Pero, señor Silva, siempre lo ayudamos.

1. señor Barrios / escuchar
2. señora Ríos y señora Marín / ayudar
3. señorita Vallejo / escuchar
4. señor Torres y señor Yáñez / mirar
5. señor Ruiz y señora López / buscar
6. señora Miranda / esperar

COMUNICACIÓN

A. ¿Con qué frecuencia? Tell how often you do the following. Use the appropriate direct object pronoun in each of your statements.

EJEMPLO mirar las noticias
A veces las miro.
Nunca las miro.

1. mirar películas en la tele
2. lavar el coche
3. ayudar a tus padres
4. arreglar el cuarto
5. escuchar la radio
6. estudiar español

B. Entrevista. Answer the following questions or use them to interview another student. Use the appropriate direct object pronoun in each answer.

EJEMPLO ¿Cuándo haces la tarea?
La hago por la noche.

1. ¿Cuándo miras la tele?
2. ¿Cuándo lees tus revistas?
3. ¿Invitas a tus amigos a casa a veces?
4. ¿Ayudas a tus padres en casa?
5. ¿Lavas los platos a veces?
6. ¿Cuidas a tus hermanos a veces?
7. ¿Comes muchos dulces?
8. ¿Traes el almuerzo al colegio?
9. ¿Cuándo haces la tarea?
10. ¿Permiten tus padres la música rock?

C. Planes de fin de semana. Using the chart, plan your weekend schedule. Then, tell when you will do each activity. You may wish to add another activity or substitute one on the chart. Use the direct object pronouns.

EJEMPLO comprar discos
Los voy a comprar el sábado por la mañana.

ACTIVIDADES	SÁBADO			DOMINGO		
	por la mañana	por la tarde	por la noche	por la mañana	por la tarde	por la noche
comprar [discos]	x					
practicar [el tenis]						
arreglar mi cuarto						
ver una película						
hacer la tarea						
ir de compras						
tocar el piano						
visitar a los amigos						
?						

RINCÓN CULTURAL

La televisión es universal. ¿Cuántas horas miras tú la televisión? ¿Una? ¿dos? ¿tres? ¿O no la miras nunca? ¿Cuáles son tus programas favoritos? ¿Te gusta mirar las comedias o prefieres los documentales? ¿Prefieres los deportes o los concursos? En Latinoamérica y en España la televisión es una diversión popular también. Allí los programas norteamericanos son populares y se presentan en español. ¿Cuántos programas reconoces *(do you recognize)*?

15.35 VACACIONES EN EL MAR:
"Segunda vez"

A los ojos de sus colaboradores, el capitán Stubing aparece como un auténtico rompecorazones.

16.20 SABADO CINE:
"CASABLANCA"

Una pareja para la historia del cine: Ingrid Bergman y Humphrey Bogart.

18.15 TENIS: COPA DAVIS
ESPAÑA-YUGOSLAVIA

19.00 HAWAI 5-0: Jack Lord, protagonista de la serie policíaca.
"Hace mucho tiempo"

20.05 LAS DESVENTURAS DEL SHERIFF LOBO
"UNA BOMBA EN LOS AIRES"
(ULTIMO EPISODIO)

La inseparable pareja, Claude Akins y Mills Watson, se despiden hoy de nosotros.

21.00 FAMA:
"UN SITIO ESPECIAL"

Debbie Allen y Gene Anthony Ray.

EXPLORACIÓN

Using numbers
Numbers above 100; the ordinals

PRESENTACIÓN

A. Here are the numbers from 100 to 1,000,000.

100	cien, ciento	700	setecientos, as
200	doscientos, as	800	ochocientos, as
300	trescientos, as	900	novecientos, as
400	cuatrocientos, as	1000	mil
500	quinientos, as	2500	dos mil quinientos, as
600	seiscientos, as	1.000.000	un millón (de)

1. **Cien** is used before any noun, including **mil**.

   100 — cien estudiantes
   100,000 — cien mil dólares

   Cien becomes **ciento** when followed by another number.

   103 — ciento tres
   135 — ciento treinta y cinco

2. Two hundred to nine hundred agree in gender with the nouns they modify.

   398 — trescient**os** noventa y ocho **pesos**
   564 — quinient**as** sesenta y cuatro **pesetas**

3. **Uno** becomes **un** before a masculine singular noun; **una** is used before a feminine singular noun.

   121 — ciento veinti**ún** dólares (*masc.*)
   1.941 — mil novecientas cuarenta y **una** pesetas (*fem.*)

B. To talk about the order in which things or events are placed (first, second, third, etc.), use ordinal numbers.

1º, 1ª	primero, primera	6º, 6ª	sexto, sexta
2º, 2ª	segundo, segunda	7º, 7ª	séptimo, séptima
3º, 3ª	tercero, tercera	8º, 8ª	octavo, octava
4º, 4ª	cuarto, cuarta	9º, 9ª	noveno, novena
5º, 5ª	quinto, quinta	10º, 10ª	décimo, décima

Es la cuarta clase del día.
Tenemos que leer el segundo capítulo.

Before a masculine singular noun, **primero** and **tercero** become **primer** (1er) and **tercer** (3er).

Es su primer álbum en español.
Mañana vamos a estudiar el tercer capítulo.

A. In spoken Spanish, ordinal numbers are seldom used after 10. Cardinal numbers are used instead.

la Avenida Once	Eleventh Avenue
en el piso doce	on the twelfth floor

B. Ordinal numbers are commonly used with **vez** (*time, instance*). The word for *last* is **último**.

Es la primera vez que voy a España.
Es la última vez que salgo con ustedes.

C. Here are some vocabulary items often used with numbers: **piso** (*floor*); **avenida** (*avenue*); **calle** (*street*).

PREPARACIÓN

A. ¿En qué cuarto? People are asking the clerk at a hotel in Seville the room number of various guests. What does he answer?

MODELO El señor García / 240
El señor García está en el doscientos cuarenta.

1. La señorita Durán / 415
2. Los señores Campos / 923
3. El señor Martí / 162
4. La señora Abella / 788
5. Los señores Ramos / 551
6. La señorita Calderón / 275
7. El señor Torres / 344
8. Los señores Beltrán / 604

B. La independencia. Students are learning the year that the following countries celebrate as their year of independence. What do they say?

MODELO Ecuador / 1830
Ecuador, mil ochocientos treinta

1. Cuba / 1898
2. México / 1822
3. los Estados Unidos / 1776
4. República Dominicana / 1844
5. Panamá / 1903
6. Argentina / 1810

C. ¿En qué curso estás? In Latin America, each high school year is designated by an ordinal number. A student starts in **primero** then proceeds to **segundo**, **tercero**, and **cuarto**. How do these students indicate what grade they are in?

MODELO Mirna / 3º
Mirna está en tercero.

1. Pepe y Carlos / 2º
2. Yo / 1º
3. Marcela / 4º
4. Julia / 1º
5. Manolo y Josefa / 2º
6. Usted / 3º

D. ¿Dónde viven? Ricardo is updating his address book. Help him by supplying some missing information about where his friends live.

MODELO Juan Manuel / Calle 4
Juan Manuel vive en la Calle Cuatro.

Teresa / 8ª Avenida
Teresa vive en la Octava Avenida.

1. Cristina / 5ª Avenida
2. José Luis / Calle 54
3. Esteban / 3er piso
4. Carlos / 1ª Avenida
5. Rosa María / 1er piso
6. Yolanda / Calle 18
7. Rafael / 9º piso
8. Isabel / 7ª Avenida

E. Experiencias. Pepe is a tour guide in Spain and is talking about the number of times he's visited the following cities. What does he say?

MODELO 4ª / Barcelona
Es la cuarta vez que visito Barcelona.

1. 3ª / Valencia
2. 6ª / Córdoba
3. 7ª / Sevilla
4. 9ª / Madrid
5. 2ª / Salamanca
6. 5ª / Toledo

COMUNICACIÓN

A. Genios matemáticos. Using hundreds and thousands, dictate math problems to other students. See who can get the answer first and say it in Spanish.

EJEMPLO ¿Cuánto son trescientos cuarenta y tres y quinientos ochenta y uno?
Son novecientos veinticuatro.

B. ¿Cuál es tu selección? List the following types of television programs according to your preferences.

EJEMPLO Primero, las comedias
Segundo, las películas policíacas

RINCÓN CULTURAL

Música y baile

Cuando vas a un baile, ¿hay una banda o discos? ¿Qué instrumentos hay? ¿Guitarras eléctricas, tambores (*drums*), saxofón, trompeta, piano? Todos estos instrumentos existen en Latinoamérica y son populares. Pero a los hispanos también les gusta escuchar otros instrumentos de origen indígena (*native origin*), y bailar con esa música. Aquí ves algunos de estos instrumentos. ¿Puedes imaginarte qué sonidos (*sounds*) producen?

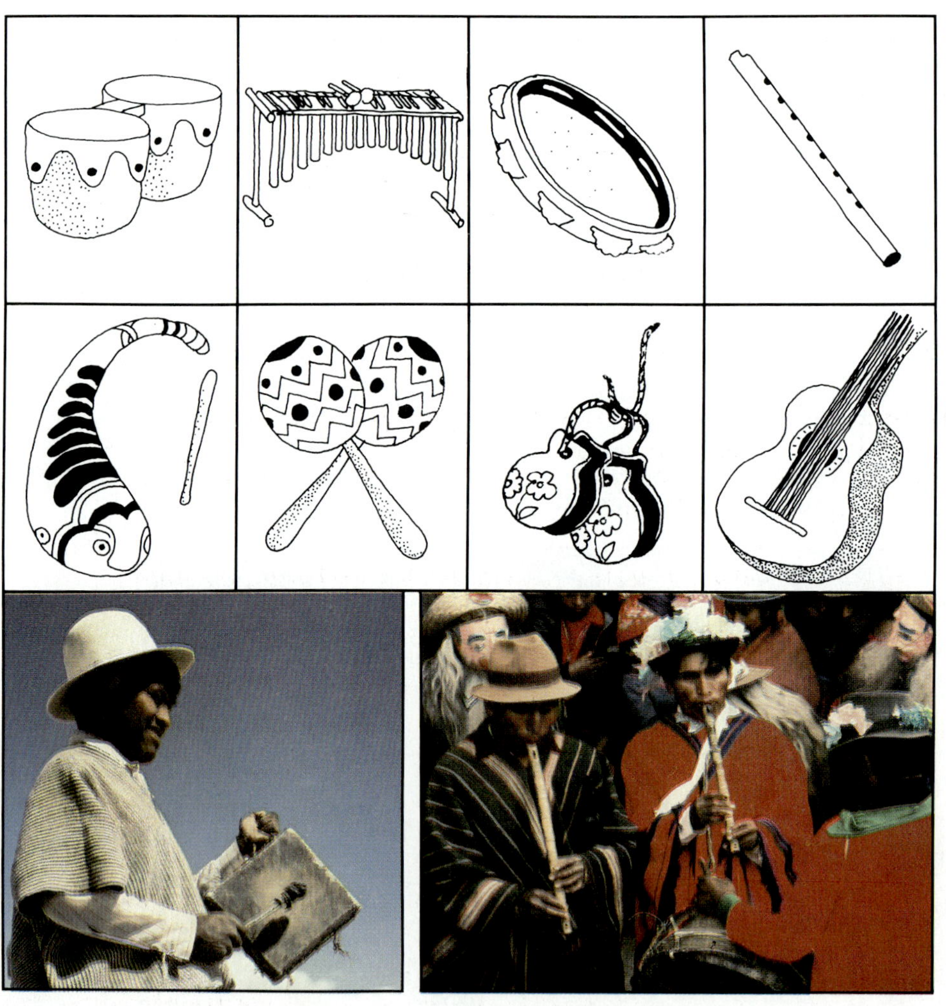

EXPLORACIÓN

Pointing out things or people
Using demonstrative adjectives

PRESENTACIÓN

To point out a particular person, thing, or group in English, we use *this*, *that*, *these*, or *those*. Spanish demonstrative adjectives express these same meanings and, like all adjectives, agree with the nouns they modify.

	Singular		Plural	
	Masculine	Feminine	Masculine	Feminine
this/these	este niño	esta niña	estos niños	estas niñas
that/those	ese niño	esa niña	esos niños	esas niñas
that/those	aquel niño	aquella niña	aquellos niños	aquellas niñas

A. The demonstrative adjective used depends on the location of the person or object with respect to the speaker.

Este and its forms refer to persons or things near the speaker (*this, these*).
Ese and its forms refer to persons or things not far from the speaker or person being spoken to (*that, those*).
Aquel and its forms refer to persons or things that are far away from both the speaker and the person being spoken to (*that, those*).

B. The adverb **aquí** (*here*) corresponds to **este**, **ahí** (*there*) to **ese**, and **allí** (*over there*) to **aquel**.

el bolígrafo que tengo aquí = este bolígrafo
el lápiz que tú tienes ahí = ese lápiz
el libro que está allí = aquel libro

PREPARACIÓN

A. El Corte Inglés. Friends shopping in a Madrid department store are asking the prices of things. What do they say?

MODELO televisor
¿Cuánto es este televisor?

dulces
¿Cuánto son estos dulces?

1. calculadora
2. radio
3. discos
4. cintas
5. grabadora
6. relojes
7. álbum
8. carteras

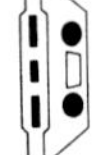

B. En la heladería. Several friends are sitting in an ice cream parlor and are making comments about what they see. Tell what they say.

MODELO coche / formidable
Ese coche es formidable.

1. bicicleta / cara
2. calle / interesante
3. helados / formidables
4. familia / simpática
5. chicos / delgados
6. juegos electrónicos / emocionantes
7. equipo / popular
8. supermercado / nuevo

C. Opiniones. A group of students is touring Mexico City. Tell what their guide says.

MODELO cine / popular
Aquel cine es popular.

1. casas / caras
2. parques / interesantes
3. iglesia / vieja
4. estadio / muy pequeño
5. banco / nuevo
6. la biblioteca / grande

COMUNICACIÓN

A. ¿Qué ves? Pick out three items in the classroom and say something about them. Be sure to use demonstrative adjectives.

EJEMPLO Esta calculadora es nueva.
Me gustan esos carteles.
Aquel bolígrafo es pequeño.

B. En el Rastro. Imagine you're standing in front of the flea market in Madrid and are pointing to various objects while asking their price.

EJEMPLO ¿Cuánto es aquel reloj?

RINCÓN CULTURAL

Where would you go to buy a new watch—to a jewelry store or to a department store in a large shopping mall? In Latin America, there are other possibilities. Although shopping malls and department stores do exist, you more likely would look for a watch in a **relojería** (*watch shop*), or you might even purchase one from a **vendedor en la calle** (*street vendor*). But your most colorful choice would be **el mercado** (*the local market*), a large space, either open or enclosed, where hundreds of vendors set up stands, selling items ranging from watches and jewelry to guitars and fresh produce. There are no store windows, often no display signs, not even a cash register. And although haggling or bargaining (**regateo**) is becoming a lost art, it is still possible to get a better deal at the **mercado** than in the stores.

EXPLORACIÓN

Talking about things we hear and say
Using the verbs **oír** *and* **decir**

PRESENTACIÓN

We often need to talk about things we hear or say. In Spanish, **oír** means *to hear* and **decir** *to say* or *to tell.*

Here are the forms of **oír** and **decir**.

oír

oigo	oímos
oyes	
oye	oyen

decir

digo	decimos
dices	
dice	dicen

Note that the **yo** form is irregular for both verbs and that in the case of **oír**, the **i** changes to **y** between two vowels.

Here are some things we hear or say:

oír
- **el ruido** noise
- **el sonido** sound
- **la voz, las voces** voice(s)
- **la canción** song
- **los pájaros** birds

decir
- **la verdad** truth
- **mentiras** lies
- **tonterías** nonsense
- **que sí** yes
- **que no** no

PREPARACIÓN

A. ¡Pobre Pepe! Pepe is on vacation, but he's having a hard time falling asleep because of the noise. What does he say?

MODELO un perro
¡Dios mío! Ahora oigo un perro.

1. la radio
2. el teléfono
3. una novela en la tele
4. una máquina de escribir
5. voces de niños
6. el ruido de los coches

B. En un campamento. Some people are camping out. As it gets dark, they tell each other what they hear. What do they say?

MODELO Pedro / una voz
Pedro oye una voz.

1. Julieta / los pájaros
2. Ellos / los animales
3. Yo / un radio
4. Tú / unos ruidos
5. Celia / un sonido
6. Ana y Eva / un perro
7. Nosotros / voces
8. Usted / una canción
9. Yo / unos gatos

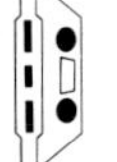

C. ¿Quién tiene razón? A group of friends is having a disagreement. Joaquín is reporting who, in his opinion, says what. Tell what he says.

MODELO Raquel / que sí
Raquel dice que sí.

1. Arturo / que no
2. Celia y Juan / tonterías
3. Yo / la verdad
4. Nosotros / que sí
5. Tú / mentiras

D. Casa de fantasmas. What scary things do friends in a haunted house tell each other?

MODELO José Antonio / decir / que oye voces
José Antonio dice que oye voces.

1. Marina / decir / que ve algo
2. Roberto y Luis / decir / que oyen ruidos
3. Tú / decir / que hay sonidos de animales
4. Nosotros / decir / que oímos el viento
5. Yo / decir / que veo un científico loco en su laboratorio

COMUNICACIÓN

A. Preferencias. Using the suggestions below, form sentences that express how often you like or don't like to hear the following things.

A mí me gusta oír	siempre a veces nunca muchas veces pocas veces todos los días	el sonido de la guitarra las canciones de Roberto Carlos ruidos en la noche la voz de mis padres el sonido del agua ruidos en el aeropuerto las explicaciones de mis profesores el pío-pío de los pájaros el sonido del tocadiscos la música de los años 60 el tictac del reloj

B. Oír y escuchar. You hear a lot of things, but it is up to you to listen to them. How do you react to these things?

EJEMPLO la opinión de mi hermana
Oigo la opinión de mi hermana y la escucho.
Oigo la opinión de mi hermana pero no la escucho.

1. el pronóstico del tiempo
2. la opinión de mis padres
3. las noticias
4. la opinión de mis profesores
5. la explicación de matemáticas
6. la opinión de mis amigos

C. Encuesta. Take a survey of the entertainment preferences (television, radio, concerts, records) of the people in your class and then report back to the class.

EJEMPLO Pablo dice que mira muchas películas policíacas.

PERSPECTIVAS

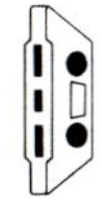

Un sueño

dream

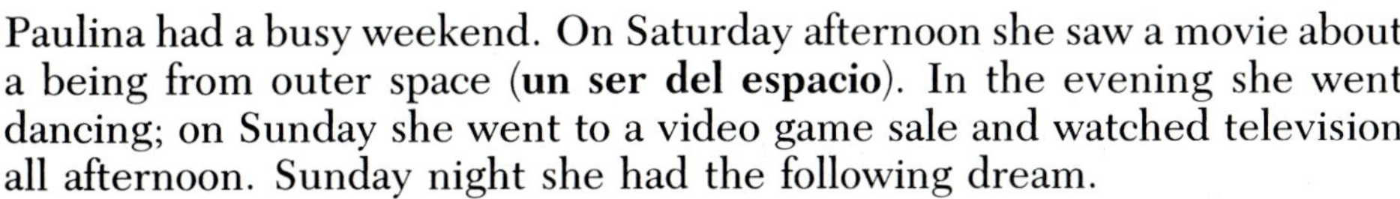

Paulina had a busy weekend. On Saturday afternoon she saw a movie about a being from outer space (**un ser del espacio**). In the evening she went dancing; on Sunday she went to a video game sale and watched television all afternoon. Sunday night she had the following dream.

"¿Dónde estoy? ¿Qué es esto? Estoy en una casa muy rara. Oigo una música electrónica muy bonita y veo mucha gente que baila. Debe ser un baile de máscaras. ¿Y estas computadoras? ¿Qué hacen aquí? ¡Y allí está aquel ser del espacio!"

strange
people
costume ball

El ser me llama y dice "¿Quieres bailar?"

Yo digo que sí y bailamos. Pronto, él desaparece y veo que está dentro de un juego electrónico. Ahora él baila con el Comilón. (*El Comilón* es un juego electrónico en que una figura con mucha hambre—un comilón—come a las otras figuras.)

disappears / inside of
glutton

Una voz dice "¿Quieres comprar este juego?"

Yo digo "¿Cuánto es?"

El vendedor responde "tres millones de dólares."

salesperson

Ahora estoy en casa y veo al Comilón en el televisor. Primero él toca la guitarra y después canta una canción. "¿Qué haces ahí?" pregunto.

El Comilón canta "Mañana es lunes. No olvides la tarea. Mañana es lunes, mañana es lunes, mañana es lunes," repite la voz del Comilón.

Después oigo otra voz "Paulina, arriba, ya es tarde, es hora de ir a la escuela." Abro los ojos y veo a mi madre que entra alegre en mi cuarto.

it's time
eyes

COMPRENSIÓN

Answer the following questions based on **Un sueño**.

1. ¿Dónde está Paulina en su sueño?
2. ¿Qué oye y qué ve?
3. ¿Qué dice el ser del espacio cuando la llama?
4. ¿Con quién baila el ser después?
5. ¿Cuánto cuesta este juego?
6. ¿A quién ve en la televisión?
7. ¿Qué canta el Comilón?
8. ¿Por qué abre Paulina los ojos?

COMUNICACIÓN

A. Costumbres y preferencias. Answer the following questions about your habits and preferences or use them to interview another student.

1. ¿Miras la tele durante la semana? ¿Y durante el fin de semana?
2. ¿Qué te gusta mirar en la tele?
3. ¿Cuál es tu programa favorito?
4. ¿Te gustan más las novelas o las películas?
5. ¿Miras las noticias todos los días?
6. ¿Hay algo interesante en la tele esta noche?
7. ¿Te gusta más mirar la tele o ir al cine?
8. ¿Vas mucho al cine?
9. ¿Cuál es tu película favorita?
10. ¿Hay una película emocionante este fin de semana?

B. **Juego de las 20 preguntas.** Decide what your favorite television program is. Other students will try to guess what program you have chosen by asking you yes-or-no questions.

> **EJEMPLO** ¿Ese programa es interesante?
> ¿Es a las nueve de la noche los lunes?
> ¿Es una novela?

C. **¿Cuál es tu puntaje?** Use the following questions as a guide to discuss computers, your score (**puntaje**), and electronic games with your fellow students.

1. ¿Cuáles son tus juegos electrónicos favoritos? ¿Cuál es tu puntaje en estos juegos? ¿Y de tus amigos?
2. ¿Quién es el primero de la clase en estos juegos? ¿El segundo, tercero, último, etc.?
3. ¿Qué clase de computadora tienes en el colegio? ¿En casa?
4. ¿Qué tienda la tiene? ¿Es cara?
5. Cuando trabajas con tu computadora, ¿oyes ruidos?

VOCABULARIO DEL CAPÍTULO

NOUNS

la avenida avenue
el baile de máscaras costume ball
la calle street
la canción song
el comilón glutton
el espacio space
la figura figure
la gente people
la máscara mask
la mentira lie
la niña child, girl
el niño child, boy
los niños children
la opinión opinion
el pájaro bird
el piso floor
el puntaje score
el punto point
el ruido noise
el ser being
el sonido sound
el sueño dream
la tontería nonsense
el total total
el vendedor salesperson
la vez time, instance
la primera (última) vez the first (last) time
la voz voice

NOUNS RELATING TO TELEVISION

el anuncio commercial
la comedia comedy
el concurso quiz show
los dibujos animados cartoons
el documental documentary
las noticias news
la novela soap opera
la película de ciencia-ficción science fiction film
la película policíaca detective film
el pronóstico del tiempo weather forecast
el reportaje deportivo sports report
las variedades variety shows

VERBS

decir to say, tell
decir que sí to say yes
decir que no to say no
desaparecer to disappear
enseñar to teach
oír to hear
olvidar to forget
preguntar to ask (a question)
repetir to repeat
responder to answer

ADJECTIVES

extra extra
raro strange
último last

ADVERBS

ahí there, right there
allí over there
dentro de inside
sólo only (*short for* **solamente**)

OTHER EXPRESSIONS

Baja la voz. Lower your voice.
¡Caramba! Wow!
Déjalos . . . Let them . . .
es hora de it's time to
Está bien. Okay.
Me encanta I love . . .
No es para tanto. Big deal.
¿Qué es esto? What's this?
Ya basta. That's enough.

Capítulo ocho

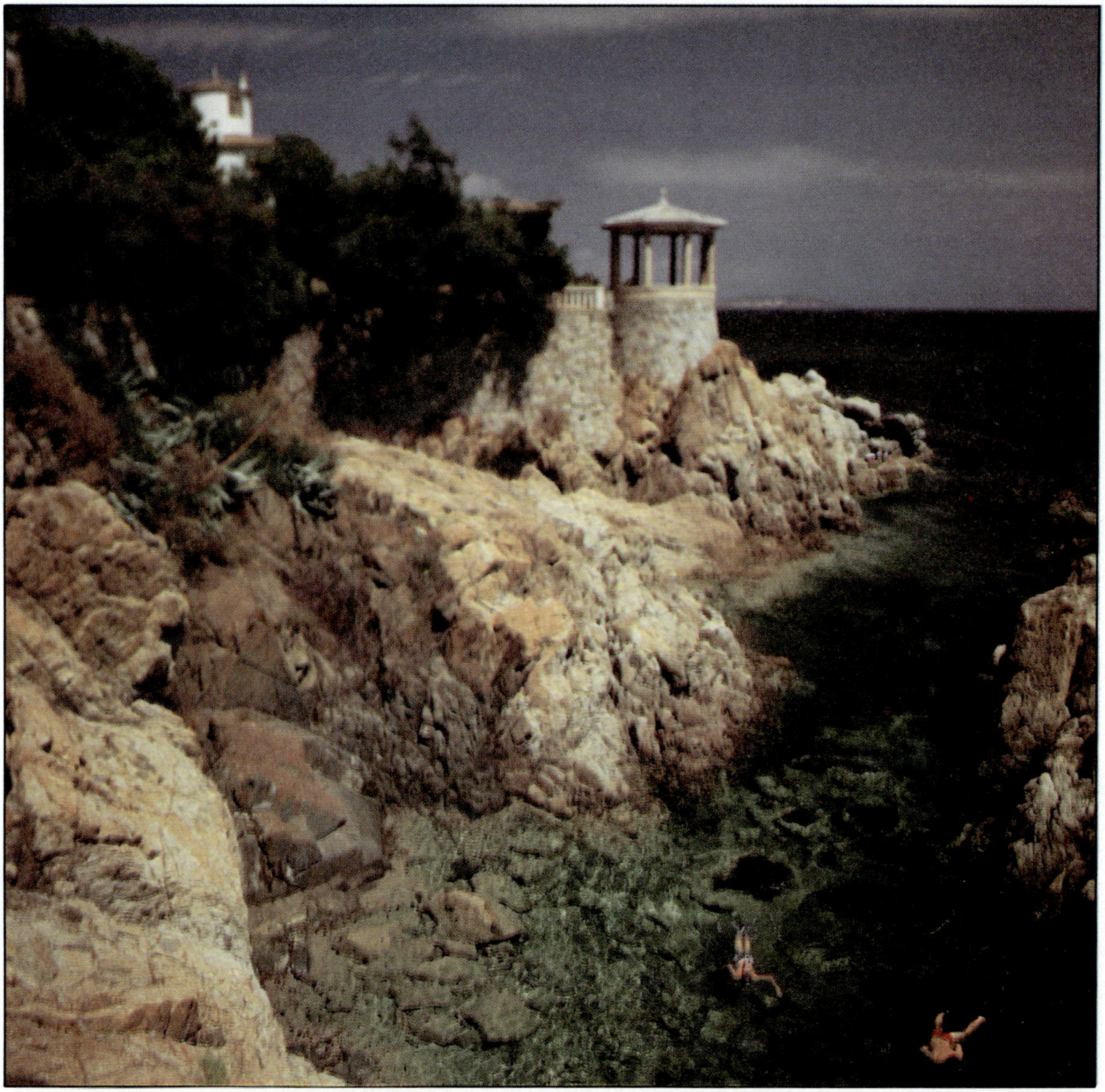

VACATION AND TRAVEL

8

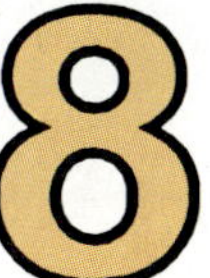

INTRODUCCIÓN

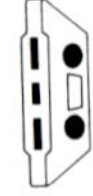

Las vacaciones ideales

Todo el mundo tiene una idea de cómo deben ser las vacaciones ideales. (todo el mundo: everyone)

Hay personas que buscan el calor de la playa y la brisa del mar. Algunos quieren practicar el esquí acuático. Otros prefieren tomar el sol y escuchar música tropical en una isla del Caribe. (playa: beach / mar: sea / algunos: some; isla: island)

Otras personas prefieren ir a las montañas para acampar o esquiar. Les gusta la naturaleza. (acampar: to camp; naturaleza: nature)

Para otra gente, la vida agitada de las grandes ciudades es emocionante. Hay museos, monumentos, teatros, tiendas . . . en fin, mil cosas que hacer. (vida: life / ciudades: cities; en fin: all in all / cosas: things)

¿Qué clase de vacaciones prefieren estas dos personas?

Juan Carlos Casals, España

Soy estudiante de la Universidad de Barcelona. A mí me gustan mucho los deportes acuáticos, sobre todo la natación. Mi idea de unas vacaciones perfectas es pasar unas semanas en la Costa del Sol con amigos. Y como soy un estudiante pobre, quiero hacerlo sin gastar mucho dinero. (natación: swimming; pobre: poor; sin gastar: without spending)

Luisa Speroni Carreras, Argentina

Trabajo en un estudio de televisión en Buenos Aires. Tengo mucha tensión en el trabajo y la vida aquí es muy agitada. Como no me dan* mucho tiempo libre, prefiero hacer viajes cortos, por ejemplo, a Bariloche. Allí, descanso y admiro la naturaleza.

since / give
short

*Dar is irregular only in the yo form: **doy**, **das**, **da**, **damos**, **dan**.

COMPRENSIÓN

Answer the following questions based on **Las vacaciones ideales**.

1. Si una persona pasa las vacaciones en la playa, ¿qué es posible hacer?
2. ¿Qué prefieren las personas que van a las montañas?
3. ¿Por qué son emocionantes las grandes ciudades para otra gente?
4. ¿Adónde le gusta ir de vacaciones a Juan Carlos? ¿Por qué?
5. ¿Por qué no tiene Juan Carlos mucho dinero?
6. ¿Dónde trabaja y vive Luisa?
7. ¿Qué clase de vacaciones le gustan a ella?

COMUNICACIÓN

¿Y tus vacaciones? Everyone has different vacation preferences. What are yours?

1. ¿Cómo prefieres viajar?

en avión en barco en tren en coche en autobús

2. ¿Dónde te gustaría pasar las vacaciones?

en la playa — en las montañas — en un campamento de verano

en el campo — en la ciudad — en el extranjero

3. ¿Cuáles son tus actividades favoritas?

visitar los museos — visitar las catedrales — ver los monumentos

comprar recuerdos — ir de compras — ir a una corrida de toros

EXPLORACIÓN

Indicating when
Seasons, months, and dates

PRESENTACIÓN

When talking about travel plans, we need to know seasons, months, and dates.

A. Las estaciones del año

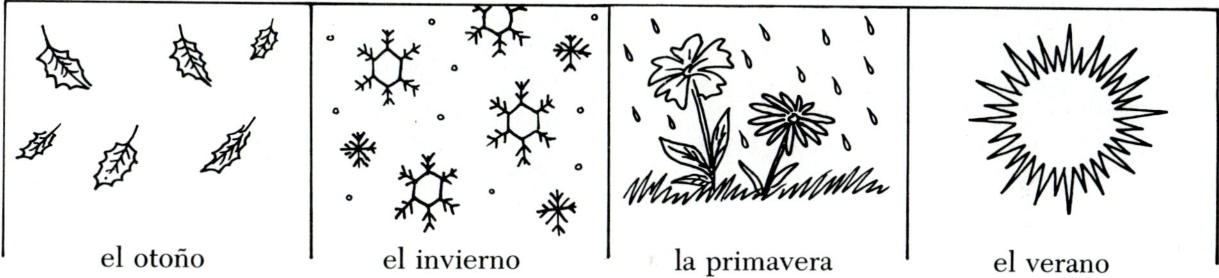

el otoño | el invierno | la primavera | el verano

Es invierno.
La primavera es mi estación favorita.
En el verano vamos a la playa.

B. Los meses del año

enero	marzo	mayo	julio	septiembre	noviembre
febrero	abril	junio	agosto	octubre	diciembre

Febrero es el mes más frío aquí.
En junio ellos van a las montañas.

Note that to say that something happens in a particular month or season, you use the preposition **en**: **en noviembre**, but **en el otoño**.

C. La fecha. To ask the date, say:

¿Qué fecha es hoy? *or* ¿Cuál es la fecha de hoy?

To give a particular date, use the following construction.

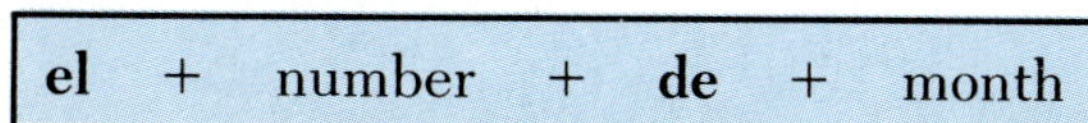

el + number + **de** + month

Hoy es el cuatro de diciembre. La fiesta es el cinco de diciembre.

However, for the first day of the month, use **el primero** (1^{ero}).

Vamos a Madrid el primero de abril.

PREPARACIÓN

A. El clima de Sudamérica. An exchange student is telling how the seasons are reversed in South America. What does he say?

MODELO verano / diciembre
Es verano en diciembre.

1. invierno / julio
2. primavera / octubre
3. otoño / abril
4. verano / febrero
5. primavera / noviembre
6. invierno / agosto

B. De vacaciones. Students at an international school are planning to go home for the summer. Where are they going and when do they plan to leave?

MODELO Marta / España / 2–8
Marta sale para España el dos de agosto.

1. Esteban / Argentina / 17–7
2. Susana y yo / la República Dominicana / 3–6
3. Miguel y Roberto / Chile / 14–8
4. Tú / Venezuela / 1–7
5. Ustedes / Panamá / 6–8
6. Leonardo / Puerto Rico / 5–6

C. ¿Cuándo es tu santo? Use the calendar to tell in which month and on what day each of the following people celebrate his or her **santo**.

MODELO Inés
Mi santo es el 21 de enero.

1. José
2. Carmen
3. Vicente
4. Ricardo
5. Carlos
6. Concepción
7. Miguel
8. Marcela
9. Ana
10. Lourdes
11. Luis
12. Cristina

ENERO	
1	Sta Martina
2	Sto Esteban
3	Sto Daniel
4	Beata Ángela
5	Sta Amelia
6	San Andrés
7	San Raimundo
8	San Severino
9	Sto Adriano
10	San Aldo
11	San Higinio
12	Beato Bernardo
13	San Hilario
14	Beato Odorico
15	San Mauro
16	San Marcelo
17	San Antonio
18	Sta Margarita
19	San Mario
20	San Sebastián
21	Sta Inés
22	San Vicente
23	Sta Brígida
24	San Francisco
25	San Pablo
26	San Timoteo
27	Sta Ángela
28	Sto Tomás de Aquino
29	San Constancio
30	Sta Julieta
31	Sta Marcela

FEBRERO	
1	Sta Brígida
2	Sta Caterina
3	San Blas
4	San José
5	Sta Águeda
6	San Gastón
7	Sta Coleta
8	San Jerónimo
9	Sta Apolonia
10	Sta Escolástica
11	Lourdes
12	Sta Eulalia
13	Sta Beatriz
14	San Cirilo
15	Sta Jovita
16	San Isaias
17	San Alejo
18	San Claudio
19	San Conrado
20	Sta Amanda
21	San Jorge
22	San Pedro
23	San Celso
24	San Sergio
25	San Lucio
26	San César
27	Sta Honorina
28	San Román

MARZO	
1	San Albino
2	Beata Inés
3	San Mariano
4	San Casimiro
5	San Adrián
6	Sta Rosa
7	Sta Felicidad
8	San Juan
9	Sta Francisca
10	San Dionisio
11	San Ramiro
12	San Maximiliano
13	San Rodrigo
14	Sta Matilde
15	San Clemente María
16	San Heriberto
17	San Patricio
18	San Salvador
19	San José
20	San Guillermo
21	San Sergio
22	San Basilio
23	San Toribio
24	Beato Diego José
25	Sta Lucía
26	San Manuel
27	San Mateo
28	San Juan
29	Sta Gladys
30	San Pedro
31	San Benjamin

ABRIL	
1	Sta Caterina
2	Sta María
3	San Ricardo
4	San Benito
5	Sta Irene
6	San Armando
7	San Juan Bautista
8	Beata Julia
9	Sta Mónica
10	San Miguel
11	San Estanislao
12	San Julio
13	San Hermenegildo
14	San Lamberto
15	San Marón
16	Sta Bernadette
17	Beata Clara
18	San Nebemias
19	Sta Ema
20	San Cesareo
21	San Conrado
22	San Teodoro
23	San Jorge
24	San Fidel
25	San Marcos
26	San Isidro
27	San Pedro
28	San Gerardo
29	Sta Catalina
30	San Pío

MAYO	
1	San José Obrero
2	San Atanasio
3	San Felipe
4	San Silvano
5	San Eulogio
6	Sto Domingo
7	Sta Flavia
8	San Víctor
9	Sta Catalina
10	San Mamerto
11	San Ignacio
12	San Émilio
13	San Pedro
14	San Matías
15	Sta Berta
16	Sta Margarita
17	San Pascual
18	San Félix
19	San Teófilo
20	San Bernardino
21	San Timoteo
22	Sta Rita
23	San Miguel
24	San Gerardo
25	San Bede
26	San Felipe
27	San Agustín
28	Sta María Ana
29	Beato Ricardo
30	Beato Bautista
31	Sta Ángela

JUNIO	
1	San Justino
2	San Eugenio
3	San Carlos
4	San Francisco
5	Sta Marcía
6	San Norberto
7	San Roberto
8	San Maximiliano
9	San Efrén
10	San Zacarías
11	San Bernabé
12	Sta Antonia
13	San Antonio
14	San Eliseo
15	San Abrahán
16	San Aureliano
17	Sta Marina
18	San Venancio
19	Sta Juliana
20	Beata Micaela
21	San Luis
22	San Juan
23	San José
24	San Juan Bautista
25	San Guillermo
26	Beata Teresa
27	San Cirilo
28	Sta Alicia
29	San Pablo
30	Beato Raimundo

JULIO	
1	Sta Ester
2	San Martín
3	Sto Tomás
4	Sta Isabel
5	Sta Filomena
6	Sta María
7	San Fermín
8	San Gregorio
9	San Nicolás
10	San Pedro
11	San Benito
12	San Juan
13	Beata Angelina
14	San Rolando
15	San Buenaventura
16	Carmen
17	Sta Marcela
18	San Edmundo
19	San Arsenio
20	San Elías
21	San Lorenzo
22	Sta María Magdalena
23	Sta Brígida
24	Sta Cristina
25	Sta Valentina
26	Sta Ana
27	Sta Julia
28	San Celso
29	Sta Marta
30	Beato Leopoldo
31	San Ignacio

AGOSTO	
1	San Alfonso
2	San Alfonso María
3	San Pedro Julian
4	San Juan María
5	San Osvaldo
6	Sto Esteban
7	Sto Alberto
8	Sto Domingo
9	San Marcelino
10	San Lorenzo
11	Sta Clara
12	San Macario
13	San Hipólito
14	Beato Antonio
15	Sto Alfredo
16	San Roque
17	San Jacinto
18	Sta Elena
19	San Luis
20	San Bernardo
21	Beato Gilberto
22	San Andrés
23	San Felipe
24	San Bartolomé
25	San Luis
26	San Víctor
27	Sta Mónica
28	San Agustín
29	San Juan Bautista
30	Sta Rosa
31	San Ramón

SEPTIEMBRE	
1	Sta Beatriz
2	Beato Severino
3	San Gregorio
4	San Rosa
5	San Justiniano
6	San Fausto
7	Sta Regina
8	Sta Adela
9	San Pedro
10	San Nicolás
11	San Vicente
12	*Nombre de María*
13	Beato Francisco
14	San Juan
15	Dolores
16	San Rogelio
17	San Justino
18	Sta Sofía
19	San Genaro
20	San Franciso María
21	San Mateo
22	San Mauricio
23	San Lino
24	Mercedes
25	San Alberto
26	San Cosme
27	San Daniel
28	San Wenceslao
29	Sto Rafael
30	San Jerónimo

OCTUBRE	
1	Sta Teresa
2	San Cirilo
3	San Remigio
4	San Francisco
5	San Apolinar
6	Sta María Francisca
7	Rosario
8	San Nestor
9	San Luis Bertrand
10	San Francisco
11	Sta Soledad
12	San Serafín
13	San Eduardo
14	San Calixto
15	Sta Teresa
16	San Gerardo
17	San Ignacio
18	San Lucas
19	San Pedro
20	Beato Contardo
21	Sta Úrsula
22	Beata Josefina
23	San Ignacio
24	San Antonio
25	San Crispín
26	Beato Buenaventura
27	San Florencio
28	Sto Simón
29	San Narciso
30	San Víctor
31	San Alfonso

NOVIEMBRE	
1	Sta Juliana
2	San Justo
3	San Martín
4	San Carlos
5	Sta Beatriz
6	San Leonardo
7	San Edalberto
8	San Godoféo
9	San Alejandro
10	San León
11	San Martín
12	San Josafat
13	San Eugenio
14	San Gerardo
15	San Alberto
16	San Edmundo
17	Sta Isabel
18	San Pedro
19	Sta Inés
20	San Gregorio
21	San Brocardo
22	Sta Cecilia
23	Sta Lucrecia
24	San Alejandro
25	Sta Catalina
26	San Leonardo
27	San Alberto
28	San Jaime
29	Beato Federico
30	San Andrés

DICIEMBRE	
1	San Eloy
2	Sta Bibiana
3	San Francisco
4	San Clemente
5	San Humberto
6	San Nicolás
7	San Ambrosio
8	*Inmaculada Concepción*
9	Sta Valeria
10	Sta Eulalia
11	San Daniel
12	Guadalupe
13	Sta Lucía
14	San Juan
15	Sta Silvia
16	Sta Adelaida
17	San Lazaro
18	San Salvador
19	Sta Juana
20	San Julio
21	San Pedro
22	San Francisco
23	Sta Victoria
24	Sta Irma
25	*Natividad del Sr*
26	San Esteban
27	San Juan
28	Stos Inocentes
29	Sto Tomás
30	Beata Margarita
31	San Silvestre

COMUNICACIÓN

A. Preferencias. Find out if other students go to the following places or do the following things for their vacations.

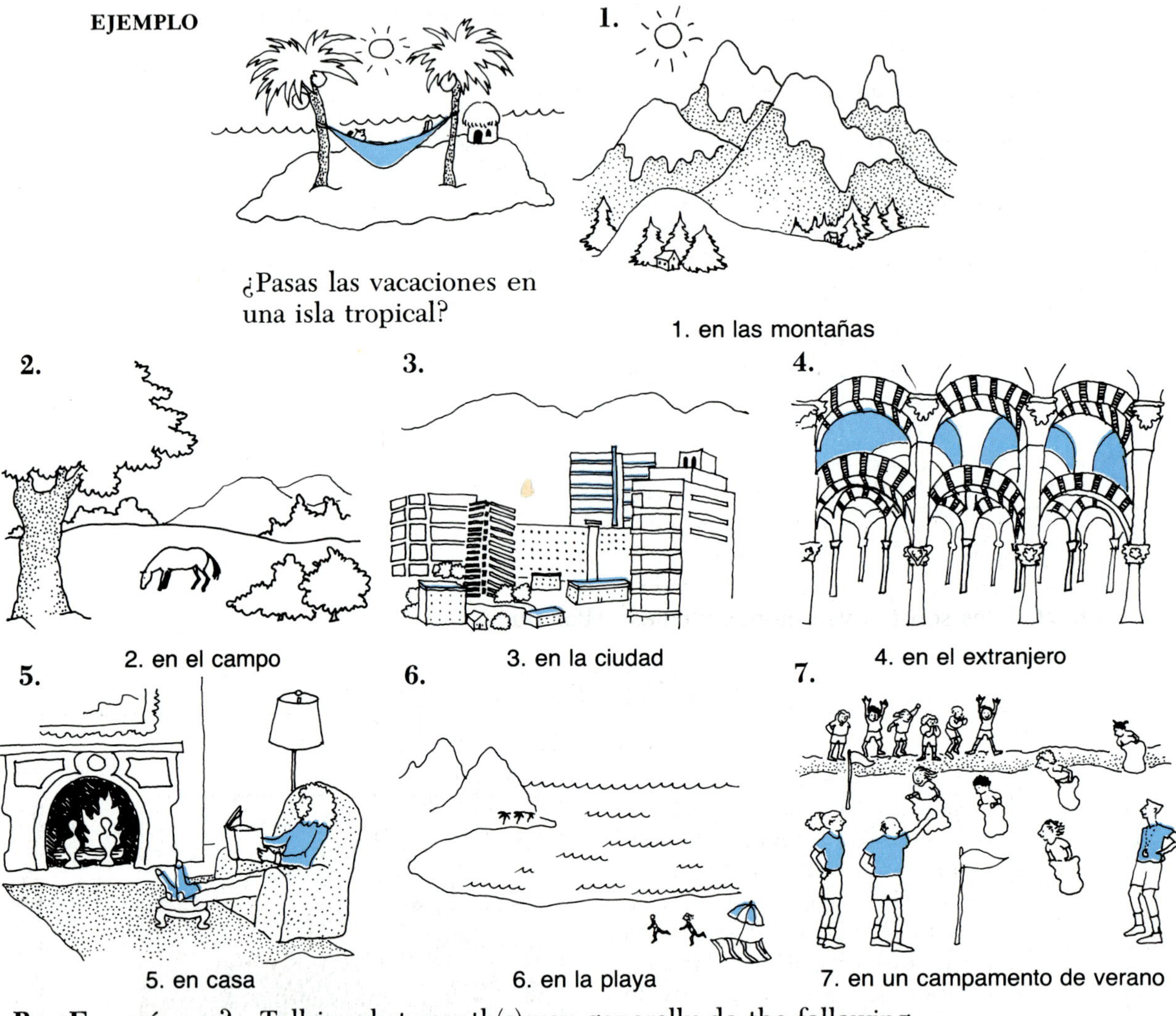

EJEMPLO ¿Pasas las vacaciones en una isla tropical?

1. en las montañas
2. en el campo
3. en la ciudad
4. en el extranjero
5. en casa
6. en la playa
7. en un campamento de verano

B. ¿En qué mes? Tell in what month(s) you generally do the following things.

EJEMPLO ir a la piscina
Voy a la piscina en junio, julio y agosto.

1. ir de vacaciones
2. ir a las montañas para esquiar
3. ir a la playa
4. practicar el esquí acuático
5. admirar la naturaleza
6. viajar a una isla del Caribe
7. regresar al colegio
8. ir a los partidos de fútbol americano

C. ¡Feliz cumpleaños! Give the birthdays of your family members and friends.

EJEMPLO El cumpleaños de mi hermana es el siete de marzo.

D. Calendario deportivo. Tell in what season you usually participate in the following sports.

EJEMPLO Practico el esquí en el invierno.

fútbol americano	tenis	béisbol
fútbol	esquí	volibol
baloncesto	esquí acuático	

E. Preguntas/Entrevista. Answer the following questions or use them to interview another student.

1. ¿Cuándo es tu cumpleaños?
2. ¿Cuál es tu mes favorito? ¿Por qué?
3. ¿Qué estación te gusta más?
4. En general, ¿en qué mes viajas?
5. ¿Con quién viajas?
6. En general, ¿cómo viajas? ¿En coche o en avión?
7. ¿Vas a veces a un campamento de verano?
8. ¿Te gustaría ir a una isla tropical?
9. ¿Te gustan los deportes acuáticos?
10. ¿Cuáles son tus vacaciones ideales? ¿Por qué?

RINCÓN CULTURAL

¿Sabes que las estaciones del año en el sur de Sudamérica son **opuestas** (*opposite*) a las estaciones aquí? Por ejemplo, cuando nosotros estamos en verano, es invierno en Argentina. Para los argentinos octubre es un mes de primavera. También hay países que tienen, como los Estados Unidos, diferentes climas en una misma estación.

¿Que tiempo hace en las diferentes estaciones donde vives tú?

EXPLORACIÓN

Expressing wishes, preferences, and opinions
Using stem-changing verbs: **e ⟶ ie**

PRESENTACIÓN

You have already learned the endings for all three groups of regular verbs (**ar**, **er**, and **ir**). Some verbs have regular endings but have changes in their stems.

A. Here is a model for **e ⟶ ie** stem-changing verbs. Study the forms of **comenzar** (*to begin*).

comenzar

comienzo	comenzamos
comienzas	
comienza	comienzan

Note that **comenzar** has regular endings, but the **e** of the stem becomes **ie** in all persons except in the **nosotros** form.

B. Here are other **e ⟶ ie** stem-changing verbs.

			yo	nosotros
ar	empezar (a) pensar (en)	to begin (to) to think (about)	emp**ie**zo p**ie**nso	empezamos pensamos
er	querer entender perder	to want, love to understand to lose, waste, miss (train, etc.)	qu**ie**ro ent**ie**ndo p**ie**rdo	queremos entendemos perdemos
ir	preferir	to prefer	pref**ie**ro	preferimos

Comenzar and **empezar** require **a** before an infinitive.

Empieza a llover. It's beginning to rain.

C. **Pensar** plus an infinitive means **to plan on** or **intend**. **Pensar en** means **to think about** someone or something.

¿Piensas viajar en mayo? Are you planning on traveling in May?
Piensan en ella. They are thinking about her.

PREPARACIÓN

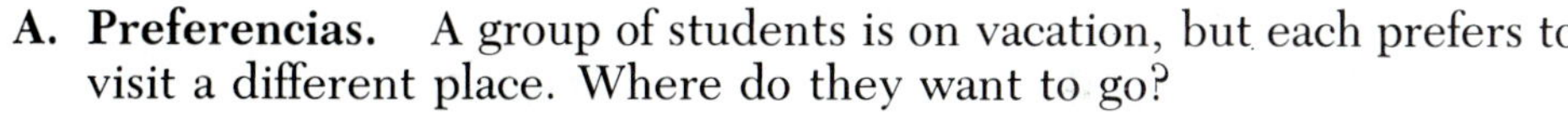

A. Preferencias. A group of students is on vacation, but each prefers to visit a different place. Where do they want to go?

> **MODELO** Roberto / el museo
> **Roberto prefiere ir al museo.**

1. las chicas / la catedral
2. César y José / el teatro
3. Yo / la corrida de toros
4. Rita y yo / el estadio
5. Margarita / la piscina
6. Felipe y Rosa / el parque

B. Desorganizados. Señora Molina is exasperated because her family is so disorganized. What does she say?

> **MODELO** Mi familia / todo
> **Mi familia siempre pierde todo.**

1. Papá / el tren
2. Mariana / la mochila
3. Yo / los lentes
4. Luis y Anita / el autobús
5. Tú / el dinero
6. Nosotros / tiempo

C. ¿A qué hora empiezas . . . ? Some friends vacationing in Puerto Vallarta are eager to get a suntan. They tell each other at what time they usually start sunbathing.

> **MODELO** Cecilia / 10:00
> **Cecilia empieza a las diez de la mañana.**

1. Federico / 9:30
2. Tú / 1:30
3. Bárbara y yo / 11:45
4. Ustedes / 12:00
5. Yo / 10:15
6. Manuel y Linda / 11:00

D. El gallego. On a trip to northern Spain, the Pérez family stops at a restaurant in La Coruña. They soon find out that the waiter speaks only **Gallego** (*Galician*), a language related to Portuguese. What do señor Pérez and his family say?

MODELO Mi familia
Mi familia no entiende gallego.

1. Nosotros
2. Gisela y Cristina
3. Yo
4. Mis hijos
5. Tú

E. ¿Qué hacemos? Based on the illustrations, tell what the following people plan to do on their first day of vacation.

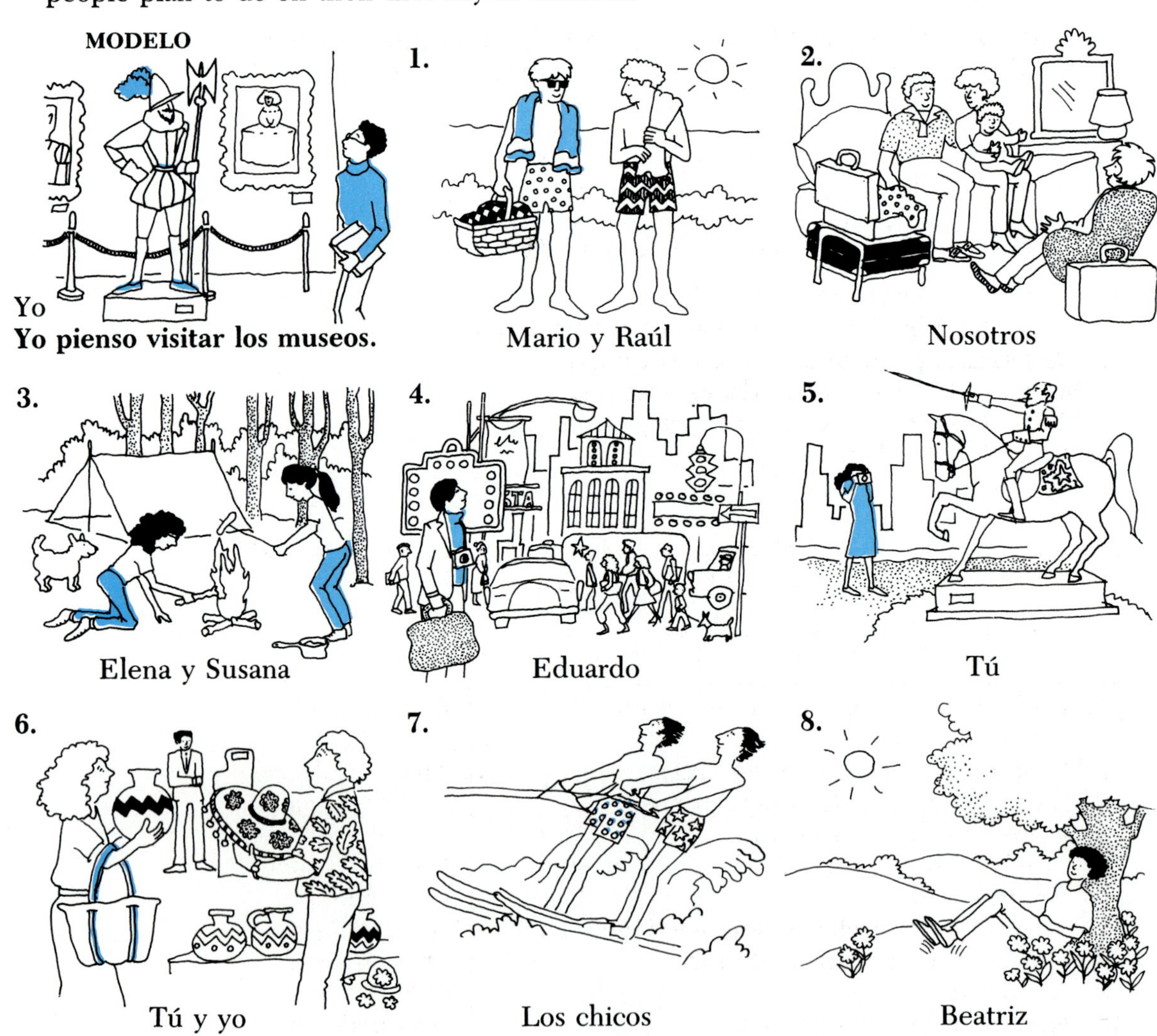

MODELO Yo
Yo pienso visitar los museos.

1. Mario y Raúl
2. Nosotros
3. Elena y Susana
4. Eduardo
5. Tú
6. Tú y yo
7. Los chicos
8. Beatriz

F. ¡Qué desastre! Some American students are camping in Cataluña, but everything seems to be going wrong. Tell what they say.

MODELO comenzar a / llover
Comienza a llover.

1. empezar a / hacer frío
2. Nosotros / no entender / catalán
3. Tú / perder / las llaves del coche
4. Raúl / querer / llamar por teléfono
5. Ustedes / olvidar la comida
6. Yo / preferir / ir a un hotel

COMUNICACIÓN

A. Un viaje a los Estados Unidos. A Spanish friend is planning a trip to the United States. Indicate if you think his ideas are good or bad and say why.

EJEMPLO Me gustaría visitar Nueva York.
Pienso que es una buena idea.
Es una ciudad interesante.
Pienso que es una mala idea. Hay mucha gente.

1. Me gustaría viajar en tren de Nueva York a California.
2. Me gustaría hablar con los estudiantes americanos.
3. Me gustaría pasar unos días en el campo.
4. Me gustaría visitar las ciudades grandes.
5. Me gustaría comer hamburguesas y pasteles.
6. Me gustaría comprar discos americanos.
7. Me gustaría ir a un partido de béisbol.

B. ¿Cuál es tu reacción? Use these expressions to tell how you would react if one of your friends said the following.

EJEMPLO Pienso viajar mucho.
¡Qué bueno!

1. Prefiero pasar mis vacaciones en una isla del Caribe.
2. Quiero ganar un millón de dólares.
3. Entiendo mucho de computadoras.
4. Pierdo mi dinero a veces.
5. Prefiero estudiar los viernes por la noche.
6. Empieza a nevar.
7. Pienso que el profesor siempre tiene razón.
8. Quiero ir a una corrida de toros.
9. Comienza a llover.
10. No entiendo a mis padres.

¡Qué pesado!
¡Fantástico!
¡Me alegro!
¡Qué tontería!
¡Qué suerte!
¡Cuánto lo siento!
¡Qué bueno!
¡No me digas!
¡Qué importa!
¡Qué pena!
¡No puede ser!

RINCÓN CULTURAL

Have you ever seen **una corrida de toros** (*bullfight*) and felt the excitement as the crowd roared **olé**? **Olé** means *bravo* and is shouted out enthusiastically when the **matador** (*bullfighter*) displays his courage in dangerously close passes with an angry charging bull.

Bullfighting is a ritual art. This art celebrates the victory of humanity over the forces of nature while recognizing, in the power of the bull, the dignity of nature itself. Although this ritual has its roots in the ancient civilizations of the Mediterranean, Spain developed this art more than other nations and then brought it to the New World. It is still celebrated in Mexico, Colombia, Venezuela, and Peru.

Although not all Spaniards are interested in bullfighting, **plazas de toros** (*bullfighting rings*) are common in Spanish cities and towns—there are about 400 of them in Spain. The largest **plaza de toros** is in Mexico and seats 35,000 spectators.

Bullfighting is also known as the **fiesta brava** (*festival of bravery*). All of the participants are dressed in brightly colored costumes, the most brilliant of which is worn by the **matador** and is called a **traje de luces** (*suit of lights*).

The **fiesta brava** is divided into three parts or **tercios**. The first **tercio** is that of the **picadores**, men on horseback who prod the bull to make it ready to fight. They are followed by the **matador**, who uses a **capa** (*large red and yellow cape*) to display his skill in a series of **pasos** (*passes*).

A trumpet call announces the second **tercio**, that of the **banderilleros**. These men race on foot at the angry bull, jumping aside as they place their colorful **banderillas**.

A third trumpet blast signals the final **tercio**, known as **la hora de la verdad** (*moment of truth*). Now the **matador**, representing intelligence, faces death alone in a battle against the beast, which represents brute force. Here he displays his courage, skill, and grace in the face of death. He must seek out danger and not avoid it. Once he masters the bull, he then kills it with his **estoque** (*sword*).

Do you know that this ancient festival of a man against a beast came to the United States from Spain and Mexico in the form of the **rodeo**, which is the Spanish word for *roundup*? What similarities do you see between the American rodeo and the Spanish **corrida**?

EXPLORACIÓN

Talking about location
Using prepositions

PRESENTACIÓN

To talk about where people or things are located, we use the verb **estar**, often with a preposition. Learn these prepositions and phrases:

cerca de	near, close to
lejos de	far from
al lado de	next to, beside
frente a	facing, opposite
enfrente de	in front of
detrás de	behind
entre	between
encima de	on top of, above
debajo de	under, beneath

¿Está el hotel lejos del aeropuerto?
Hay un parque entre el museo y el teatro.
Hay un cine al lado de mi casa.

Remember that **de** contracts with **el** to form **del**.

Here are some other expressions that are useful in asking for information or in directing someone to a place:

¿Dónde queda(n) . . . ?	Where is (are) . . . located?
Siga derecho.	Go straight ahead.
Doble a la derecha.	Turn right.
Doble a la izquierda.	Turn left.

PREPARACIÓN

A. ¿Dónde está mi pasaporte? Ángela has lost her passport, and Carmen is helping her look for it. What does Carmen ask?

MODELO encima del televisor
¿Está encima del televisor?

1. entre los papeles
2. cerca del teléfono
3. detrás de la cámara
4. encima del radio
5. debajo del suéter
6. al lado de la grabadora

B. Guardia civil. Some American tourists in Spain are asking a Guardia Civil for directions. What do they say?

MODELO ¿Queda el hotel lejos del aeropuerto? (no / cerca)
No, queda cerca del aeropuerto.

1. ¿Queda el cine detrás del teatro? (no / enfrente de)
2. ¿Queda el correo cerca del banco? (sí / al lado)
3. ¿Queda la catedral cerca de aquí? (no / lejos)
4. ¿Está el museo al lado de la iglesia? (no / frente a)
5. ¿Está la biblioteca frente a la escuela? (no / detrás de)
6. ¿Está la plaza de toros lejos de aquí? (no / cerca)

C. Álbum de fotos. Caridad is describing some photos she took while on vacation at her aunt and uncle's home. Complete her statements by adding the appropriate prepositions.

MODELO

Mi tío y mi tía viven en Valencia. Queda ___lejos___ de Madrid.

1. Aquí estamos ________ su casa.

2. Su casa está ________ correo.

3. Hay una tienda ________ la casa de mis tíos.

4. Aquí mi primo David está ________ tío y mi tía.

5. Mi hermana está ________ tía Estela.

COMUNICACIÓN

A. En la parada del autobús. At a bus stop, people ask you for directions. Using the map below, tell what directions you would give them.

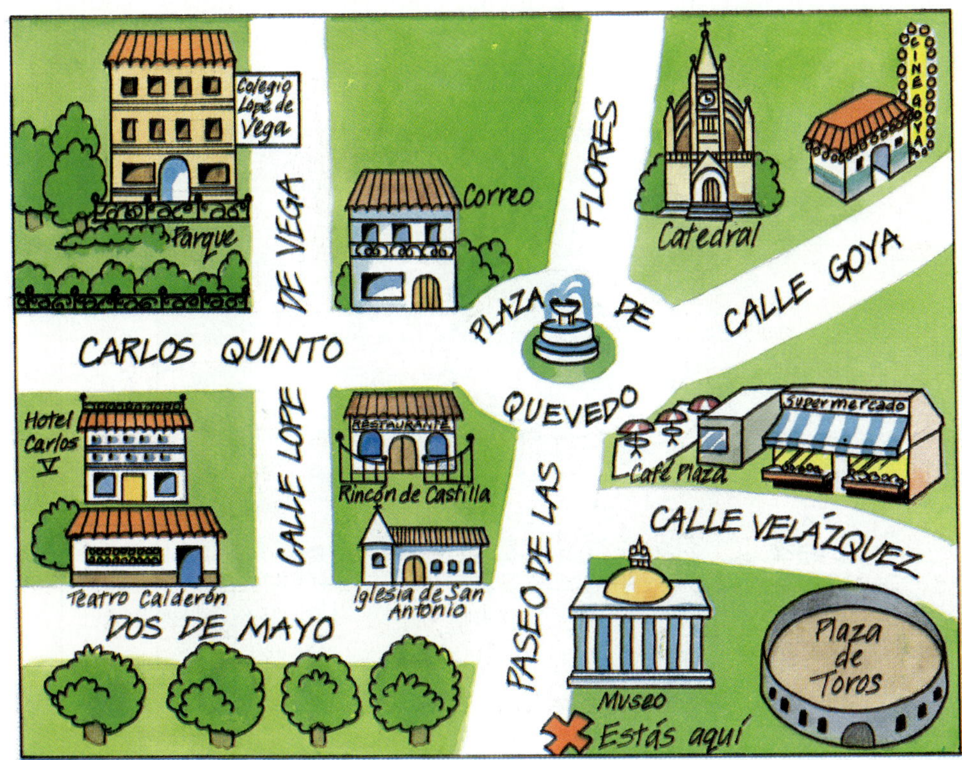

EJEMPLO ¿Dónde está la calle Dos de Mayo, por favor?
Siga derecho y doble a la izquierda en la primera calle.

1. Me gustaría ir al correo. ¿Dónde queda, por favor?
2. ¿Dónde está el hotel Carlos Quinto, por favor?
3. Tengo que ir al supermercado. ¿Dónde queda, por favor?
4. ¿Dónde está la catedral, por favor?
5. ¿Y el museo? ¿Dónde queda, por favor?
6. ¿Dónde queda la calle Goya, por favor?

B. ¿Quién es? Choose another student in your class. The rest of the class will ask questions to find out whom you have chosen.

EJEMPLO ¿Está detrás de Gloria?
¿Está entre Camilo y Lorenzo?

RINCÓN CULTURAL

Madrid es la capital y la ciudad más grande de España. Es también una de las capitales europeas más interesantes. Imagínate que es la primera vez que visitas Madrid. Tú le haces preguntas a tu guía (*guide*) sobre los puntos de interés turístico. ¿Qué contesta el guía a tus preguntas? Consulta el plano de la ciudad (*city map*) para contestar.

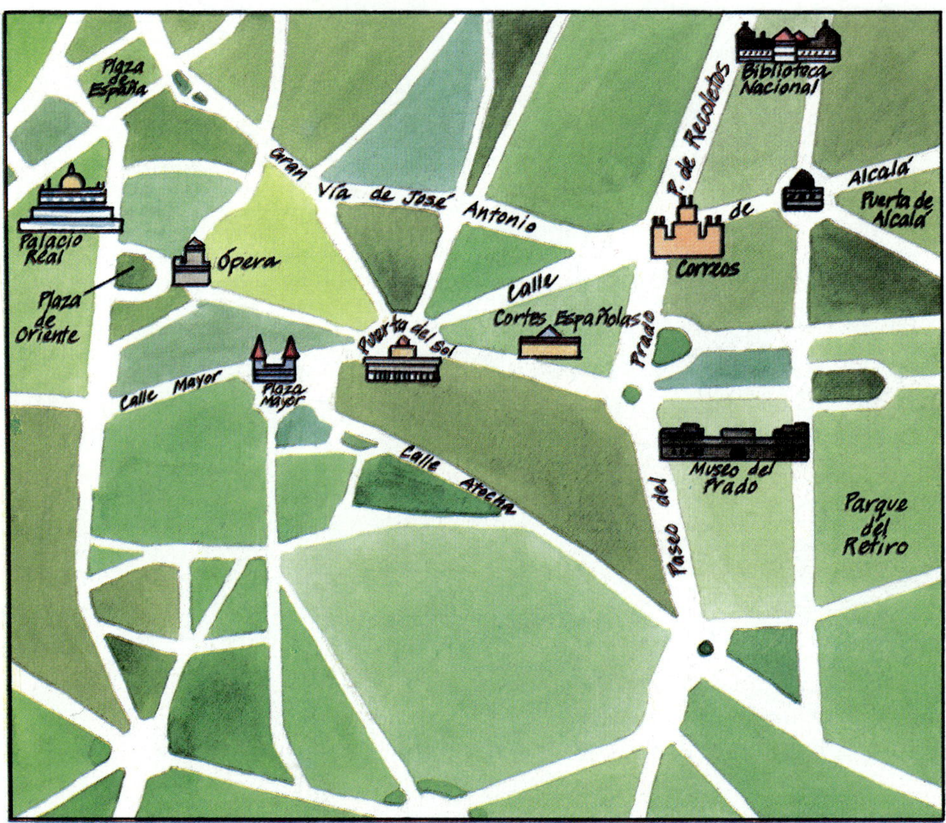

1. ¿La Plaza Mayor está cerca de la Puerta del Sol?
2. ¿El Museo del Prado está lejos del Parque del Retiro?
3. ¿La Gran Vía empieza en la Plaza de España?
4. ¿Es el Retiro un buen lugar (*place*) para comer?
5. ¿La Plaza Mayor es moderna o antigua?

EXPLORACIÓN

Talking about people already mentioned
Object pronouns **me, te, nos**

PRESENTACIÓN

You have already learned to use **lo**, **la**, **los**, and **las** as direct object pronouns to avoid repeating nouns.

Conozco a Juan.	**Lo** conozco.
Miran las revistas.	**Las** miran.

The pronouns for *me*, *you* (familiar), and *us* are **me**, **te**, and **nos**. They may replace direct or indirect object nouns. Notice that object pronouns are placed before the conjugated verb.

Ella **me** llama.	She calls me.
Yo **te** comprendo.	I understand you.
Nuestros padres **nos** ayudan.	Our parents help us.

When the object pronoun is used with an infinitive, it is attached to the infinitive.

Voy a tu casa para ayudar**te**.

If the infinitive is used with another verb, the pronoun may be attached to the infinitive or placed before the conjugated verb.

Quiero ver**la**. ⟶ **La** quiero ver.
Van a invitar**nos**. ⟶ **Nos** van a invitar.

Notice that when the pronouns are used as indirect objects, they often mean *to* or *for me*, *you*, *us*.

Ella **me** enseña español.	She teaches *me* Spanish. She teaches Spanish *to me*.
¿**Te** compran una bicicleta?	Are they buying a bike *for you*? Are they buying *you* a bike?

PERSPECTIVAS

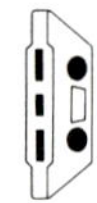

Un verano en México

Silvia Jiménez, a Mexican-American student, has visited Mexico for the first time. Here are some of the postcards she wrote her friends and family in Texas.

Querida Diana, 1º de junio

¡Por fin estoy en México! ¡Y hasta agosto — todavía no lo creo! Las clases empiezan mañana. Ya entiendo bastante español, pero hablarlo — vivirlo — no es lo mismo que oírlo en casa de mis abuelos o estudiarlo.

Por la noche estoy tan cansada que no puedo más. Pero estoy muy contenta. Un abrazo de tu amiga

Silvia

finally
until
I can't take any more
hug

Querida profesora, 10 de julio

Ya estamos en la última semana de clases. ¡Me encanta la vida de la ciudad! Ya conocemos a unos estudiantes mexicanos que nos llevan a ver los monumentos y a comer en restaurantes típicos. Me dicen que ahora casi hablo como mexicana. ¡Pienso que voy a sacar buenas notas en el otoño!

Saludos de

Silvia

take
get
grades
regards

16 de julio

Queridos abuelos,

Mañana salgo para Yucatán. Si no pierdo el avión, llego temprano por la mañana. ¡Qué suerte tener a tía Elsa y tío Paco de vacaciones allí! Este viaje es como un sueño.

Es el mejor regalo de mi vida. ¡Mil gracias!

Los quiere
Silvia

I'll arrive
early
like
best

ruins
Mayan
from

21 de julio

Querido Rafael,

Después de un viaje de dos horas en autobús, estamos en Chichén-Itzá. ¡Las ruinas son fabulosas!

Voy a comprar recuerdos, quizás unas reproducciones de Quetzalcóatl y del Chac-mool. Mañana vamos a Uxmal para ver más ruinas mayas. Te escribo desde la isla de Cozumel donde vamos a pasar unos días en la playa. Pienso en ti. Hasta pronto,

Silvia

COMPRENSIÓN

Based on **Un verano en México**, tell whether each statement is **verdadero** or **falso**.

1. Silvia va a pasar dos meses en México.
2. No entiende nada de español.
3. Está demasiado cansada y no está contenta.
4. Sus amigos mexicanos la llevan a ver la ciudad.
5. Va a sacar buenas notas en el otoño.
6. Sus tíos están en Yucatán y ella va a verlos.
7. No tiene tiempo para ver las ruinas de Chichén Itzá y Uxmal.
8. Silvia pasa su última semana en Cozumel.

COMUNICACIÓN

A. Cartas mexicanas. One of Silvia's postcards got wet, and the ink ran. Help her parents read it by filling in the missing words. Refer to the **Perspectivas** and use other words you know.

Queridos mamá y papá, 30 de agosto

Hoy es el último día de mis dos _____ en México. Ahora hablo y _____ mucho español. Me encanta la _____ de aquí y quiero _____ pronto. Me gustan las _____ mayas, pero también es bueno tomar el _____ en la _____ !Este viaje de verdad es _____ un sueño!

Un abrazo de su hija, Silvia ♡

B. Proyectos de viaje. Imagine you are planning a vacation. Using the questions below as a guide, tell about your trip.

1. ¿Cuándo sales de viaje?
2. ¿Cuántos días piensas pasar de vacaciones?
3. ¿Adónde quieres ir?
4. ¿Cómo prefieres viajar?
5. ¿Con quién vas a viajar?
6. ¿Qué ciudades vas a visitar?
7. ¿Qué otras actividades quieres hacer?

C. Agencia de viajes. Imagine you are a travel agent. Based on the information the following people give, choose the vacation best suited to their situation or make a suggestion of your own.

1. Somos estudiantes pobres pero queremos hacer un viaje a España este verano.
   a. Deben buscar los hoteles y restaurantes más caros.
   b. Deben viajar en bicicleta y acampar.
   c. Deben olvidar este viaje.
   d. ?

2. Me gustan el mar, el esquí acuático y la natación.
   a. Usted debe pasar las vacaciones en las montañas.
   b. Usted debe ir a una ciudad grande.
   c. Usted debe ir a una isla del Caribe.
   d. ?

3. A nosotros nos gusta la historia, la música clásica, el arte y el teatro.
   a. Deben pasar sus vacaciones en una ciudad grande.
   b. Deben ir al campo.
   c. Deben pensar en la playa para sus vacaciones.
   d. ?

4. Quiero viajar y hablar español mejor, pero no quiero ir al extranjero.
   a. Debes visitar una isla del Caribe.
   b. Debes pasar unos meses en una comunidad hispana en los Estados Unidos.
   c. Debes mirar programas de televisión en español.
   d. ?

VOCABULARIO DEL CAPÍTULO

NOUNS

el abrazo hug
la actividad activity
el aire air
el atletismo athletics
el autobús bus
el avión plane
el barco boat
la brisa breeze
el campamento de verano summer camp
el campo country (countryside)
la catedral cathedral
la ciudad city
la corrida de toros bullfight
la cosa thing
la derecha right
el esquí acuático waterskiing
la estación season
el estudio studio
el extranjero; en . . . in a foreign country, abroad
la fecha date
la isla island
la izquierda left
el mar sea
el mes month
la montaña mountain
el monumento monument
la naturaleza nature
la playa beach
el recuerdo souvenir
la reproducción reproduction, copy
la ruina ruin
el sol sun
la suerte luck
la tensión tension
el trabajo work, job
el tren train
la vida life

PRONOUNS

algunos some
todo el mundo everyone, everybody

ADJECTIVES

acuático water, aquatic
agitado hectic, agitated
atlético athletic
corto short
fabuloso fabulous
ideal ideal
libre free
maya Mayan
mejor best
mexicano Mexican
perfecto perfect
pobre poor
típico typical, characteristic
tropical tropical

VERBS

acampar to camp
admirar to admire
comenzar (a) (ie) to begin (to)
creer to believe
dar to give
empezar (a) (ie) to begin (to)
entender (ie) to understand
gastar to spend
hacer un viaje to take a trip
llegar to arrive
llevar to take (along someone or something)
pensar (ie) to think
pensar + *inf.* to plan on, intend
pensar en to think about
perder (ie) to lose, waste, miss (a bus, plane)
preferir (ie) to prefer
quedar to be located
tomar el sol to take a sunbath

PREPOSITIONS AND PREPOSITIONAL PHRASES

al lado de next to, beside
cerca (de) near (to)
debajo de under, beneath
desde from
detrás (de) behind
encima (de) on (top of), above
enfrente de in front of
entre between
frente a facing, opposite
hasta until
lejos (de) far (from)
sin without

OTHER WORDS AND EXPRESSIONS

como since, because
¿Cuál es la fecha de hoy? *or* **¿Qué fecha es hoy?** What's today's date?
Doble . . . Turn . . .
en fin all in all
no puedo más I can't take it any more.
por fin finally
sacar . . . notas to get . . . grades
saludos regards, greetings
Siga derecho. Go straight ahead.
temprano early

Capítulo nueve

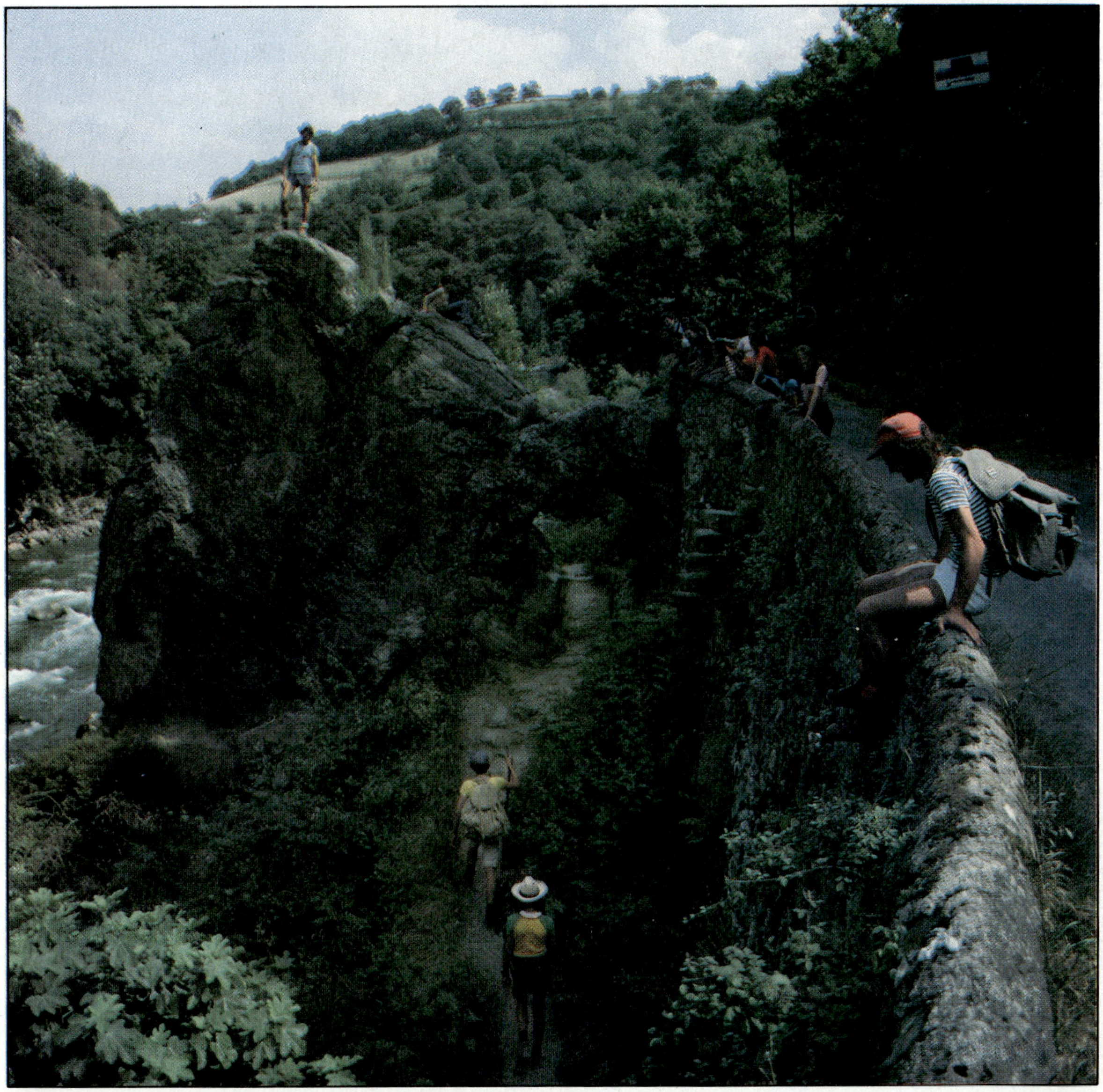

RECREATION AND HOBBIES

9

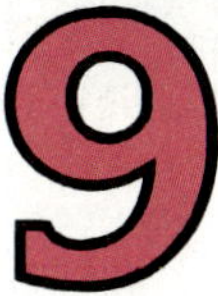

INTRODUCCIÓN

El anuario

yearbook

Members of the Spanish Club have been asked to write about their extra-curricular activities for the school yearbook. Here is what some of them wrote.

Phil "Felipe" Williams
Yo soy coleccionista. Colecciono todo—monedas, juegos electrónicos, historietas. Juego también ajedrez, un pasatiempo muy exigente. Para estar en buena forma, corro todas las mañanas antes de ir a la escuela.

coins
chess / hobby
demanding
I jog (run)

Raquel Salamanca
A mí me interesan las artes.* Tomo clases de baile moderno y de jazz y soy miembro del grupo de teatro. En los pocos ratos libres que tengo me gusta leer y dibujar.

free time
draw

*__Interesar__ and **encantar** are like **gustar**. They are usually used in the third person singular or plural with indirect object pronouns: **Me interesan los deportes. Nos encanta el teatro.**

Frank "Paco" Anderson
Como saben, los deportes son mi vida. Cuando no es el fútbol, es el baloncesto o el béisbol. En el verano siempre voy a acampar con los exploradores. (scouts)

Miriam "Mimi" Roth
Me encanta la fotografía y acabo de ganar un premio (just won / prize) por una de mis fotos. También estoy en el club de cocina (cooking) internacional donde preparamos platos de otros países (countries). No soy muy atlética, pero me encanta patinar (to skate) y montar bicicleta.

COMPRENSIÓN

Tell to whom each statement refers.

1. Le gusta bailar y dibujar.
2. Le interesa la cocina de otros países.
3. Va a las montañas con los exploradores.
4. Colecciona muchas cosas.
5. Es miembro de un grupo de teatro.
6. Es fanático de los deportes.
7. A veces gana premios por sus fotografías.
8. Corre antes de ir a la escuela.

COMUNICACIÓN

A. Pasatiempos favoritos. Which of the following pastimes and hobbies do you enjoy?

B. Los ratos libres. Now you know how to talk about pastimes. Using the suggestions below, give reasons why you are or are not interested in some of these activities.

EJEMPLO Me gusta patinar porque es muy bonito.
No me interesa el ajedrez porque es muy difícil.

PASATIEMPOS

Los deportes	el fútbol americano el esquí (acuático) el baloncesto el fútbol la gimnasia	el tenis el boliche la lucha libre el volibol el béisbol	patinar nadar correr levantar pesas
Las artes	bailar cantar escribir dibujar tocar un instrumento participar en un grupo de teatro		
Los juegos	el ajedrez las damas el dominó los rompecabezas		
Otras actividades	hacer yoga sacar fotos cocinar cantar en el coro acampar programar computadoras colaborar en un periódico participar en un equipo de debate leer novelas, poesía, ciencia-ficción, historia, revistas coleccionar monedas, estampillas, carteles, insectos, etc.		

YOGA
TERAPIA
Enfermedades reumáticas y respiratorias
Yoga físico y mental
Director: Doctor M. FRAILE SANCHEZ
(Unico centro de yoga en Madrid dirigido por un médico)
ASANGA. C/ Alcalá, 155 - 1.º Tel. 431 71 32

RAZONES

porque es/son	emocionante exigente aburrido interesante	difícil fatigoso* divertido bonito	bueno para la salud* caro barato
para	aumentar de peso bajar de peso	sacar músculos* descansar	aprender

***Vocabulario nuevo**
fatigoso tiring **la salud** health
sacar músculos to develop muscles

EXPLORACIÓN

Discussing what we do
Using stem-changing verbs:
o ⟶ ue; u ⟶ ue

PRESENTACIÓN

A. You have already learned one type of stem-changing verb—the **e** to **ie**. Another group of stem-changing verbs is the **o** to **ue** type.

Study the forms of **recordar** (*to remember*), **poder** (*can, to be able, may*), and **dormir** (*to sleep*).

recordar

recuerdo	recordamos
recuerdas	
recuerda	recuerdan

poder

puedo	podemos
puedes	
puede	pueden

dormir

duermo	dormimos
duermes	
duerme	duermen

Note that the verbs have regular endings, but the **o** of the stem becomes **ue** in all persons except the **nosotros** form. Here are other **o** ⟶ **ue** stem-changing verbs.

almorzar to have lunch
costar to cost
encontrar to find, meet
mostrar to show
volver to return

¿Puedo mirar la tele?
Encontramos a José después de clase.
Los niños duermen mucho.
¿Cuánto cuesta un coche nuevo?

B. Jugar has a stem change from **u** to **ue**, except in the **nosotros** form.

jugar

juego	jugamos
juegas	
juega	juegan

Juego fútbol todos los sábados. Nunca jugamos los domingos.

PREPARACIÓN

A. Dormilones. Several friends are telling how late they sleep on weekends. Tell what they say.

MODELO Enrique / 10:00
Enrique duerme hasta las diez.

1. Nosotros / 11:00
2. Mi hermano / 9:30
3. Usted / 12:00
4. Los niños / 9:00
5. Tú / 10:45
6. Yo / 11:15

B. ¿Quién puede? A yoga teacher is asking her class who can do certain postures. What do the students answer?

MODELO Cristina
Cristina puede hacerlo.

1. Rosa María y Marta
2. Nosotras
3. Yo
4. Teresita
5. Tú
6. Ustedes

C. Reunión de coleccionistas. The Collectors Club is having a meeting today. Tell what each person is showing.

MODELO Luisa / sus carteles
Luisa muestra sus carteles.

1. Roberto / su colección de insectos
2. Juanita y Clara / sus muñecas
3. Tú / tus tarjetas de béisbol
4. Nosotros / nuestros discos viejos
5. La profesora / sus anuarios
6. Yo / mis estampillas

D. ¿Cómo lo encuentras tú? Students are telling what they think of different pastimes. What do they say?

MODELO Vicente / difícil el yoga
Vicente encuentra difícil el yoga.

1. Elena / bonito el baile moderno
2. Paco / exigente el ajedrez
3. Lucía y Tomás / emocionantes los deportes
4. Tú / fatigoso levantar pesas
5. Tú y yo / difícil el yoga
6. Yo / aburrida la cocina

E. Recreo. Tell what the following people are playing.

MODELO

los estudiantes
Los estudiantes juegan baloncesto.

COMUNICACIÓN

A. ¿Verdad o mentira? Are the following statements true or false for you? If a statement is false, reword it to make it true.

EJEMPLO Yo puedo nadar bien.
Yo no puedo nadar muy bien.

1. Yo siempre encuentro mis cosas.
2. Yo siempre duermo bien.
3. Yo encuentro difícil el yoga.
4. Yo juego ajedrez bastante mal.
5. Mis amigos y yo siempre recordamos los cumpleaños.
6. Yo vuelvo a casa temprano después de la escuela.
7. Yo siempre almuerzo bien en la cafetería.
8. Yo siempre muestro mi colección de . . .

B. ¿Quién puede . . . ? Make questions to ask other students in order to find out who in your class is able to do the following things.

EJEMPLO tocar un instrumento
José, ¿puedes tocar un instrumento?

1. sacar buenas fotografías
2. preparar platos de otros países
3. dibujar bien
4. escribir poesía
5. hacer yoga
6. levantar pesas
7. bailar o cantar

C. Los planes de fin de semana. Listed below are possible activities for the coming weekend.

1. Give the activities that you can do this weekend.

   EJEMPLO Yo puedo ir al cine.

2. Identify the activities you are not able to do and give the reason why.

   EJEMPLO Yo no puedo invitar a mis amigos porque no tengo tiempo.

Actividades	**Razones**
practicar un deporte	No tengo tiempo.
levantar pesas	Mis padres no quieren.
leer un buen libro	No tengo dinero.
comprar algo para mi colección	Hace mal tiempo.
patinar	Va a llover.
ir a un partido de fútbol	Estoy cansado(a).
volver a medianoche	No quiero hacerlo.
ir a una fiesta con mis amigos	Lo encuentro fatigoso.
dormir hasta el mediodía	Tengo mucho que hacer.
ir a un concierto de rock	Tengo que estar en casa.
esquiar	Cuesta mucho.

RINCÓN CULTURAL

En Europa y en Latinoamérica, el fútbol es el deporte más popular y todos lo practican—ricos y pobres, jóvenes y viejos. Hay todas clases de equipos, escolares (*school*), clubes privados y, por supuesto, profesionales. La competencia (*competition*) entre los equipos profesionales es feroz. El fútbol es realmente una pasión nacional. Cuando hay un juego entre dos países, como entre Brasil y Uruguay, por ejemplo, todos consideran a su equipo como un símbolo nacional y todo el mundo habla de la competencia con mucho entusiasmo patriótico. Aquí están las banderas de países que participaron en la Copa Mundial, España 1982. ¿Puedes identificar el país?

EXPLORACIÓN

Talking about someone already mentioned
Indirect object pronouns le *and* les

PRESENTACIÓN

You have used **lo**, **la**, **los**, and **las** to replace direct objects. You have also used **me**, **te**, and **nos** both as direct and indirect objects to refer to people already mentioned.

The third person object pronouns have different forms, depending on whether they are direct or indirect objects.

INDIRECT OBJECT PRONOUNS		DIRECT OBJECT PRONOUNS	
me	nos	me	nos
te		te	
le	**les**	**lo**	**los**
		la	**las**

A. The indirect object pronouns meaning *to* or *for him, her,* and *you* are **le** and **les**. Like all indirect object pronouns, they tell *to whom* or *for whom* the action of the verb is performed. The meaning of **le** and **les** is usually clear from the context.

Le escribo.	I write	to him. / to her. / to you.
Va a comprar**les** algo.	He's going to buy something	for you (*all*). / for them (*m/f*).

B. When the meaning is not clear or when we wish to add emphasis, **a** plus a prepositional pronoun may be used *in addition to* the indirect object pronouns.

me . . .	a mí	nos . . .	a nosotros/nosotras
te . . .	a ti		
le . . .	a él / a ella / a usted	les . . .	a ellos / a ellas / a ustedes

FOR CLARITY: Quiere dar**les** las noticias **a ustedes**.
A ella no **le** muestro mis fotos.

FOR EMPHASIS: **A mí** no **me** hablan.
¿**Nos** traen algo **a nosotros**?

C. In Spanish it is common to express the indirect object twice in the same sentence. Even though it isn't translated, the indirect object pronoun cannot be omitted.

Le digo la verdad **a Daniel**.	I tell Daniel the truth.
¿**Les** hablas español **a tus amigos**?	Do you speak Spanish to your friends?

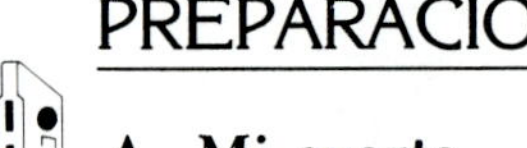

PREPARACIÓN

A. Mi cuarto. It's the day before an exchange student arrives at the Bonilla's. Little Cristina is telling everyone what she is going to show her. What does Cristina say?

MODELO mis libros y discos
Voy a mostrarle mis libros y discos.

1. mis juegos electrónicos
2. mis anillos y pulseras
3. mi perro
4. mis fotos
5. mi colección de muñecas
6. mi osito de felpa

B. Hermano mayor. Mario never has time to learn his role in the school play because of the things he does for his little brothers. Tell what he says.

MODELO arreglar el cuarto
Les arreglo el cuarto.

1. leer libros
2. preparar el almuerzo
3. enseñar inglés
4. tocar discos
5. comprar muchas cosas
6. enseñar a jugar fútbol

C. Poco cooperativo. Students are talking about a club member who is of no help to anyone else. What do they say?

MODELO A ellos / no decir nada
A ellos no les dice nada.

1. a él / no enseñar nada
2. a mí / no prometer nada
3. a ustedes / no dar nada
4. a ti / no preguntar nada
5. a ella / no traer nada
6. a nosotros / no decir nada

D. Padres estrictos. Marisol thinks her parents are strict. What does she say her friends' parents permit them to do?

MODELO A Luis / llevar el coche
A Luis le permiten llevar el coche.

1. A Elena / tener fiestas en casa
2. A Juan y a Pedro / tocar música rock
3. A Betina / salir los sábados por la noche
4. A mis amigos / volver a medianoche
5. A Luisa / dormir en casa de sus amigas

COMUNICACIÓN

A. Entrevista. Answer the following questions or use them to interview another student. Be sure to use direct object pronouns in your answers.

EJEMPLO ¿Ayudas mucho a tus padres?
Sí, los ayudo mucho.

1. ¿Coleccionas estampillas? ¿insectos?
2. ¿Juegas ajedrez? ¿dominó?
3. ¿Escuchas jazz? ¿rock? ¿música clásica?
4. ¿Practicas fútbol? ¿lucha libre? ¿volibol?
5. ¿Ayudas al equipo de debate? ¿al grupo de teatro?
6. ¿Lees el periódico de la escuela? ¿el anuario?
7. ¿Lees novelas? ¿poesía? ¿revistas? ¿historietas?
8. ¿A veces preparas el desayuno? ¿el almuerzo? ¿la cena?
9. ¿Tocas el piano? ¿la guitarra?
10. ¿Sabes cocinar bistec? ¿vegetales? ¿pescado?
11. ¿Quieres llevar a tus amigos al cine?
12. ¿Piensas tocar música clásica para una fiesta?

B. ¿Recuerdas? Try to remember the interests, likes, and dislikes of other people in your class.

EJEMPLO A Juan le gustan el fútbol y el béisbol, ¿verdad?
Sí, a él le gustan.
No, a él le encanta el fútbol, pero no le interesa el béisbol.

C. ¿A quién? Using indirect object pronouns, tell to or for whom you usually do the following things.

EJEMPLO A mis amigos les escribo tarjetas.

1. comprar un regalo
2. escribir tarjetas
3. dar noticias
4. decir la verdad
5. mostrar la tarea
6. arreglar la casa
7. preparar el desayuno
8. traer chocolates

RINCÓN CULTURAL

Los latinoamericanos practican toda clase de deportes al aire libre porque la geografía del continente es muy diversa. Hay costas con playas fabulosas para la pesca o el esquí acuático en casi todos los países, desde México a la Argentina, y especialmente en el Caribe. Hay ríos grandes como el Amazonas, el Orinoco y el Río de la Plata. Hay montañas altísimas, como los Andes, donde es posible esquiar todo el año, y hay desiertos, como el Atacama en Chile, donde hace un calor imposible. Hay llanuras (*plains*) como la pampa argentina, buenas para la agricultura; y hay selvas (*jungles*) enormes con ciudades grandes como Iquitos en el Perú.

Consulta el mapa en las páginas 7 y 8. ¿Dónde crees que practican estos deportes en Latinoamérica?

el buceo	skin diving	**el acuaplanismo**	surfing
el esquí	skiing	**la pesca**	fishing
la equitación	horseback riding	**la caza**	hunting

EXPLORACIÓN

Avoiding repetition of nouns
Prepositional pronouns

PRESENTACIÓN

As you have already seen, there are certain pronouns used with the preposition **a** for emphasis or for clarity.

A mí me interesa la lucha libre.
Le encanta la música rock a él.
Voy a darles a ustedes estampillas para su colección.

A. Remember that the prepositional pronouns are the same as the subject pronouns, except for *me* (**mí**) and the familiar *you* (**ti**).

PREPOSITIONAL PRONOUNS	
mí	nosotros, nosotras
ti	
él	ellos
ella	ellas
usted	ustedes

These pronouns may be used after the prepositions **a**, **de**, **en**, **para**, **por**, **sin**, or after prepositional phrases (**cerca de**, **lejos de**, **enfrente de**, etc.)

No queremos salir sin ti.
Es un regalo para ella.
Viven cerca de ustedes.

B. There are two exceptions. When **mí** and **ti** are used with **con**, they become **conmigo** and **contigo**.

¿Quieres jugar damas conmigo?
No, no quiero jugar contigo.

C. Note that prepositional pronouns also replace things.

Hablan de los deportes.
Hablan de **ellos**.

Piensan en la fiesta.
Piensan en **ella**.

PREPARACIÓN

A. ¡No quiero problemas! Lola is asking Santiago what he and his friends always talk about. Santiago does not want to give her any information. What does he say?

MODELO ¿Hablan de las chicas?
No, no hablamos de ellas.

1. ¿Hablan de los profesores?
2. ¿Hablan de la señorita Álvarez?
3. ¿Hablan de la clase de gimnasia?
4. ¿Hablan de mí?
5. ¿Hablan de nosotros?
6. ¿Hablan del baile?

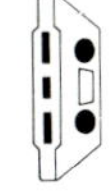
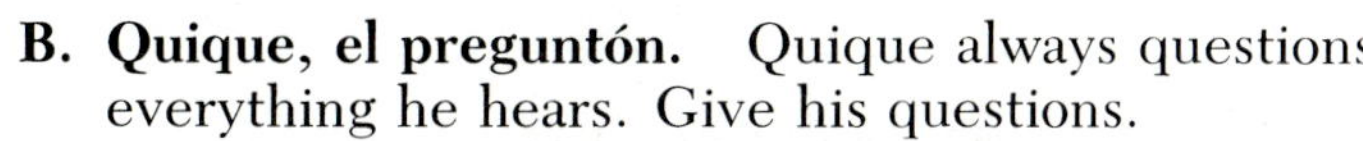

B. Quique, el preguntón. Quique always questions everything he hears. Give his questions.

MODELO Salgo con los otros chicos.
¿Sales con ellos?

1. Estudio con Marianela.
2. Voy al cine con Eduardo.
3. Aprendo con el profesor Moreno.
4. Vivo con mis abuelos.
5. Quiero hablar contigo.
6. Veo televisión con Carlos.
7. Prefiero trabajar con ustedes.
8. Corro con Jaime todos los días.

JUVENTUD
Y NATURALEZA
ACTIVIDADES EN COLABORACION CON COMUNIDADES AUTONOMAS

C. Una tarde de teatro. The Spanish Club is going to a play. Members are looking at a theater plan to see where they are sitting. How do they answer the club president's questions?

MODELO ¿Quién está al lado de Marta? (el profesor)
El profesor está al lado de ella.

1. ¿Quién está al lado de Luis? (María)
2. ¿Quién está enfrente de Alicia? (Juan)
3. ¿Quién está detrás de Miguel y José? (Pilar)
4. ¿Quién está cerca de ustedes? (tú)
5. ¿Quién está cerca de ti? (Esteban)

COMUNICACIÓN

A. Preferencias. Indicate your feelings by completing the following.

EJEMPLO ¿Canto en el coro?
Sí, me gusta cantar en él.

1. ¿Estudio con ________ ?
   ¡Sí! Siempre estudio con ________ .
2. ¿Hablo de ________ ?
   Pues sí, a veces hablo de ________ .
3. ¿Juego baloncesto con ________ ?
   ¡Por supuesto! Juego muchas veces con ________ .
4. ¿Trabajo en ________ ?
   ¡Qué pesado! Nunca trabajo en ________ .
5. ¿Voy a colaborar en el periódico con ________ ?
   ¡Me alegro! Me gusta mucho trabajar en el periódico con ________.
6. ¿Hago la tarea sin ________ ?
   ¡Ay, no! No puedo hacer la tarea sin ________ .

COMBOTICKET
REPERTORIO ESPAÑOL
COMBOTICKET

Música y Danza
La zarzuela en todo su esplendor: la zarzuela española y la zarzuela latinoamericana . . . clásica y moderna, cómica y dramática. Además conciertos y espectáculos de danza, música y canto.

Drama
El drama romántico, el drama de costumbres, el drama psicológico y el satírico. Drama para todos los públicos.

Latinoamericano
Obras dinámicas y vitales de la actualidad latinoamericana. Lo mejor de lo mejor para los latinos de Nueva York.

Español
Desde el teatro renacentista de Fernando de Rojas, pasando por García Lorca, hasta lo más representativo de la escena española de hoy.

B. Entrevista. Answer the following questions or use them to interview another student. Be sure to use the appropriate prepositional pronoun in your answers.

EJEMPLO ¿Juegas damas con tus amigos?
Sí, juego damas con ellos.

1. ¿Practicas un deporte con otros estudiantes?
2. ¿Lavas el coche para tu papá?
3. ¿Hablas mucho de tu familia?
4. ¿Colaboras en el periódico?
5. ¿Cantas en el coro?
6. ¿Vas de compras sin dinero?
7. ¿Participas en el grupo de teatro?
8. ¿Juegas baloncesto con el equipo?
9. ¿Pasas tu tiempo libre con tus amigos?
10. ¿Vas a acampar con los exploradores?
11. ¿Patinas con tus amigos a veces?
12. ¿Piensas mucho en tu familia?

RINCÓN CULTURAL

¿Te gustan las películas extranjeras? Hoy en día España y varios países de Latinoamérica, sobre todo México y Argentina, producen películas famosas en el mundo entero. A pesar de (*in spite of*) tener excelentes industrias cinematográficas, los españoles y latinoamericanos ven muchas películas francesas y norteamericanas. Ésta es una buena manera de practicar el francés o el inglés. ¿Reconoces el título español de estas películas?

1. *El extraterrestre*
2. *Oficial y caballero*
3. *El imperio contraataca*
4. *Carros de fuego*
5. *Rebelión a bordo*
6. *Lo que el viento se llevó*

EXPLORACIÓN

Giving advice or orders
The familiar commands

PRESENTACIÓN

To give advice or orders, to request, or to tell someone not to do something, we use the command forms. The familiar commands are used for people with whom you would use the **tú** form of the verb.

A. The affirmative singular command of regular and stem-changing **ar**, **er**, and **ir** verbs is the same as the **tú** form of the verb minus the final **s**.

¡Ayuda a tu hermano!	Help your brother!
¡Vuelve pronto!	Return soon!
¡Abre el libro!	Open your book!

The following verbs have irregular affirmative **tú** commands.

decir	**di**	ir	**ve**
salir	**sal**	tener	**ten**
hacer	**haz**	poner	**pon**
ser	**sé**		

B. To form a negative **tú** command, use the following formula:

yo form minus **o**	plus opposite vowel **ar ⟶ e, er ⟶ a, ir ⟶ a**	add **s**
no mirø	e	no mires
no veø	a	no veas
no duermø	a	no duermas
no salgø	a	no salgas

The following verbs have irregular negative **tú** commands.

dar	**no des**	ir	**no vayas**
estar	**no estés**	ser	**no seas**

Mira la revista.	No mires el periódico.
Piensa en mí.	No pienses en ella.
Di la verdad.	No digas mentiras.
Sé buena.	No seas mala.

PREPARACIÓN

A. En el estadio Cibao. Some Dominican students are at a baseball game. The teacher wants to keep things organized. What does he say to each student?

MODELO comprar los programas ahora
¡Compra los programas ahora!

1. sacar fotos de los jugadores
2. hablar con las chicas más tarde
3. buscar unos helados para nosotros
4. traer los refrescos ahora
5. escuchar la radio también
6. poner la cámara aquí

B. Precauciones. Miguel is about to leave for his first performance with the **Tuna**, and his parents are giving him some last-minute advice. Tell what they say.

MODELO no olvidar tus llaves
¡No olvides tus llaves!

1. no olvidar la guitarra
2. no ir en la moto
3. no comer antes del concierto
4. no estar nervioso
5. no olvidar mirar a la gente
6. no tener miedo
7. no salir con los amigos
8. no volver muy tarde

C. ¿Qué voy a hacer? Marisa is planning her summer vacation at the beach and would like her friend's opinion. What does her friend say to her?

MODELO Pienso pasar el verano en la playa. (sí)
Sí, pasa el verano en la playa.

1. Pienso ir a la Florida. (sí)
2. Pienso viajar en coche. (no)
3. Pienso dar paseos por la playa. (sí)
4. Pienso descansar en el hotel. (no)
5. Pienso hacer el esquí acuático con los amigos. (sí)
6. Pienso nadar todos los días. (sí)
7. Pienso ir a bailar todas las noches. (no)
8. Pienso llamar a mis padres por teléfono. (sí)

COMUNICACIÓN

A. Consejos. Some new students are interested in finding out about extracurricular activities. What advice would you give them?

EJEMPLO ser miembro de muchos grupos
No, no seas miembro de muchos grupos.

levantar pesas
Sí, levanta pesas.

1. estudiar computadoras
2. cantar en el coro
3. participar en el grupo de teatro
4. tomar una clase de guitarra
5. participar en el equipo de debate
6. hacer yoga
7. coleccionar monedas
8. ir a los conciertos
9. colaborar en el periódico
10. patinar por la noche

B. ¡Vamos a jugar en San Juan! Your school soccer team has been invited to play in San Juan. Give each player advice by selecting the most appropriate suggestion below.

EJEMPLO	**Situación**	Hay un jugador que no puede ir en avión.
	Sugerencia	¡No vayas en avión! ¡Ve en barco!

Situaciones

1. Hay un jugador que habla español.
2. Hay un jugador que no habla español.
3. Hay un jugador que no quiere gastar mucho en comidas.
4. Hay un jugador a quien le gustan el arte y la historia.
5. Hay un jugador a quien le encanta la cocina hispana.
6. Hay un jugador que quiere comprar recuerdos.
7. Hay un jugador a quien no le gusta salir solo por la noche.
8. Hay un jugador que es fotógrafo aficionado.

Sugerencias

hablar español con el equipo puertorriqueño
estudiar español antes de ir
ir de compras a las tiendas
comer en restaurantes típicos
llevar la cámara
salir con los jugadores puertorriqueños
comer en la escuela
visitar los museos de San Juan
¿ . . . ?

PERSPECTIVAS

La vida al aire libre — outdoors

Los muchachos exploradores y las muchachas guías de aquí y de los países hispanos tienen más o menos las mismas experiencias. Por ejemplo, si eres explorador o guía, probablemente conoces la vida al aire libre. Vamos a ver si sabes las reglas que observa un buen acampador o una buena acampadora.

boy, girl scouts

rules / camper

1. Lleva tu equipo en una mochila. ¡No lleves demasiado! ¡No olvides tu saco de dormir!
2. Levanta la tienda cuando todavía es de día. No esperes hasta la noche.
3. Haz una fogata, pero ten cuidado con el fuego.
4. Aprende a cocinar sobre la fogata. No tengas miedo de comer algo nuevo.
5. Respeta la naturaleza. Observa los animales, los pájaros y las plantas, pero no les hagas daño.

equipment / too much
bag
tent
campfire / be careful / fire
harm

6. Muestra consideración hacia los otros acampadores y los animales. No hagas ruido.
7. Explora el bosque. Da caminatas, pero ten cuidado de no perder el camino. — woods / go for hikes; way
8. No nades solo ni camines solo en el bosque. Ve siempre con otra persona. — walk
9. Conserva nuestros recursos naturales.
10. Al volver a casa, deja todo limpio. No dejes papeles y otra basura. — leave / clean / garbage

Con estas reglas puedes pasar unas semanas muy agradables al aire libre, conocer a nuevos amigos y aprender a ser responsable de ti mismo. ¡Buena suerte!

COMPRENSIÓN

Tell whether these statements are true (**verdadero**) or false (**falso**).

1. No hay exploradores ni guías en los países hispanos.
2. Las reglas para acampadores no son importantes.
3. No debes llevar demasiado en la mochila.
4. Puedes hacer una fogata si tienes cuidado.
5. Está bien hacer mucho ruido en el bosque.
6. Es difícil perder el camino en el bosque.
7. No es una buena idea nadar o dar caminatas solo.
8. Tenemos que respetar la naturaleza, especialmente las plantas y los animales.
9. Si no sabes levantar una tienda, tienes que dormir al aire libre.
10. Debemos dejar todo limpio al regresar a la ciudad.

COMUNICACIÓN

A. Cartel de tareas. Imagine your group leader is making a chart of camp chores. Tell what you prefer to do, what you can do, and what you don't want to do.

EJEMPLO Puedo levantar la tienda, pero prefiero cocinar. No quiero traer agua.

levantar la tienda
hacer la fogata
cuidar el fuego
cocinar
hacer el almuerzo para la caminata
lavar los platos
traer agua
arreglar el campamento
hacer un cartel de reglas
llevar el equipo durante la caminata
sacar la basura

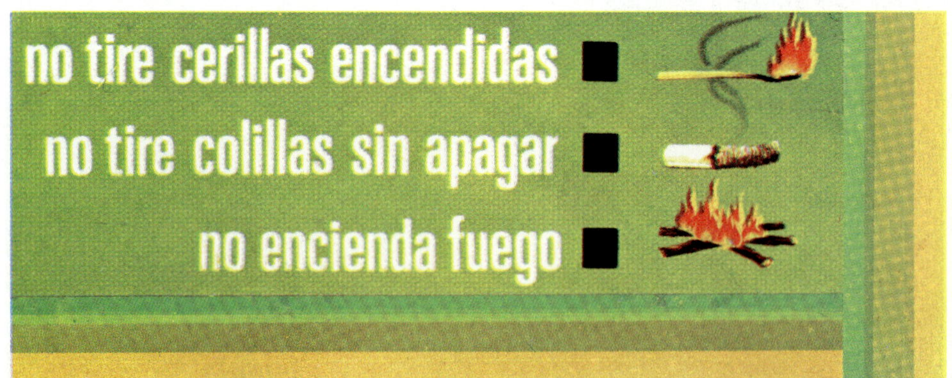

B. Un día de lluvia. It's a rainy day at camp. Tell what you do to pass the time.

EJEMPLO Les escribo tarjetas a mis amigos.
Jugamos damas.

Sugerencias

jugar ajedrez	escribir tarjetas
jugar damas	leer un libro
dibujar	hacer gimnasia
cantar	hacer una comida especial
arreglar el equipo	?

C. Perfil de un acampador. Use the questions below to find out how you or another student feel about camping.

1. ¿Cuesta mucho ir a un campamento de exploradores o guías?
2. ¿Hay un bosque cerca de tu ciudad?
3. ¿Prefieres dormir en un saco de dormir o en casa?
4. ¿Sabes hacer una fogata?
5. ¿Tienes miedo de perder el camino cuando das caminatas?
6. ¿Coleccionas insectos o plantas cuando vas a acampar?
7. Cuando das una caminata, ¿siempre vuelves cuando todavía es de día?
8. ¿Te gusta dibujar plantas o animales?
9. ¿Siempre dejas limpio el campamento?
10. ¿Encuentras divertida la vida de un acampador?

D. Entrevista. Interview students about their pastimes. Then report back to the class.

EJEMPLO ¿Qué haces en tus ratos libres?

VOCABULARIO DEL CAPÍTULO

NOUNS RELATING TO CAMPING

el acampador camper
la basura garbage
el bosque woods, forest
la caminata hike
el camino way, path
el equipo equipment
la fogata campfire
el fuego fire
el (muchacho) explorador boy scout
la (muchacha) guía girl scout
la planta plant
el saco de dormir sleeping bag
la tienda tent

NOUNS

el ajedrez chess
el anuario yearbook
las artes arts
el club club
la cocina cooking, cuisine
el coleccionista collector
la consideración consideration
el coro chorus
los damas checkers
el debate debate
el dominó domino, dominoes
la estampilla stamp
la experiencia experience
el insecto insect
el instrumento instrument
el miembro member
la moneda coin
la muñeca doll
el país country, nation
el pasatiempo pastime, hobby
las pesas weights
el premio prize
los ratos libres free time
los recursos resources
la regla rule
la salud health
el yoga yoga

PRONOUNS

todo everything

ADJECTIVES

atlético athletic
estudiantil student
exigente demanding
fatigoso tiring
internacional international
limpio clean
moderno modern
solo alone

VERBS

acabar de + inf. to have just
almorzar (ue) to have lunch
caminar to walk
colaborar to work on
coleccionar to collect
conservar to conserve
correr to run, jog
costar (ue) to cost
dejar to leave (something or someone behind)
dibujar to draw
dormir (ue) to sleep
encantar to like a lot
encontrar (ue) to meet, to find
interesar to be interested in
levantar to lift, to raise
levantar una tienda to pitch a tent
mostrar (ue) to show
observar to observe
participar (en) to participate (in)
patinar to skate
poder (ue) to be able to, can
recordar (ue) to remember
respetar to respect
sacar músculos to develop muscles
volver (ue) to return

ADVERBS

demasiado too much
probablemente probably

EXPRESSIONS

al aire libre outdoors
dar una caminata to go on a hike
Es de día. It's daytime.
estar en buena forma to be in good shape
hacer(le) daño to harm (someone)
por ti mismo for yourself
tener cuidado (de) to be careful

Capítulo diez

LOOKING GOOD 10

INTRODUCCIÓN

Seguir la moda: ¿a qué precio?

Keeping up with fashion

Inés, a new student from Chile, and Rita are shopping for school clothes in Los Angeles.

RITA	Mira, esta tienda tiene mucha ropa en venta.	clothing / on sale
INÉS	¡Qué bueno! Me gustan mucho esos jeans franceses. Señorita, ¿tiene usted estos jeans en la talla treinta y ocho?	French size
VENDEDORA	¿Treinta y ocho? ¡No puede ser! Usted es delgada.	
RITA	Señorita, creo que ella habla de las tallas europeas y no de las americanas.*	
VENDEDORA	¡Ah, ya entiendo! La señorita debe usar la talla diez. Aquí los tiene usted.	use, wear
INÉS	¡Qué bien me quedan! ¿Cuánto son?	fit
VENDEDORA	Cuarenta y cinco dólares.	
INÉS	¿Cuarenta y cinco? A ese precio, ¿quién quiere estar a la moda?	in style

*To use an adjective as a noun, simply omit the noun: **las [tallas] americanas** *the American ones*; **los [zapatos] baratos** *the cheap ones*; **el [coche] grande** *the big one*.

COMPRENSIÓN

Answer the questions based on **Seguir la moda: ¿a qué precio?**

1. ¿Dónde están Inés y Rita?
2. ¿Qué tipo de jeans quiere Inés?
3. ¿Qué talla usa Inés en Chile?
4. ¿Tiene la tienda esta talla? ¿Cuál es el problema?
5. ¿Qué talla le trae la vendedora?
6. ¿Cómo le quedan los jeans?
7. ¿Por qué no va a comprarlos?

COMUNICACIÓN

Here are some articles of clothing you might buy.

LOS COLORES

A. Mi ropa favorita. Tell what kind of clothing you prefer to wear and what kind you don't.

> **EJEMPLO** Prefiero usar pantalones cortos en el verano.
> No me gustan los sombreros.

B. Mis colores preferidos. Tell what your favorite color is and what other colors you like.

> **EJEMPLO** Mi color preferido es el azul, pero me gusta el rojo también.

C. Galanterías. Using adjectives you know, make up compliments to give other students about what they are wearing.

> **EJEMPLO** ¡Qué bien te queda esa camisa, César!

D. La ropa apropiada. Tell what you would wear in the following situations.

> **EJEMPLO** Para ir a la playa, . . .
> Para ir a la playa uso un traje de baño.

1. Para ir a la escuela, . . .
2. Para salir con mis amigos, . . .
3. Cuando hace mucho calor, . . .
4. Cuando hace mucho frío, . . .
5. Para ir a un concierto de rock, . . .
6. Para ir a acampar a las montañas, . . .
7. Cuando está lloviendo, . . .
8. Para hacer un viaje en tren, . . .

EXPLORACIÓN

Discussing what we buy
Stem-changing verbs **e ⟶ i** *and* **venir**

PRESENTACIÓN

A. You have already learned three types of stem-changing verbs (**e ⟶ ie**, **o ⟶ ue**, and **u ⟶ ue**). Another group of stem-changing verbs is the **e ⟶ i** type. Study the forms of the verb **pedir** (*to ask for, to order, to request*).

pedir

pido	pedimos
pides	
pide	piden

Pedir has regular endings, but the **e** of the stem becomes **i** in all persons except the **nosotros** form. Note that "for" is not expressed because it is included in the meaning of the verb.

Siempre piden bistec.	They always order steak.
A veces le pido dinero a mi papá.	Sometimes I ask my dad for money.
¿Pides ropa para tu cumpleaños?	Do you ask for clothes for your birthday?

B. Here are other **e ⟶ i** stem-changing verbs:

repetir to repeat, to have a second helping of food
servir to serve
servir para to be good for, to be useful
seguir to follow, to continue

repetir

repito	repetimos
repites	
repite	repiten

servir

sirvo	servimos
sirves	
sirve	sirven

seguir

sigo	seguimos
sigues	
sigue	siguen

Notice that the **u** in the **yo** form of **seguir** is omitted.

Siempre seguimos el mismo camino.	We always follow the same road.
El profesor repite la pregunta.	The teacher repeats the question.
Estos zapatos no sirven para jugar tenis.	These shoes are no good for playing tennis.

C. Like **tener**, **venir** (*to come*) is an **ie** stem-changing verb with an irregular **yo** form.

venir

vengo	venimos
vienes	
viene	vienen

Sus abuelos vienen de España. — His grandparents come from Spain.
¿Quién viene ahora? — Who's coming now?

PREPARACIÓN

A. ¿Quién sigue la moda? Patricia, the fashion editor of the school newspaper, knows who keeps up with the latest styles. What does she say about the following people?

MODELO Julia (sí)
Julia sigue la moda.

1. El señor Montero (sí)
2. Emilia y tú (no)
3. Yolanda y Alba (sí)
4. Todos nosotros (sí)
5. Tú (no)
6. Yo (no)

B. Lo mío es tuyo. Mario's friends are always asking for things. What do they ask him for?

MODELO Luis / los zapatos de boliche
Luis le pide los zapatos de boliche.

1. Paco / el guante de béisbol
2. Nosotros / el sombrero de playa
3. Marcela / los lentes de sol
4. Ustedes / el suéter del colegio
5. Tú / el impermeable
6. Yo / la corbata

C. Restaurante de lujo. El Crillón, a luxury restaurant in Lima, has various waiters serving different courses. The head waiter is telling the staff what they will be serving. What does he say?

MODELO José Luis / el agua
José Luis sirve el agua.

1. Tú / el pan
2. Santiago / la sopa
3. Manolo y Pepe / las ensaladas
4. Gonzalo y yo / el primer plato
5. Ustedes / el segundo plato
6. Yo / los postres

D. La familia Rodríguez. Members of the Rodríguez family are coming home. What do they say?

MODELO Ana María / la escuela
Ana María viene de la escuela.

1. Tú / el partido de fútbol
2. Nosotros / la tienda
3. Carmen / el supermercado
4. Yo / el correo
5. Ustedes / el trabajo
6. Mis abuelos / la iglesia

COMUNICACIÓN

A. Comidas familiares. When your mother or father serves the family meal, you often want to ask for a larger or smaller portion or a second helping. Use the following suggestions to describe meals in your home.

Sugerencias pedir: mucho, [un] poco, más, bastante
repetir: siempre, nunca, dos veces

carne asada, pollo, pescado, bistec, habichuelas, papas, pastel, manzanas, fresas, ?

EJEMPLO Cuando mi mamá sirve bistec, siempre repito. Cuando mi papá sirve tortilla, sólo pido un poco.

SEÑORAS
Lavado y Planchado

Prenda	Precio
Camisas	236
Camisones	210
Blusas	236
Pijamas	263
Faldas	315
Vestidos	420
Pantalones	394
Pañuelos	79
Abrigos	694

Entregue su ropa a la camarera o valet, quien se la devolverá terminada en el tiempo mínimo posible.

CABALLEROS
Lavado y Planchado

Prenda	Precio
Camisas	236
Camisas etiqueta	315
Camisetas	116
Pañuelos	79
Calcetines	79
Pijamas	263
Pantalones	394
Chaquetas	594
Corbatas	74

No aceptamos responsabilidad por ropa que encoja o destiña.

B. Entrevista. Answer the following questions or use them to interview another student.

1. En general, ¿sigues la moda? ¿Por qué?
2. ¿A quién le pides dinero para comprar ropa?
3. ¿A quién le pides dinero para ir al cine?
4. ¿Qué vas a pedir como regalo de cumpleaños?
5. ¿Te queda bien la ropa del año pasado?

RINCÓN CULTURAL

A los jóvenes hispanos les gusta vestir (*dress*) bien. La moda de los jóvenes norteamericanos (bluejeans viejos, camiseta y un par de tenis [*sneakers*]) no les parece elegante. Los bluejeans son muy populares en España y en Latinoamérica, pero los jóvenes se visten más elegantemente para ir al cine, a una fiesta o para ir de compras. Y para ir a la escuela muchos tienen que usar uniforme. Generalmente, consiste en una blusa blanca, una falda oscura (*dark*) y calcetines para las chicas; y para los chicos, una chaqueta y pantalones oscuros, una camisa blanca y una corbata.

Imagínate que estás de visita en casa de unos amigos en Colombia. ¿Qué usas para estas ocasiones?

para ir al colegio, a la fiesta de quinceañera de una amiga, a pasar un fin de semana en el campo, de compras, a un restaurante, al cine

EXPLORACIÓN

Talking about physical characteristics Parts of the body and use of the definite article

PRESENTACIÓN

A. To talk about looks and health, you have to know the parts of the body. Below, **el hombre mecánico**, a Spanish-speaking robot, describes the parts of his body.

*__Doler__ (*to hurt*) is an **o ⟶ ue** stem-changing verb that follows the same pattern as **gustar**: **Me duele el estómago. ¿Te duelen los pies?**

El hombre mecánico is made up of the following parts:

la boca	mouth	**el diente**	tooth	**el ojo**	eye
el brazo	arm	**el estómago**	stomach	**la oreja**	ear (outer)
la cabeza	head	**la garganta**	throat	**el pelo**	hair
la cara	face	**la mano**	hand	**el pie**	foot
el corazón	heart	**la nariz**	nose	**la pierna**	leg

B. Instead of the possessives, the definite articles **el**, **la**, **los**, **las** are used with parts of the body when it is clear whose body you are talking about.

Tengo **el** pelo largo.	My hair is long.
¿Te duelen **los** ojos?	Do your eyes hurt?
Tienes **las** manos frías.	You have cold hands.

But, to avoid confusion, a possessive adjective can be used.

Mis ojos son azules.	My eyes are blue.

C. To talk about hair color and length, use these adjectives.

Tiene el pelo rubio	blond
castaño	brown
negro	black
largo	long
corto	short

PREPARACIÓN

A. El primo del hombre mecánico. A Spanish robot is describing his cousin. Tell what he says.

B. Mala memoria. Gilberto can never remember what other people look like. Whenever he makes a comment about someone, his friend Roberto corrects him. What does Roberto say?

MODELO Juan tiene el pelo rubio. (No, . . . castaño)
No, Juan tiene el pelo castaño.

1. Felipe tiene los ojos azules. (No, . . . verdes)
2. Raúl tiene el pelo castaño. (No, . . . negro)
3. Dulce tiene los ojos grises. (No, . . . azules)
4. Marcos tiene el pelo largo. (No, . . . corto)
5. La señora Álvarez tiene el pelo negro. (No, . . . rubio)
6. Teresa tiene los ojos pardos. (No, . . . verdes)

C. ¡Ay qué dolor! People with all kinds of aches and pains are at the doctor's office. What does the doctor ask each patient?

MODELO

COMUNICACIÓN

A. Imaginación sin límites. Create your own robot or creature from outer space. Describe its body or clothing to another student who will try to draw it.

B. Adivina quién es. Choose a person in your class and give students three clues about that person's appearance. They will ask questions to guess who the person is.

EJEMPLO Tiene el pelo largo, los ojos azules
y la nariz pequeña.
¿Usa lentes? Sí.
¿Es Emilio? No . . . .

C. Entrevista. Answer the following questions about your best friend.

1. ¿De qué color tiene el pelo? ¿Es largo?
2. ¿De qué color tiene los ojos? ¿Son grandes?
3. ¿Cómo tiene la boca, grande o pequeña?
4. ¿Cómo tiene la nariz?
5. ¿Tiene las piernas largas o cortas?
6. ¿Tiene los pies grandes o pequeños?

RINCÓN CULTURAL

Como en inglés, el español tiene muchas expresiones con las partes del cuerpo (*body*). Las usamos para describir situaciones y la personalidad o la conducta de las personas. ¿Puedes adivinar (*guess*) qué expresión corresponde a cada dibujo?

a. to perk up one's ears **b.** to lend a hand **c.** to stick your nose in somebody else's business **d.** to cost an arm and a leg **e.** to give someone the cold shoulder **f.** to put your foot in your mouth **g.** from head to toe **h.** to be armed to the teeth **i.** to wear your heart on your sleeve

EXPLORACIÓN

Talking about yourself
Reflexive verbs

PRESENTACIÓN

In Spanish, to talk about things you do to or for yourself, like combing your hair, you have to use reflexive verbs.

A. A reflexive verb requires a reflexive pronoun that refers back to the subject: I wash **myself**. The reflexive pronouns are the same as direct and indirect object pronouns, except in the third person, where **se** is used. Like other object pronouns, they are placed either before the verb or attached to the infinitive.

lavarse

me lavo	**nos** lavamos
te lavas	
se lava	**se** lavan

Quiero lavar**me** las manos.
Me quiero lavar las manos. — I want to wash my hands.

B. Learn the following reflexive verbs.

acostarse (ue) to go to bed
bañarse to take a bath
despertarse (ie) to wake up
dormirse (ue) to fall asleep
lavarse los dientes to brush one's teeth
levantarse to get up
peinarse to comb one's hair
ponerse to put on
probarse (ue) to try on
vestirse (i) to get dressed

Me acuesto siempre a las diez.	I always go to bed at ten.
José se baña por la mañana.	José takes a bath in the morning.
¿A qué hora te despiertas?	What time do you wake up?
Los niños se duermen temprano.	Children go to sleep early.
Olvida lavarse los dientes.	He forgets to brush his teeth.
¿Te gusta levantarte tarde?	Do you like to get up late?
Se peina con la mano.	He uses his hand to comb his hair.
¿Se ponen corbata todos los días?	Do they put on a tie every day?
¿Por qué no te pruebas estos jeans?	Why don't you try on these jeans?
Nos vestimos antes del desayuno.	We get dressed before breakfast.

PREPARACIÓN

A. Un día típico. Luis Alberto, a student at the Colegio San Martín, is describing his typical morning activities. Tell what he says.

MODELO despertarse a las seis y media
Me despierto a las seis y media.

1. levantarse a las siete
2. bañarse con agua fría
3. lavarse los dientes
4. peinarse un poco
5. vestirse en cinco minutos
6. ponerse la mochila

B. Carmen, la dormilona. On weekends Carmen avoids what she has to do during the week. Tell what she does not do on weekends.

MODELO levantarse temprano
No se levanta temprano.

1. despertarse a las seis y media
2. levantarse a las siete
3. vestirse rápido
4. peinarse bien
5. ponerse perfume
6. acostarse temprano

C. La vida de internado. Students at a boy's boarding school are talking about each other's personal habits. What do they say?

MODELO Ustedes / despertarse a las cinco y media
Ustedes se despiertan a las cinco y media.

1. Mario y Vicente / dormirse en clase
2. Yo / siempre / acostarse tardísimo
3. Pepe y Carlos / siempre / ponerse un sombrero
4. Nosotros / bañarse dos veces al día
5. Tú / nunca / peinarse con cuidado
6. Juan / levantarse a las cinco

D. Un hermano autoritario. Juan is always telling his little brother what to do. Tell what Juan says.

MODELO bañarse
Tienes que bañarte ahora.

1. lavarse los dientes
2. dormirse ahora
3. ponerse esos pantalones
4. levantarse ya
5. vestirse más rápido
6. acostarse ahora

E. ¿Qué vas a ponerte? Students going to a concert at the Coliseo Roberto Clemente are talking about what others are going to wear. What do they say?

MODELO Alicia / vestido
Alicia se va a poner un vestido.

1. Tú / unos jeans
2. Ustedes / unos zapatos de tenis
3. Pedro y yo / una corbata
4. Yo / un sombrero
5. Rosa / unos lentes de sol
6. Los otros / unos pantalones

COMUNICACIÓN

A. Obligaciones y preferencias. Using the following suggestions, tell how you feel about having to do some of the things listed below.

Obligaciones:	tengo que	debo	necesito
Preferencias:	me encanta	me gusta	prefiero

EJEMPLO Tengo que levantarme a las seis de la mañana pero no me gusta.

1. acostarse temprano / tarde
2. vestirse bien para salir
3. peinarse todos los días
4. bañarse por la mañana / noche
5. probarse ropa en las tiendas
6. lavarse los dientes después de comer
7. despertarse temprano el fin de semana
8. ?

B. Día tras día. At what time do you do the following activities on a typical school day?

RINCÓN CULTURAL

Más que **cualquier** otro continente, Latinoamérica es un verdadero **crisol** de razas. Por eso se habla de un **mestizaje** racial y cultural. En la base de este mestizaje figuran tres razas: la india, la negra y la blanca (principalmente españoles y portugueses). En países como México, Guatemala, Perú, Ecuador, Bolivia y Paraguay, gran parte de la **población** es india. En otros, como Colombia, Panamá, Brasil y las islas del Caribe, gran parte de la población es negra. Al mismo tiempo, además de los españoles y portugueses, hay mucha gente de otros países europeos (**Alemania**, Italia e **Inglaterra**) que viven mayormente en Argentina, Uruguay y Chile. Hay, pues, una gran variedad de razas en Latinoamérica. Por eso, no podemos hablar de unas características raciales "típicas" con referencia a los latinoamericanos.

cualquier any
crisol melting pot
mestizaje mixture
población population
Alemania Germany
Inglaterra England

EXPLORACIÓN

Talking about past events
The preterite of **ar** *verbs*

PRESENTACIÓN

You have used the present tense to talk about the present and **ir a** to talk about the future.

A. To talk about the past, you may use a past tense called the *preterite*. To form the preterite, drop the **ar** of the infinitive and add the endings shown in the chart.

comprar

compr**é**	compr**amos**
compr**aste**	
compr**ó**	compr**aron**

B. Most stem-changing verbs (**e** ⟶ **ie**, **o** ⟶ **ue**) are regular in the preterite. They do not have a stem change.

pensar

pens**é**	pens**amos**
pens**aste**	
pens**ó**	pens**aron**

C. In the preterite, verbs ending in **car**, **gar**, and **zar** change the spelling of the **yo** form to maintain the sound of the stem. Compare the **yo** and **él** forms of these verbs.

			yo	**él**
bus**car**	car	c ⟶ qu	bus**qué**	buscó
comen**zar**	zar	z ⟶ c	comen**cé**	comenzó
ju**gar**	gar	g ⟶ gu	ju**gué**	jugó

Here are some familiar spelling-change verbs:
car: sacar, tocar, practicar
zar: empezar, almorzar
gar: llegar, pagar

D. Here are some expressions frequently used with the preterite.

ayer	yesterday	**el verano pasado**	last summer
anoche	last night	**la semana pasada**	last week
esta mañana	this morning	**el mes pasado**	last month
el año pasado	last year	**el viernes pasado**	last Friday

Ayer compré una corbata nueva.	Yesterday I bought a new tie.
Pensaste en ellos anoche.	You thought about them last night.
Comenzó a llover esta mañana.	It started to rain this morning.
Toqué el piano el mes pasado.	I played the piano last month.

PREPARACIÓN

A. ¡Qué mala suerte! Julia went to a sale but did not find anything. Her friends try to find out why. What do they ask?

MODELO mirar bien
¿Miraste bien?

1. preparar una lista
2. llegar temprano a la tienda
3. mirar en el segundo piso
4. hablar con las vendedoras
5. pasar mucho tiempo en la venta
6. buscar con cuidado

B. Gran venta. Julia's friends are telling her all the things they bought at the big sale. What do they say?

MODELO Alicia / un traje de baño negro
Alicia compró un traje de baño negro.

1. Yo / un impermeable azul
2. Tú / un sombrero de playa
3. Ellas / unos lentes de sol
4. Rosita y yo / unos zapatos blancos
5. Los muchachos / unas corbatas rojas
6. Emilia / un vestido verde

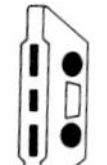

C. Quejas. Gabriel has been taking care of his three younger cousins. What complaints does he have for their parents when they return?

MODELO Tito / no jugar con sus hermanos
Tito no jugó con sus hermanos.

1. Luisa / no practicar el piano
2. Juanito y Luisa / no almorzar
3. Ellos / no arreglar su cuarto
4. Tito / no sacar la basura
5. Juanito / no bañarse
6. Los niños / no acostarse temprano
7. Luisa / no lavarse los dientes
8. Yo / no descansar un minuto

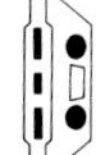

D. Penas de amor. Pilar is accusing her boyfriend Miguel of giving her the cold shoulder. What does he say to her?

MODELO No me hablaste durante el recreo.
Sí te hablé durante el recreo.

1. No me esperaste después de clase.
2. No me llamaste anoche.
3. No me buscaste en la biblioteca.
4. No almorzaste conmigo ayer.
5. No jugaste ajedrez conmigo.
6. No pensaste en mí hoy.
7. No llegaste a tiempo para el cine.
8. No me pagaste los cinco dólares.

COMUNICACIÓN

A. Entrevista. Answer the following questions or use them to interview another student.

1. ¿Miraste la televisión anoche? ¿Qué programa?
2. ¿Hablaste por teléfono anoche? ¿Con quién?
3. ¿Ayudaste a lavar los platos anoche?
4. ¿A qué hora te acostaste?
5. ¿A qué hora te levantaste esta mañana?
6. ¿Preparaste el desayuno hoy?
7. ¿Sacaste al perro esta mañana?
8. ¿A qué hora llegaste a clase?
9. ¿Olvidaste algo en casa?
10. ¿Practicaste un deporte?

B. Ayer. Describe what you did (or did not do) yesterday at various times.

EJEMPLO Ayer me acosté a las diez.

Sugerencias

comprar ropa	ayudar a mis padres
hablar con mis amigos	escuchar discos
lavarse el pelo	visitar las tiendas
pensar en mis problemas	trabajar mucho
mirar la televisión	sacar fotos
preparar la cena	tocar un instrumento
jugar ajedrez	regresar tarde a casa
patinar con mis amigos	?

PERSPECTIVAS

México de ayer y hoy

Ricardo Estévez, a young Californian, is in Mexico City with his family. He is writing to a friend about the excitement he felt during his first few days.

Querido Emilio,

Mi familia y yo llegamos a México el domingo pasado. Desde el primer momento me impresionó la mezcla de cosas modernas y antiguas que hay en esta ciudad. Caminar por ella es como viajar por el tiempo. Primero llegamos a un aeropuerto ultramoderno, y después para ir al hotel tomamos un taxi—un coche del año 60 creo—que nos llevó a la zona colonial. Nuestro hotel está cerca del Zócalo, una plaza del siglo XVI.

Ayer por primera vez caminé solo por la ciudad. Comencé por visitar la Plaza de las Tres Culturas. Allí me encontré con tres culturas diferentes: las ruinas de un gran mercado

mezcla: mixture
por: through
me encontré: I found

azteca, una iglesia colonial y un edificio moderno que representa el México de hoy. ¡Qué pena que no llevé mi cámara!

También visité la Lagunilla, un mercado de ropa, artesanía, libros y muchas otras cosas a precios baratos. ¡Esto realmente me encantó! Allí compré un vestido típico mexicano para mi hermana. ¡Qué colores tan bonitos usan en la ropa—morados con amarillos y rojos! Ya sabes que a mí casi no me gusta comprar ropa, pero me compré una camisa fabulosa con cabezas de pájaros aztecas. También busqué el disco que quieres, pero no lo encontré. Regresé al hotel tarde y muy cansado. Mañana pienso levantarme temprano para ir al Museo de Antropología. Bueno, me voy a acostar ahora.

Saludos para todos,
Ricardo

edificio: building
artesanía: crafts

COMPRENSIÓN

Answer the following questions based on **México de ayer y hoy.**

1. ¿Dónde está Ricardo?
2. ¿Cuándo llegaron Ricardo y su familia a esta ciudad?
3. ¿Qué lo impresionó desde el primer momento?
4. ¿Qué encontró en la Plaza de las Tres Culturas?
5. ¿Qué compró para su hermana en el mercado?
6. ¿Qué se compró él?
7. ¿Qué buscó para su amigo Emilio?
8. ¿Cuándo regresó al hotel?
9. ¿Qué piensa hacer Ricardo mañana?

COMUNICACIÓN

A. ¿Cómo te vistes? Tell what you would like to wear in the following situations and then tell what you usually wear.

EJEMPLO a la iglesia . . .
Cuando voy a la iglesia, me gustaría usar pantalones, pero generalmente me pongo mi vestido azul.

1. a un restaurante . . .
2. a la escuela . . .
3. a bailar . . .
4. a las tiendas . . .
5. a una fiesta . . .
6. ?

B. La semana pasada. Tell what you and your friends or family did last week.

EJEMPLO Ayer gasté mucho dinero.
El domingo montamos bicicleta en el parque.

Sugerencias

esta mañana	jugar . . .	buscar
ayer	trabajar	descansar
anoche	visitar	invitar a . . .
la semana pasada	comprar	arreglar . . .
el lunes	ayudar a . . .	encontrar
(jueves . . .)	gastar	acostarse
un día	practicar . . .	levantarse
	empezar (a)	?

C. Vacaciones. Tell some of the places you and your family visited, the things you did, and what you bought on your vacation.

EJEMPLO Visitamos un zoológico.
Compré muchos recuerdos.

D. Entrevista. Answer the following questions or use them to interview another student.

1. ¿A qué hora empezaste la tarea ayer por la tarde?
2. ¿Cuándo te acostaste anoche?
3. ¿Cuándo te levantaste hoy?
4. ¿Te bañaste esta mañana?
5. ¿Escuchaste la radio para oír el pronóstico del tiempo?
6. ¿Almorzaste en la escuela?
7. ¿Con quién(es) hablaste durante el recreo?
8. ¿Encontraste difícil la lección hoy?
9. ¿Buscaste a tus amigos después de la clase?

VOCABULARIO DEL CAPÍTULO

NOUNS RELATING TO THE BODY

la boca mouth
el brazo arm
la cabeza head
la cara face
el corazón heart
el diente tooth
la mano (*f*) hand
la nariz nose
la oreja ear
el pelo hair
el pie foot
la pierna leg

NOUNS RELATING TO CLOTHING

los calcetines socks
la blusa blouse
la corbata necktie
la chaqueta jacket
la falda skirt
el impermeable raincoat
los jeans jeans
los lentes de sol sunglasses
la moda style, fashion
los pantalones pants
la ropa clothes, clothing
el sombrero hat
la talla size
el traje de baño swimsuit
el vestido dress
el zapato shoe

OTHER NOUNS

la artesanía crafts
el edificio building
el hombre man
el mercado market
la mezcla mixture
el taxi taxi
el técnico technician
el transistor transistor
la venta sale
la zona zone, district

ADJECTIVES OF COLOR

amarillo yellow
azul blue
blanco white
castaño brown (hair, eyes)
gris gray
morado purple
negro black
pardo brown
rojo red
rosado pink
rubio blond
verde green

OTHER ADJECTIVES

antiguo ancient, old
colonial colonial
estereofónico stereo
europeo European
francés French
largo long

REFLEXIVE VERBS

acostarse (ue) to go to bed
bañarse to take a bath
despertarse (ie) to wake up
dormirse (ue) to fall asleep
lavarse to wash, get washed
lavarse los dientes to brush one's teeth
levantarse to get up
peinarse to comb one's hair
ponerse to put on
probarse (ue) to try on
vestirse (i) to get dressed

OTHER VERBS

doler (ue) to ache, hurt
encontrar (ue) to find
impresionar to impress
pedir (i) to ask for, order
representar to represent
seguir (i) to follow, continue
servir (i) to serve
servir para to be good for, useful
usar to use, wear
venir to come

OTHER WORDS AND EXPRESSIONS

en venta on sale
estar a la moda to be in style
no importa it doesn't matter
me (le) queda(n) bien it fits me (her) well, it looks good on me (her)
por through
seguir la moda to keep up with the styles

Capítulo once

CHOOSING A CAREER

11

INTRODUCCIÓN

Profesión para una mujer moderna

woman

Isabel va a acabar pronto sus estudios de escuela secundaria. Ella le habla a su papá sobre sus planes para el futuro.

finish / studies

SEÑOR SELIS — Bueno, hija, ¿Ya sabes qué quieres hacer después de graduarte en junio?

ISABEL — Sí, papá. Quiero estudiar para ingeniera electricista. *(electrical engineer)*

SEÑOR SELIS — ¿Ingeniera . . . ? ¿Lo dices en serio? ¡Ya sé! Quieres tomarle el pelo a tu papi, ¿verdad? *(to kid)*

ISABEL — No papá, hablo muy en serio.

SEÑOR SELIS — Vamos, Isabel, sé que te fascinan todas las cosas eléctricas, ¡pero la ingeniería no es profesión para una mujer!

ISABEL — ¿Y por qué no? Hay buenos puestos, es un trabajo interesante y paga bien. *(jobs / it pays)*

SEÑOR SELIS — Las mujeres no sirven para eso.

ISABEL — ¿Ah no? ¿Y quién te arregló el televisor ayer?

COMPRENSIÓN

Indicate if the following statements are true or false. If a statement is false, reword it to make it true.

1. Isabel le habla a su mamá sobre sus estudios.
2. Ella quiere ser profesora.
3. Su papá cree que es una mala idea.
4. Su papá piensa que las mujeres no sirven para ser ingenieras.
5. Isabel le arregló la bicicleta a su papá.

COMUNICACIÓN

A. ¿Qué profesión te interesa más? Tell which profession interests you and which does not.

EJEMPLO Me gustaría ser abogado pero no me interesa ser actor.

Some professions have the same form for both the masculine and the feminine.

el, la dentista	dentist
el, la periodista	journalist
el, la artista	entertainer

Some professions have different masculine and feminine forms.

el abogado, la abogada	lawyer
el actor, la actriz	actor, actress
el hombre (la mujer) de negocios	businessman (woman)
el enfermero, la enfermera	nurse
el ingeniero, la ingeniera	engineer
el médico, la médica	doctor
el policía, la mujer policía	police officer
el programador de computadoras, la programadora de computadoras	computer programmer
el secretario, la secretaria	secretary

B. Profesión preferida. Tell why you prefer a certain profession. You may use the suggestions below or give your own reasons.

EJEMPLO Me gustaría ser programador porque paga bien.

es un trabajo fácil
me gusta hablar
me gusta viajar
me encanta la física
es un trabajo divertido
me encantan las computadoras
me gusta cuidar a los enfermos
es un trabajo interesante
me gusta escribir
me gusta ayudar a la gente
?

Luis Manuel García
Director Gerente
JIMENEZ Y REY, S.A.
Editores

Aragón, 800
Teléfono (85) 312 78 96 BARCELONA–8

C. Tele-examen. Imagine that you are your favorite television or movie character. Give only your profession and see if the class can guess who you are by asking questions.

EJEMPLO Soy periodista.
¿Dónde trabajas?
En el Daily Planet.
Eres Clark Kent.

EXPLORACIÓN

Describing people and things
ser *and* **estar**

PRESENTACIÓN

You have already learned to use the verbs **ser** and **estar**. Although both mean *to be*, they have very different uses and are not interchangeable.

A. Ser indicates an identifying trait, such as:

identification	Yo soy María Cristina. Buenos Aires es una ciudad grande.
nationality	Roberto es cubano.
origin	Es de La Habana.
profession	Usted es periodista, ¿no?
personality	¿Eres muy exigente?
characteristic traits	Juan es joven y guapo. La casa es grande y muy bonita.
possession	Estas cosas son de Rosa.
time	¿Qué hora es? Son las tres.
material	La muñeca es de papel.

B. Estar indicates location or changeable conditions—how something or someone looks, seems, or feels. **Estar** is used when talking about:

location	El médico ya está en casa.
physical condition	Los actores están cansados. El agua está fría.
feelings	Pablo está preocupado hoy.
health	Nuestra abogada está enferma.
appearance	Mi tío está gordo en esta foto.

PREPARACIÓN

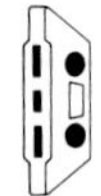

A. Expedición. A team has been formed in Iquitos, Peru, for an expedition to the Amazon. The guide is introducing everyone. What does he say?

MODELO El señor Muñoz / fotógrafo
El señor Muñoz es fotógrafo.

1. La señorita Aponte / ingeniera
2. El señor Frías / periodista
3. Julia y Manuel / enfermeros
4. La señora Moreno / científica
5. Amelia y Pablo Ríos / médicos
6. Y yo / profesor de biología

B. La prueba final. Some actresses are auditioning for the role of Dulcinea in *El hombre de la Mancha*. As they wait for the results, how do they feel?

MODELO María / nerviosa
María está nerviosa.

1. Julia / deprimida
2. Tú / seria
3. Ustedes / emocionadas
4. Yo / cansada
5. Ellas / preocupadas
6. Lola / aburrida
7. Rita / contenta
8. Elena y Laura / nerviosas

C. Presentación. Antonio Vargas is at an international youth conference. Tell how he introduces himself to the other delegates by supplying the correct form of **ser** or **estar**.

Muy buenas noches a todos. Me llamo Antonio Vargas. ___1___ de Lima, Perú, pero mis padres ___2___ de Ayacucho. Ayacucho ___3___ en los Andes.

Tengo 21 años, ___4___ estudiante de la Universidad de San Marcos y quiero ___5___ periodista. Hablo inglés, español y quechua. Mi pasatiempo favorito ___6___ seguir las noticias internacionales y de mi país.

Ahora ___7___ secretario para el periódico *La Prensa*. Cuando ___8___ en mi trabajo, ___9___ muy responsable, paciente y serio. Pero cuando voy a fiestas siempre ___10___ muy simpático, divertido y a veces un poco loco.

Yo ___11___ muy aficionado a los deportes. Cuando mi familia y yo ___12___ de vacaciones, practico deportes acuáticos.

___13___ muy contento de ___14___ aquí con ustedes.

¡Elige hoy, tu opción profesional!

COMUNICACIÓN

A. Cualidades personales. Give at least two personality traits that these groups of people usually have.

EJEMPLO Los profesores
Los profesores son serios y pacientes.

1. los médicos
2. los periodistas
3. los abogados
4. los programadores
5. los artistas
6. los estudiantes

B. Descripciones. Using the suggestions, make up sentences to describe yourself or other people you know well. Use **ser** or **estar**, and remember to use the correct form of the adjectives.

EJEMPLO Yo estoy ocupada cuando estoy en el trabajo.

Yo	ser	rubio
Mi mejor amigo(a)	estar	enfermo
Mi papá		simpático
Mi mamá		nervioso
Mi profesor(a) de español		aquí
Nosotros		serio
Ustedes		ocupado
		guapo
		malo, bueno
		en la clase
		gordo, delgado
		en casa
		loco
		en el trabajo
		preocupado

C. Entrevista. Answer the following questions or use them to interview another student.

1. ¿Cómo estás hoy?
2. ¿Estás nervioso(a) cuando hablas español?
3. En general, ¿eres simpático(a)? ¿eres divertido(a)?
4. Cuando esperas a tus amigos, ¿eres paciente?
5. ¿Qué quieres ser en el futuro? ¿Por qué?
6. ¿Te gustaría estar en el extranjero? ¿En qué país? ¿Por qué?

RINCÓN CULTURAL

En los países hispanos, las mujeres no tienen todavía las mismas oportunidades que los hombres en el mundo profesional. Pero gracias al desarrollo económico e industrial de España y Latinoamérica, esta situación ahora comienza a cambiar. Más y más mujeres asisten a la universidad para seguir profesiones que no se limitan a la enseñanza, la enfermería o la asistencia social. Hoy en día podemos encontrar un mayor número en las ciencias, la abogacía, los negocios, etc., pero estas profesiones continúan principalmente en manos de los hombres.

Ahora que las mujeres empiezan a trabajar fuera de la casa, la familia tiene que pensar en un nuevo problema: la crianza de los hijos. Esto puede representar un obstáculo para la mujer que trabaja. Pero ahora existen guarderías y los hombres también participan más y más en el cuidado de los hijos. Sin embargo la verdad es que esta responsabilidad descansa todavía sobre la mujer.

Si el hombre y la mujer trabajan fuera de la casa, ¿qué crees tú que uno puede hacer con respecto a la crianza de los hijos, las tareas de la casa, etc.?

desarrollo development
cambiar change
fuera outside
crianza raising
guarderías day-care centers

EXPLORACIÓN

Talking about the past
The preterite of regular **er** *and* **ir** *verbs*

PRESENTACIÓN

You have already learned to talk about the past using **ar** verbs. Now you will learn to use the past tense of regular **er** and **ir** verbs. Study the forms of **comer** and **abrir**.

comer

com**í**	com**imos**
com**iste**	
com**ió**	com**ieron**

abrir

abr**í**	abr**imos**
abr**iste**	
abr**ió**	abr**ieron**

A. Here are some other regular **er** and **ir** verbs you have already learned.

aprender	decidir	prometer
asistir	escribir	recibir
comprender	insistir (en)	salir
correr	permitir	vivir
cumplir		

El señor Campos aprendió inglés.	Mr. Campos learned English.
¿Ya abrieron los regalos?	Did they open the presents yet?
Prometí ayudarte lavar el coche.	I promised to help you wash the car.
Decidieron estudiar para médicos.	They decided to study to be doctors.

B. Like stem-changing **ar** verbs, stem-changing **er** verbs are regular in the preterite.

perder

perdí	perdimos
perdiste	
perdió	perdieron

Volver (**ue**), **doler** (**ue**), and **entender** (**ie**) are like **perder**.

Perdí mi trabajo de verano.	I lost my summer job.
¿A qué hora volviste a casa?	At what time did you return home?
Me dolió la cabeza ayer.	I had a headache yesterday.
No entendí al profesor.	I didn't understand the teacher.

PREPARACIÓN

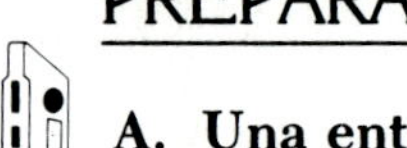

A. Una entrevista difícil. Alberto is interviewing for a job with *Iberia*, the national airline of Spain. What does the personnel officer ask him?

MODELO cuándo / vivir en los Estados Unidos
¿Cuándo vivió usted en los Estados Unidos?

1. dónde / asistir a la universidad
2. cuándo / salir de la universidad
3. cuándo / aprender programación
4. cuándo / aprender inglés
5. por qué / decidir venir aquí

B. ¡Qué profesor! Doctora Pérez is asking her friend Carlos Marín, a retired science teacher, about his career days. What does she ask?

MODELO aprender biología en el instituto
Aprendiste biología en el instituto, ¿verdad?

1. escribir algunos libros de ciencia
2. cumplir 20 años de trabajo en la clase
3. asistir a muchas entrevistas
4. recibir un premio de física
5. vivir en Buenos Aires por unos años
6. volver a la universidad

C. Ya es tarde. Felipe has lots of ideas for things to do today, but his brothers have already done them. What do they say?

MODELO ¿Comemos a las seis?
No, ya comimos.

1. ¿Salimos a dar un paseo?
2. ¿Le escribimos al abuelo?
3. ¿Corremos por el parque?
4. ¿Aprendemos las canciones nuevas?
5. ¿Comemos los chocolates?

D. Reunión. At a reunion, Colegio Santa Ana graduates are talking about what's happened to everyone. What do they say?

MODELO Rodrigo / decidir ser ingeniero
Rodrigo decidió ser ingeniero.

1. Úrsula / volver a España a estudiar
2. Julia / aprender inglés
3. Ellos / vivir tres años en el extranjero
4. Yo / asistir a dos universidades
5. María Elena / recibir un premio de química
6. Tú / abrir una tienda de regalos
7. Carlos y yo / escribir un libro de historia
8. Jacinto / perder su puesto en el laboratorio

COMUNICACIÓN

A. ¿Qué pasó en la clase? Ask your teacher and other students what they did in class this past week. Change or make additions to the expressions in the list.

EJEMPLO asistir a clase
Ricardo, ¿asististe a clase todos los días?

perder la tarea
Profesor, ¿perdió usted nuestra tarea?

escribir los ejercicios
aprender el vocabulario nuevo
responder a todas las preguntas
prometer estudiar más
asistir a clase
insistir en hablar español
perder la tarea
entender nuestros problemas
comprender la lección
recibir buenas notas
permitir ruido en la clase
?

B. Entrevista. Answer the following questions or use them to interview another student.

1. ¿Dónde aprendiste español?
2. ¿Entendiste a la profesora hoy?
3. ¿Qué escribiste en la clase de español hoy?
4. ¿Saliste con tus amigos el fin de semana pasado? ¿Volviste tarde a casa?
5. ¿Comiste en un restaurante bueno?
6. ¿Corriste mucho ayer? ¿Te dolieron los pies después?
7. ¿Cuándo cumpliste años? ¿Qué regalo(s) recibiste?

RINCÓN CULTURAL

INGENIERO DE MINAS

Para trabajos en Cerro de Pasco; sueldo 800,000 soles; pagamos viaje, vivienda, alimentación, servicios médicos. Currículum vitae a Domingo Ponte 573, Magdalena. 9 a 11 de la mañana.

URGENTE Necesitamos hombres y mujeres jóvenes y de buena presencia para propaganda televisión; Av. Arenales 1487.

JEFE DE VENTAS

Compañía importadora necesita para su Departamento de Ventas Jefe de Ventas con experiencia en el negocio de libros. Presentarse con currículum documentado al Jirón Puno 485 en horas de oficina.

ELECTRICISTA: reparar instalaciones, televisores, cables, cocinas. Huascarán 1057, telf. 245174.

RECEPCIONISTA, mayor de 25 años, para atender público; sueldo y comisión. Arica 373, Miraflores.

SECRETARIA DE VENTAS; escribir a máquina, educación secundaria, experiencia en trabajo similar; presentarse a Rufino Torrico N° 882-401.

DETECTIVE PRIVADO

(CONFIDENCIAL)

Experto profesional. Banca, industria, comercio, cuidado de residencias, casos difíciles. Coche necesario. Operativo las 24 horas. Telf. 366323.

ADMINISTRADOR-PORTERO DISCOTECA

Excelente presencia, estudios secundarios, fuerte, atlético, documentos en orden. Telf. 366174.

Which of the following qualifications would be required of applicants for these positions?

a. advanced degree
b. pleasant speaking voice
c. good typing skills
d. minimum age of 25
e. willingness to work odd hours
f. previous sales experience
g. pleasant appearance

EXPLORACIÓN

Talking about the past
The preterite of **ir** *stem-changing verbs*

PRESENTACIÓN

A. The **ir** verbs with a stem change in the present tense also have a stem change in the preterite. The vowel in the stem changes from **o** to **u** or from **e** to **i** only in the **él** and **ellos** forms.

dormir (ue, u)

dormí	dormimos
dormiste	
durmió	durmieron

pedir (i, i)

pedí	pedimos
pediste	
pidió	pidieron

Generalmente se duerme temprano. Anoche se durmió tarde.
A veces pido pollo, pero anoche no lo pedí.

B. Here are some stem-changing **ir** verbs you already know. Compare the regular **yo** form with the irregular **él** form.

seguir (i, i)	seguí	siguió
preferir (ie, i)	preferí	prefirió
repetir (i, i)	repetí	repitió
servir (i, i)	serví	sirvió
vestirse (i, i)	me vestí	se vistió

C. Learn these new verbs.

conseguir (i, i)	to get, obtain	conseguí	consiguió
divertirse (ie, i)	to have fun	me divertí	se divirtió
sentirse (ie, i)	to feel	me sentí	se sintió

divertirse (ie, i)

me divertí	nos divertimos
te divertiste	
se divirtió	se divirtieron

Conseguir is like **seguir**. **Divertirse** and **sentirse** have an **e ⟶ ie** change in the present and an **e ⟶ i** change in the preterite. They are also reflexive.

Se siente mal hoy. Ayer también se sintió mal.
Siempre se divierten. No se divirtieron anoche.

PREPARACIÓN

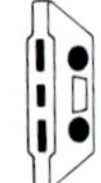

A. ¡Qué pérdida de tiempo! Javier asked his brother to go with him to buy some jeans. What happened in the store?

MODELO Javier / pedir jeans
Javier pidió jeans.

1. Ellos / pedir la talla 28
2. Mario / seguir a su hermano
3. El vendedor / conseguir los jeans
4. Javier / preferir otro color
5. Javier y Mario / seguir al vendedor
6. Los jeans / no servir
7. Javier / vestirse para salir
8. Mario / repetir la pregunta

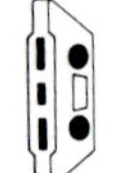

B. La España romántica. The Spanish club just arrived in Madrid. Tell how the members felt.

MODELO El profesor / cansado
El profesor se sintió cansado.

1. Carlos / contentísimo
2. Pedro y Jesús / nerviosos
3. Elena / emocionada
4. Tú / fantástico
5. Nosotros / alegres
6. Ustedes / cansados

C. ¡Qué divertido! After their first day in Madrid, the club members are talking about how much they enjoyed themselves.

MODELO Carlos / divertirse / bastante
Carlos se divirtió bastante.

1. El profesor / mucho
2. Yo / bastante
3. Tú / muchísimo
4. Pedro y Jesús / un poco
5. Nosotros / mucho

D. La Alhambra. After a tiring day in the Alhambra, a Moorish palace in Granada, everyone slept well that night. Tell what they said the next morning.

MODELO Ana / nueve horas
Ana durmió nueve horas.

1. Verónica / diez horas
2. Tú / ocho horas y media
3. Nosotros / seis horas
4. Elena y Susana / once horas
5. Yo / siete horas y media

COMUNICACIÓN

A. Críticos gastronómicos. Tell what you or someone else ordered the last time you went to a restaurant and whether or not you liked it.

EJEMPLO Yo pedí una sopa de cebolla y no me gustó nada.
Mi padre pidió chuletas y le encantaron.

B. ¿Cómo te sentiste? Imagine that you found yourself in the following situations. Tell how you felt.

EJEMPLO Dormiste toda la noche.
Me sentí bien.

bien	gordo	sorprendido	nervioso
mal	deprimido	contento	responsable
solo	enfermo	cansado	preocupado
raro	importante	fantástico	?

1. Saliste mal en un examen.
2. Conseguiste un buen trabajo.
3. No recibiste un regalo de cumpleaños.
4. Te divertiste mucho en una fiesta.
5. Perdiste las llaves de tu casa.
6. Comiste demasiado.
7. No asististe a clase ayer.
8. Te dormiste en el tren.
9. No comiste nada hoy.
10. ?

RINCÓN CULTURAL

En una encuesta (*survey*) en una revista española los jóvenes españoles expresaron sus opiniones con respecto al trabajo. ¿Qué piensas tú de los resultados (*results*)? ¿Son las opiniones de tus amigos muy diferentes?

LOS ESTUDIOS Y EL TRABAJO

Es difícil escoger* una profesión	53%
Es difícil conseguir trabajo	86%

LOS FACTORES IMPORTANTES EN EL TRABAJO

Interesante y agradable	46%
Sueldo**	34%
Oportunidad de ascenso***	27%
Ayudar a los otros	33%

*choose **salary ***promotion

Adapted from *En contacto. Lecturas intermedias* by McVey-Gil, Wegmann, and Méndez-Faith (New York: Holt, Rinehart and Winston, 1980).

EXPLORACIÓN

Giving advice or orders
The formal commands

PRESENTACIÓN

You have already learned to give advice to a family member or friend using **tú** commands. For a person you would address as **usted**, use the formal command, **usted**. In speaking to more than one person, use the **ustedes** command.

A. The affirmative and negative **usted** and **ustedes** commands of **ar**, **er**, and **ir** verbs are formed from the **yo** form of the present tense. Drop the final **o** and add the opposite vowel endings shown in the chart. (Even stem-changing verbs follow this rule.)

INFINITIVE	**yo** FORM	COMMANDS	
		usted	**ustedes**
escuchar	escucho	escuch**e**	escuch**en**
comer	como	com**a**	com**an**
escribir	escribo	escrib**a**	escrib**an**
pensar	pienso	piens**e**	piens**en**
volver	vuelvo	vuelv**a**	vuelv**an**
repetir	repito	repit**a**	repit**an**
seguir	sigo	sig**a**	sig**an**
hacer	hago	hag**a**	hag**an**
oír	oigo	oig**a**	oig**an**

Note that commands for **ar** verbs end in **e** or **en**; **er** and **ir** commands end in **a** or **an**. To form the negative command, place **no** before the verb.

No sigan por esta calle.
No escuchen esa música.
No duerma hasta el mediodía.

Usted and **ustedes**, although not required, are often added to commands for politeness.

Estudie usted estos libros de programación.
Vengan ustedes temprano.

B. Commands for verbs ending in **car**, **zar**, and **gar** have the same spelling change they have in the **yo** form of the preterite. Note also that the commands show any stem change occurring in the present.

INFINITIVE	**yo** FORM	SPELLING CHANGE	OPPOSITE VOWEL	COMMAND
buscar	busco	c ⟶ qu	e	busque
empezar	empiezo	z ⟶ c	e	empiece
jugar	juego	g ⟶ gu	e	juegue

Saque muchas fotos.
No comiencen el examen todavía.
Pague usted pronto.

C. The following verbs have irregular formal command forms.

	usted	**ustedes**
estar	esté	estén
dar	dé	den
ir	vaya	vayan
ser	sea	sean

Sean ustedes pacientes.
No esté nerviosa.
Vayan a clase ahora.
No le dé nada.

PREPARACIÓN

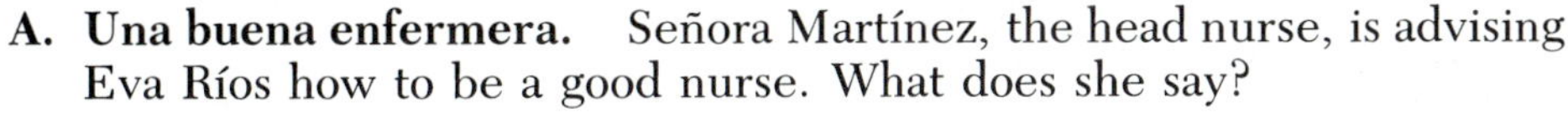

A. Una buena enfermera. Señora Martínez, the head nurse, is advising Eva Ríos how to be a good nurse. What does she say?

MODELO hablar con los enfermos.
Hable usted con los enfermos.

1. observar a las buenas enfermeras
2. escuchar a los médicos
3. cuidar bien a los enfermos
4. no olvidar lavarse las manos
5. ayudar a las otras enfermeras
6. respetar a los enfermos

B. Consejos personales. José López, the class president, is giving new students some advice. What does he say?

MODELO asistir a los partidos de volibol
Asistan a los partidos de volibol.

1. hacer las tareas
2. seguir mi ejemplo
3. aprender español
4. no dormir en clase
5. ser simpáticos con sus profesores
6. ir siempre a clase

C. Un viaje al extranjero. Martha is going to summer school in Cuernavaca. What advice does her Spanish teacher give her?

MODELO empezar a hacer planes ahora
Empiece a hacer planes ahora.

1. llegar al aeropuerto con tiempo
2. buscar un buen hotel
3. comenzar a hablar español
4. no almorzar en restaurantes caros
5. pagar en pesos mexicanos
6. sacar muchas fotos

D. Una fiesta de sorpresa. Gilberto is giving a surprise party. How does he answer his friends who want to help out?

MODELO ¿Venimos temprano? (sí)
Sí, vengan temprano.

1. ¿Compramos los refrescos ahora? (no)
2. ¿Traemos la cámara? (sí)
3. ¿Empezamos a tocar a las ocho? (sí)
4. ¿Vamos de compras ahora? (no)
5. ¿Buscamos los pasteles? (sí)
6. ¿Jugamos ajedrez? (no)
7. ¿Abrimos los regalos pronto? (sí)
8. ¿Ponemos los discos nuevos? (sí)

E. Camino a seguir. Camilo is graduating this year. What advice does the guidance counselor give him?

MODELO seguir estudios en la universidad
Siga estudios en la universidad.

1. pensar en el futuro
2. conseguir una buena educación
3. mostrar dedicación al trabajo
4. servir a la comunidad
5. comenzar a buscar puesto ahora

COMUNICACIÓN

A. Consejero. Imagine you are a counselor talking to students. Based on their interests, suggest one of the careers listed or add a suggestion of your own. Use the command form in giving your suggestions.

1. Soy una persona muy responsable. Me interesan los problemas de la salud y de la nutrición. También me gusta mucho cuidar a los demás.
   a. ser actor de cine
   b. estudiar para enfermero
   c. ir a la escuela de policía
   d. ?
2. Soy muy independiente y seria. Me encantan las matemáticas y las máquinas, y creo que me gustaría trabajar en un laboratorio.
   a. estudiar para ser abogada
   b. aprender programación
   c. trabajar como ingeniera química
   d. ?
3. Me gusta hablar delante de la gente. Me fascinan los problemas legales, preparar documentos y dar opiniones.
   a. trabajar como fotógrafa
   b. hacer estudios para abogada
   c. buscar puesto de secretaria
   d. ?
4. Me encanta viajar, conocer a mucha gente y hacer entrevistas. También me gustaría escribir.
   a. seguir cursos para periodista
   b. estudiar para dentista
   c. conseguir un trabajo como profesor
   d. ?

B. Consulta médica. Imagine you are a physician examining the following patients. Using the suggestions, what advice would you give them?

tomar jugo	tener cuidado	hacer ejercicio
dormir más	descansar	comer más/menos
correr	no salir	ir al hospital
practicar un deporte	aumentar de peso	bajar de peso
caminar		. . . ?

EJEMPLO

Coma más carne, arroz y vegetales.
Aumente de peso.

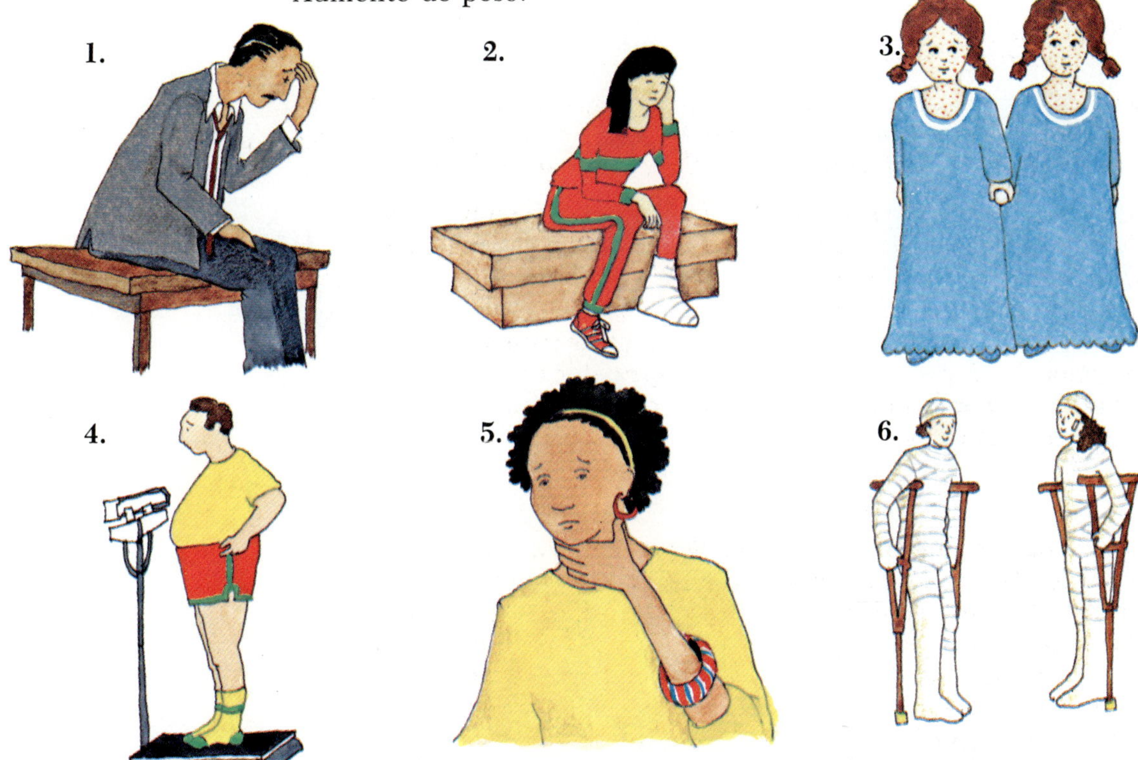

PERSPECTIVAS

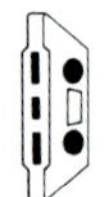

Mi profesión

The guidance counselor at the Colegio León Pinelo in Lima has invited some people to talk about their professions.

Sonia Heller
Soy médica, pero no de personas. Es decir que soy veterinaria. Un veterinario puede trabajar en un zoológico o con animales domésticos o del campo. Muchos creen que no es una profesión exigente, pero ayer, por ejemplo, le saqué una muela a un gorila, y la semana pasada operé al tigre del zoológico donde trabajo. Si siguen esta profesión, estén seguros que no van a saber qué es sentirse aburridos.

Es decir: That is to say

seguros: sure

El Colegio León Pinelo
presenta un
Día de profesiones

los invitados incluyen a:
Sonia Heller, veterinaria
Gustavo Pinzón, piloto
Patricia Ávila, agente de viajes

Salón Goya
el 15 de marzo
a las 14 h.

Gustavo Pinzón

Yo soy piloto de aviación y trabajo para Aeroperú. Para hacerme piloto estudié en la Escuela de Aviación, seguí cursos en el extranjero, y sólo después de esto conseguí mi licencia. Es una profesión difícil que exige excelentes condiciones físicas y mentales. Piensen ustedes, la vida de todos los pasajeros está en mis manos. Si deciden estudiar para ser piloto, recuerden que es una profesión de mucha responsabilidad.

hacerme: to become
exige: demands
pasajeros: passengers

Patricia Ávila

Soy agente de viajes y gerente de la agencia. Mi trabajo consiste en programar paseos turísticos, en aconsejar a los clientes y prepararles sus viajes. La preparación de un viaje es una tarea difícil que exige mucha experiencia. También hay que conocer otros países, su cultura y su idioma. Por ejemplo, yo me preparé en España, trabajé unos años en Europa y viví en varios países de Sudamérica. Si quieren ser agente de viajes, aprendan por lo menos dos idiomas extranjeros y viajen lo más posible.

gerente: manager
aconsejar: advising
idioma: language
por lo menos: at least

COMPRENSIÓN

Answer the following questions based on **Mi profesión.**

1. ¿Qué clase de médica es Sonia Heller?
2. ¿A qué animal le sacó una muela?
3. ¿Dónde trabaja Sonia?
4. ¿Qué profesión tiene el señor Pinzón?
5. ¿Dónde estudió para hacerse piloto?
6. ¿Qué exige su profesión?
7. ¿Qué hace Patricia Ávila?
8. ¿En qué consiste su trabajo?
9. ¿Qué debe conocer y aprender una persona para ser agente de viajes?

COMUNICACIÓN

A. Director de personal. Imagine you are a personnel officer interviewing candidates for some of the positions below. What questions would you ask?

EJEMPLO piloto
¿Dónde consiguió su licencia?
¿Cuántos años de experiencia tiene?

secretario	dentista	programador	camarero
fotógrafo	abogado	científico	ingeniero
veterinario	enfermero	policía	profesor
vendedor	gerente	actor	periodista

B. En veinte años. Imagine what your life is going to be like in twenty years. Describe your profession and your activities.

EJEMPLO Tengo 35 años y soy policía. Me gusta porque estoy casi todo el tiempo en la calle.

C. ¡No es verdad! You have been unfairly accused of having or of not having done certain things. How would you defend yourself?

EJEMPLO Usted no llegó a las ocho ayer.
No es verdad. Llegué a las ocho ayer.

1. Usted no llevó los libros al laboratorio.
2. Usted no practicó el diálogo.
3. Usted no acabó la lección.
4. Usted escribió mal la composición.
5. Usted perdió su libro.
6. Usted olvidó la tarea en casa.
7. Usted sacó mala nota en el examen.
8. Usted se durmió en la clase.
9. Usted no pidió permiso para hablar.

D. ¿Qué pasó? Imagine you had a summer job in one of the places listed below. Make up a story about something that happened.

un hospital	una escuela	un hotel
un laboratorio	un supermercado	un zoológico
una tienda	un periódico	un banco
un aeropuerto	un restaurante	?

EJEMPLO El verano pasado trabajé en un hospital de animales. Un día el veterinario se durmió y un gorila salió del edificio. Todo el mundo empezó a correr. Llamaron a los policías pero . . .

VOCABULARIO DEL CAPÍTULO

NOUNS RELATING TO PROFESSIONS

el abogado, la abogada lawyer
el actor, la actriz actor, actress
el (la) agente de viajes travel agent
el (la) artista entertainer
el (la) dentista dentist
el enfermero, la enfermera nurse
el (la) gerente manager
el hombre (la mujer) de negocios businessman (woman)
el ingeniero, la ingeniera engineer
el ingeniero electricista electrical engineer
el médico, la médica doctor
el periodista, la periodista journalist
el piloto de aviación, la pilota pilot
el policía, la mujer policía police officer
el programador de computadoras computer programmer (man)
la programadora de computadoras computer programmer (woman)
el secretario, la secretaria secretary
el veterinario, la veterinaria veterinary doctor

OTHER NOUNS

la agencia agency
los animales domésticos pets
la condición condition
la cultura culture
los estudios studies
el futuro future
el gorila gorilla
el idioma language
la ingeniería engineering
la licencia license
la mujer woman
el papi dad
el pasajero passenger
la profesión profession
el puesto job, position
la responsabilidad responsibility
el tigre tiger
el zoológico zoo

ADJECTIVES

eléctrico electric
mental mental
secundario secondary
seguro sure

VERBS

acabar to finish
aconsejar to advise
arreglar to fix
conseguir (i, i) to obtain
consistir en to consist of
divertirse (ie, i) to have fun
exigir to demand
fascinar to fascinate
graduarse to graduate
hacerse to become (a profession)
operar to operate on
pagar to pay (for)
programar to program, to plan
sentirse (ie, i) to feel

EXPRESSIONS

en serio seriously
es decir that is to say
estudiar para to study to be . . .
lo más posible as much as possible
por lo menos at least
seguir un curso to take a course
tomarle a alguien el pelo to kid someone, pull someone's leg

Capítulo doce

ADVENTURE AND EXPLORATION 12

INTRODUCCIÓN

Una semana en la selva

jungle

Alicia Miró, una fotógrafa venezolana, participó en una expedición al río Orinoco, en Venezuela. Después de cinco días de viaje se separó accidentalmente del grupo y pasó una semana perdida en la selva amazónica. Aquí tienen ustedes una entrevista con ella para *El Nacional* de Caracas.

lost

PERIODISTA Dígame, señorita Miró, ¿cómo se sintió usted cuando se encontró sola en la selva?

ALICIA Me sentí desesperada. Pensé: La selva es tan peligrosa que nunca voy a poder salir de aquí.

hopeless / dangerous
never

PERIODISTA ¿Por qué no buscó inmediatamente a los otros?

ALICIA Los busqué . . . los llamé muchas veces, pero ellos no me respondieron.

PERIODISTA Entonces, ¿qué pasó?

ALICIA ¿Qué vas a hacer ahora?, me pregunté. Y yo misma me respondí: Alicia, no pierdas la cabeza. Debes volver al río.

I myself

PERIODISTA ¿Lo encontró?

ALICIA	Sí, pero con mucha dificultad. Caminé, creo, unos cincuenta kilómetros. Pasé mucha hambre y muchas noches no dormí un solo minuto.	single
PERIODISTA	¿Y no consiguió nada de comer en la selva?	
ALICIA	Comí sólo frutas: plátanos, uvas . . .	
PERIODISTA	¿Y cómo llegó al río?	
ALICIA	Bueno, seguí siempre el sol. Cuando llegué al río me encontré con unos indios y ellos me llevaron en canoa hasta Canaima. Allí tomé el primer avión a Caracas . . .	
PERIODISTA	Una última pregunta: ¿piensa usted regresar algún día al Amazonas?	
ALICIA	Sí, pero primero quiero olvidar esta aventura.	

COMPRENSIÓN

Indicate whether the following statements are true or false. If a statement is false, reword it to make it true.

1. Alicia se sintió contenta cuando se encontró sola.
2. Alicia pensó: va a ser fácil salir de aquí.
3. Los otros miembros de la expedición no le respondieron.
4. Alicia se respondió: no pierdas la cabeza.
5. Alicia durmió muy bien todas las noches.
6. Ella siguió siempre el sol.
7. Alicia no encontró el río.
8. Los indios la ayudaron.
9. Alicia no piensa volver nunca al Amazonas.

COMUNICACIÓN

¿Y tú? The following things may appeal to your spirit of adventure. Tell which interest you, which do not, and why.

<table>
<tr><td>(No)</td><td>Me gustaría
Me interesa
Me fascina</td><td>porque es</td><td>muy
demasiado
bastante</td><td>peligroso, interesante,
emocionante, caro, difícil,
fatigoso, ?</td></tr>
</table>

cruzar los Estados Unidos en bicicleta

hacer un safari en África

dar la vuelta al mundo

pilotear un avión

hacer un viaje al espacio

explorar la selva amazónica

participar en una carrera de automóviles

saltar en paracaídas

explorar el mundo submarino

bajar un río en canoa

escalar una montaña

pasear en velero

EXPLORACIÓN

Talking about the past
Using irregular preterites: ir *and* ser, dar *and* ver

PRESENTACIÓN

A. In the preterite, the verbs **ir** and **ser** are identical. Note that the **yo** and **él** forms have no accent marks.

ir

fui	fuimos
fuiste	
fue	fueron

ser

fui	fuimos
fuiste	
fue	fueron

No confusion occurs because the context of the sentence makes the meaning clear. In addition, **ir** is often followed by **a**.

Ustedes fueron a Venezuela, ¿verdad?
Fuimos a explorar el río.

¿Cómo fue el viaje a Sudamérica?
Su padre fue profesor de inglés.

B. **Dar** has **er/ir** endings in the preterite. **Ver** is regular except that, like **dar**, there are no accent marks on the **yo** and **él** forms.

dar

di	dimos
diste	
dio	dieron

ver

vi	vimos
viste	
vio	vieron

Dieron la vuelta al mundo en un mes.
No les di las noticias.

¿Quién vio unos seres del espacio?
Vi unos veleros en la playa.

PREPARACIÓN

A. ¿Ya están listos? Several students are going on a canoe trip, and everyone is busy getting things ready. Tell what members of the group went to do.

MODELO Alfredo / buscar un mapa
Alfredo fue a buscar un mapa.

1. Constanza y Anita / comprar un transistor
2. Nosotros / traer la comida
3. Tú / buscar una cámara
4. Lorenzo / escuchar el pronóstico del tiempo
5. Ustedes / preparar las mochilas
6. Los chicos / arreglar las canoas

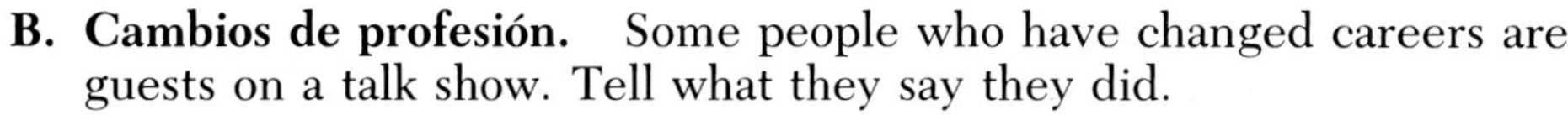

B. Cambios de profesión. Some people who have changed careers are guests on a talk show. Tell what they say they did.

MODELO Antonio / piloto
Antonio fue piloto.

1. Rafael / camarero
2. Diana y Marta / actrices
3. Usted / gerente
4. Elio y yo / policías
5. Tú / vendedor
6. Yo / abogado

C. Fiesta de graduación. At the Colegio Simón Bolívar graduation party everyone is talking about how the school year was. What do they say?

MODELO la comida / no / malo
La comida no fue mala.

1. El Sr. Velásquez / el mejor profesor
2. Nosotros / responsable
3. La clase de química / no / fácil
4. Los profesores / simpático
5. Yo / el mejor jugador de fútbol
6. Los partidos de fútbol / bueno

D. Programa de intercambio. Some Latin American exchange students brought gifts for their American host families. Tell what they gave them.

MODELO Yo / un disco de Guillermo Dávila
Yo les di un disco de Guillermo Dávila.

1. Laura / unas camisas de México
2. Nosotros / unas monedas antiguas de Chile
3. Tú / un poncho de Colombia
4. Estela y Pablo / una cartera de Argentina
5. Los hermanos Aguilar / unos carteles del viejo San Juan
6. Yo / una pulsera de Taxco

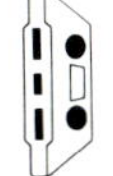

E. ¡Qué semana! Joaquín and his family went skiing in the Guadarrama Mountains north of Madrid. When it rained for several days they decided to watch TV. What did they see?

MODELO Blanca / las novelas
Blanca vio las novelas todos los días.

1. Mis padres / las noticias
2. Yo / una película policíaca
3. Mi hermano / dos películas de ciencia-ficción
4. Mis hermanitas / los dibujos animados
5. Mi mamá / las variedades
6. Tú / un documental sobre el mundo submarino
7. Nosotros / una comedia
8. Mi papá / los reportajes deportivos

COMUNICACIÓN

A. ¿Adónde fueron? Try to remember when and where your friends and family went during the past week.

EJEMPLO Mi padre fue al banco el martes.
Yo fui a mi clase de música el jueves.

Sugerencias	aeropuerto	cine	piscina
	agencia de viajes	club	supermercado
	baile	colegio	teatro
	banco	fiesta	tienda
	casa	iglesia	zoológico
	centro comercial	partido	?

B. Personas famosas. Using the following questions as a guide, describe a famous person of the past.

1. ¿Cuándo y dónde vivió?
2. ¿Cuál fue su profesión?
3. ¿Qué estudió?
4. ¿Cómo fue?
5. ¿Por qué fue famoso?
6. ¿Fue popular?

C. Entrevista. Answer the following questions or use them to interview another student.

1. ¿Fuiste al cine la semana pasada? ¿Con quién? ¿Qué viste?
2. ¿Fuiste de compras con tus amigos? ¿Qué compraste?
3. ¿Les diste regalos a tus amigos este año? ¿Por qué?
4. ¿Viste algo bueno en la televisión? ¿Qué?
5. ¿Diste una fiesta en tu casa la semana pasada? ¿Por qué?

RINCÓN CULTURAL

Mucha gente cree que en las costas del Caribe todavía existen muchos tesoros. Muchos galeones españoles se hundieron entre los siglos XVI y XVIII y también muchos piratas navegaron por toda esa región.

En 1961, por ejemplo, Kip Wagner descubrió los restos de un galeón español que se hundió durante un huracán cerca de la Florida en 1715. En ese galeón encontró un tesoro fabuloso de monedas de oro y plata.

¿Te gustaría encontrar un tesoro? Aquí tienes un mapa de piratas. Síguelo y vamos a ver si encuentras el tesoro.

1. Entra por la bahía del Esqueleto hasta la Playa Blanca en la Caleta Calavera.
2. Camina 1 km al NE, hasta llegar a la laguna del Muerto.
3. Sigue la orilla hasta encontrar la roca negra.
4. Escala la roca.
5. Ahora baja y camina hasta el primer árbol.
6. Ahora cuenta cinco pasos en dirección al segundo árbol. ¡Ahí está el tesoro!

tesoros treasures **se hundieron** sank **orilla** shore **árbol** tree

EXPLORACIÓN

Comparing things or people
The comparative: **más/menos que**

PRESENTACIÓN

In order to compare people or things, you need to know the comparative in Spanish.

A. To say that something or someone is more or less than another, use one of the following formulas.

más	+ (adjective/adverb) + **que**	more . . . than
menos	+ (adjective/adverb) + **que**	less . . . than

La selva es **más peligrosa que** el bosque.
The jungle is more dangerous than the woods.

Ecuador es **menos grande que** Brasil.
Ecuador is smaller than Brazil.

Un automóvil llega **más rápido que** el autobús.
A car arrives faster than the bus.

Remember that an adjective agrees in gender and in number with the noun. Adverbs, because they modify verbs, do not change.

B. The adjectives **bueno** and **malo** and the adverbs **bien** and **mal** share the same irregular comparative forms: **mejor** (better) and **peor** (worse).

La comida de aquí es **mala**. Es **peor** que la comida de allá.
Estas canoas son **buenas**, pero las otras son **mejores**.
Yo salí **bien** en el examen. Tú saliste **mejor** que yo.

PREPARACIÓN

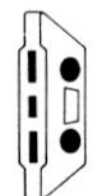

A. Comparaciones. Tía Margarita is comparing Isaac and his sister Rebeca. Tell what she says.

MODELO alto
Isaac es más alto que su hermana.

1. serio
2. cómico
3. exigente
4. independiente
5. nervioso
6. responsable

B. Todo es mejor aquí. Señor Ruiz, the director of the Campamento Juárez, thinks his summer camp is better than any other. Tell what he says.

MODELO el campamento / bonito
El campamento es más bonito.

1. el equipo / nuevo
2. los acampadores / inteligentes
3. los bosques / verdes
4. los juegos / divertidos
5. la piscina / limpia
6. las caminatas / cortas
7. las reglas / razonables
8. las tareas / fáciles

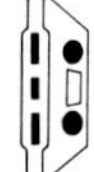

C. Todo es peor en la selva. Ángel Bordas, a research assistant on a jungle expedition, is complaining about living conditions in the tropics. What does he say?

MODELO el ruido
El ruido es peor en la selva.

1. el aire
2. el sol
3. los caminos
4. el agua
5. los insectos
6. el calor

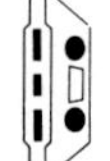

D. Un pequeño complejo de inferioridad. Silvia thinks her friend did better than she at the interscholastic sports competition. Tell what she says.

MODELO jugar volibol
Tú jugaste volibol mejor que yo.

1. correr
2. jugar béisbol
3. nadar
4. levantar pesas
5. patinar
6. esquiar

COMUNICACIÓN

A. Usted y los otros jóvenes. Are you the same as or different from other young people? Use the suggestions below to make statements that reflect your opinions.

Yo soy { más / menos } ________ que mi(s) amigo(s).

Sugerencias: alegre, alto(a), atlético(a), cómico(a), delgado(a), divertido(a), exagerado(a), independiente, inteligente, interesante, moderno(a), paciente, popular, responsable, serio(a), simpático(a), . . .

B. Aventuras para todos. Compare some of the following adventures telling which is more or less interesting, exciting, dangerous, etc.

EJEMPLO Pilotear un avión es menos emocionante que escalar una montaña.

cruzar los Estados Unidos
pilotear un avión
explorar el mundo submarino
dar la vuelta al mundo
hacer un safari en África
bajar un río en canoa
acampar en las montañas
hacer un viaje al extranjero
participar en una carrera de automóviles
hacer un viaje al espacio
explorar la selva amazónica
saltar en paracaídas
?

C. ¿Verdad o sexismo? Do you agree or disagree with the following statements? If you disagree, change the sentences so that they reflect your opinions.

EJEMPLO Las chicas son menos atléticas que los chicos.
No, las chicas son más atléticas que los chicos.

1. Las chicas cocinan mejor que los chicos.
2. Los chicos trabajan menos en la escuela que las chicas.
3. Las chicas son más exageradas que los chicos.
4. Los chicos son menos pacientes que las chicas.
5. Las chicas aprenden más rápido que los chicos.
6. Los chicos son más tacaños que las chicas.
7. Las chicas ayudan más a sus padres en casa.
8. Los chicos son menos nerviosos que las chicas.

RINCÓN CULTURAL

Usa el mapa para hablar de las atracciones turísticas de Venezuela. ¿Cuáles te interesan más?

EXPLORACIÓN

Talking about things we did
*The **i**-stem and **u**-stem preterites*

PRESENTACIÓN

As you have seen, some commonly used verbs have irregular preterites. So far most of these verbs are irregular only in the stem (**pedir–pidió**). Now you will learn some verbs that have irregular stems and endings in the preterite.

There are two groups: **i**-stem and **u**-stem preterites. Both types take the same irregular endings: **e**, **iste**, **o**, **imos**, **ieron**. Note that there are no written accents.

A. Here are some common **i**-stem preterites.

hacer

hice	hicimos
hiciste	
hizo	hicieron

querer

quise	quisimos
quisiste	
quiso	quisieron

venir

vine	vinimos
viniste	
vino	vinieron

B. Here are some **u**-stem preterites.

estar

estuve	estuvimos
estuviste	
estuvo	estuvieron

poder

pude	pudimos
pudiste	
pudo	pudieron

poner

puse	pusimos
pusiste	
puso	pusieron

saber

supe	supimos
supiste	
supo	supieron

tener

tuve	tuvimos
tuviste	
tuvo	tuvieron

¿Qué hiciste anoche? — What did you do last night?
Vino al concierto tarde. — He came to the concert late.
Supe las malas noticias. — I found out the bad news.
Tuvieron que volver a casa. — They had to return home.

PREPARACIÓN

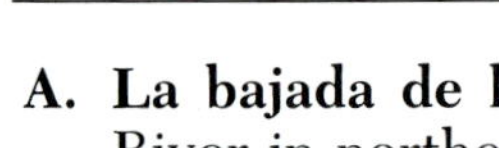

A. La bajada de la Sella. Participants in the kayak race on the Sella River in northern Spain are discussing how long it took them to complete the race. What do they say?

MODELO Alberto / 9 horas
Alberto la hizo en nueve horas.

1. Yo / 11 horas
2. Mario y Javier / 7 horas
3. Pilar / 9 horas
4. Tú / 13 horas
5. Ustedes / 10 horas
6. Nosotros / 8 horas

B. Excursión al Orinoco. Venezuelans have arrived in Caracas to begin a jungle trip to the Orinoco River. From where do they say they came and how did they travel?

MODELO Yo / Mérida / avión
Yo vine de Mérida en avión.

1. Luis / Maracaibo / coche
2. Mis amigos / Isla Margarita / barco
3. Catalina / Puerto La Cruz / autobús
4. Tú / San Antonio / taxi
5. Esteban y yo / Cumaná / avión
6. Ustedes / Macuto / coche

C. En busca de la aventura. Photographers for a television adventure series are talking about where they have gone during the past year. Tell what they say.

MODELO Yo / África / julio
Estuve en África en julio.

1. Juan Manuel / Puerto Rico / diciembre
2. Los hermanos Díaz / Sudamérica / abril
3. Marisol y yo / Europa / mayo
4. Tú / Hawaii / enero
5. Todos / India / marzo
6. Yo / Australia / octubre

D. ¿Por qué? Pedro has been so busy with his astronomy project that he has neglected his friends. His best friend Carlos is trying to find out what is happening. What does he ask?

MODELO hacer gimnasia esta mañana
¿Por qué no hiciste gimnasia esta mañana?

1. venir al partido de volibol hoy
2. hacer tu tarea anoche
3. querer dar un paseo en bicicleta
4. venir a buscarme anoche
5. querer salir con nosotros
6. hacer tus ejercicios hoy

E. ¿Dónde pusieron mis cosas? Lola is in the lobby of the Del Prado Hotel in Mexico City and cannot find her belongings. What does she ask her friends?

MODELO el muchacho / la llave
¿Dónde puso el muchacho la llave?

1. Patricia / la cámara
2. Usted / los abrigos
3. Yo / la cartera
4. Nosotros / el dinero
5. Tú / el radio
6. Ustedes / la mochila

F. La carrera del año. Everyone in town is talking about the annual car rally. What have these people found out about it?

MODELO nosotros / las reglas / nuevas
Nosotros supimos que las reglas son nuevas.

1. Yo / los coches / ultramodernos
2. Los chicos / los premios / fabulosos
3. Tú / los participantes / fenomenales
4. Adela / los hoteles / muy caros
5. Ustedes / los reportajes deportivos / excelentes

EXPLORACIÓN

Expressing negative ideas
Negative and affirmative words

PRESENTACIÓN

You have already used some negative words in Spanish such as **no** and **nada**. Study the negative words and their opposites in the chart.

NEGATIVO		AFIRMATIVO	
nada	nothing	**algo**	something
nadie	nobody	**alguien**	someone
ni . . . ni	neither . . . nor	**o . . . o, y**	either . . . or, and
nunca	never	**siempre**	always
tampoco	either, neither	**también**	also

¿**Siempre** lo hizo? — No, **no** lo hizo **nunca**.
¿Vio a **alguien** en la calle? — No, **no** vio a **nadie**.
¿Le diste **algo**? — No, **no** le di **nada**.
¿Llevaron frutas **y** queso? — No, **no** llevaron **ni** frutas **ni** queso.

A. Sentences using a negative word can be formed in two ways: (1) by placing the negative word before the verb or (2) by placing **no** before the verb and the negative word after the verb.

Nadie llamó.	**No** llamó **nadie**.	No one called.
Nada me gustó.	**No** me gustó **nada**.	I didn't like anything.
Nunca lo vimos.	**No** lo vimos **nunca**.	We never saw it.
Tampoco fue.	**No** fue **tampoco**.	He didn't go either.
Ni tú **ni** yo vamos.	**No** vamos **ni** tú **ni** yo.	Neither you nor I are going.

B. Unlike English, Spanish uses double negatives.

No le di **nada**. — I didn't give him anything.
Nunca le escribo a **nadie**. — I never write to anyone.

C. Sometimes a negative word may be used by itself in response to a question.

¿Quién te despertó esta mañana? — Nadie.
¿Qué compraron ustedes? — Nada.
Yo no fui. ¿Y tú? — Tampoco.

PREPARACIÓN

A. No hizo nada. Verónica accomplished many things yesterday. However, Roberto did nothing. Tell what he says.

MODELO Ella comprendió algo.
Yo no comprendí nada.

1. Ella supo algo.
2. Ella estudió algo.
3. Ella vio algo.
4. Ella escribió algo.
5. Ella encontró algo.
6. Ella hizo algo.

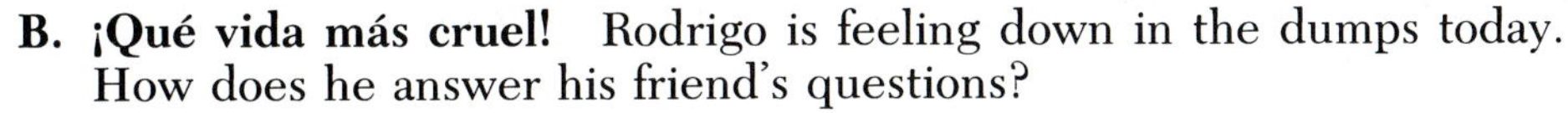

B. ¡Qué vida más cruel! Rodrigo is feeling down in the dumps today. How does he answer his friend's questions?

MODELO ¿Quién te llamó por teléfono?
Nadie me llamó por teléfono.

1. ¿Quién fue al cine contigo?
2. ¿Quién te esperó después de clase?
3. ¿Quién te vino a ver?
4. ¿Quién te ayudó a limpiar la casa?
5. ¿Quién dio un paseo contigo?
6. ¿Quién te hizo un favor?
7. ¿Quién fue a jugar contigo?

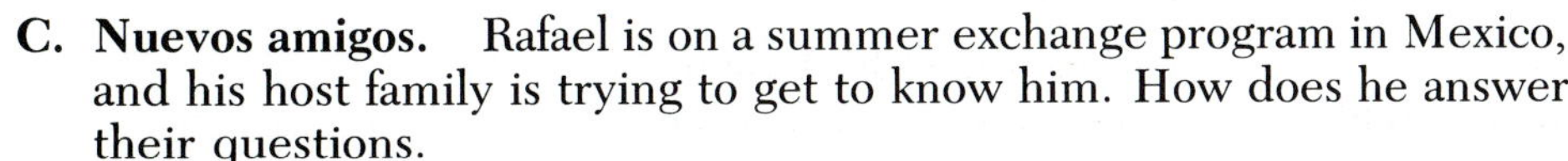

C. Nuevos amigos. Rafael is on a summer exchange program in Mexico, and his host family is trying to get to know him. How does he answer their questions.

MODELO ¿Sabes montar bicicleta o nadar?
No, no sé ni montar bicicleta ni nadar.

1. ¿Sabes jugar fútbol o tenis?
2. ¿Tomas café o té?
3. ¿Conoces Monterrey o Puebla?
4. ¿Comes carne o pescado?
5. ¿Te gusta levantar pesas o hacer yoga?
6. ¿Lees periódicos o revistas?
7. ¿Juegas damas o dominó?

D. ¡Qué aburrido! Some people are complaining that they never did anything exciting when they were young. What do they say?

MODELO Yo / hacer un viaje en moto
Yo nunca hice un viaje en moto.

1. Ricardo / nadar en un río
2. Ustedes / practicar el esquí acuático
3. Mi familia / pasear en velero
4. Tú / participar en una carrera de automóviles
5. Yo / viajar a otro país
6. Mis amigos / cruzar los Estados Unidos en bicicleta
7. Isabel / hacer un safari
8. Nosotros / pilotear un avión

E. Club de montañismo. The Mountain Climber's Club has just come back from an excursion. How do they answer a reporter's questions?

MODELO ¿Encontraron ustedes algo allí? (No . . . nada)
No, no encontramos nada allí.

1. ¿Con quién fueron ustedes a la montaña? (no . . . con nadie)
2. ¿Qué hicieron ustedes? (no . . . nada)
3. ¿Vieron pájaros o animales? (no . . . ni . . . ni)
4. ¿Vieron a otras personas allí? (no . . . tampoco)
5. ¿Escalaron la montaña de noche? (no . . . nunca)
6. ¿Sacaron fotos de alguien? (no . . . de nadie)

COMUNICACIÓN

A. Las cosas que nadie hace. In every school there are things that no one does. What are some of those things in your school?

> EJEMPLO Nadie se pone corbata para ir a un partido de fútbol.
> Nadie come las hamburguesas de la escuela.

B. ¡Quejas y más quejas! Use negative expressions to tell what you and your friends typically complain about.

> EJEMPLO No tengo nada que hacer esta noche.
> Nadie me comprende.

C. Entrevista. Answer the following questions negatively or use them to interview another student.

1. ¿Quién te ayuda con la tarea?
2. ¿Vas a hacer algo interesante este fin de semana?
3. ¿Vas al cine o al teatro?
4. ¿Vas a invitar a alguien al baile?
5. ¿Le vas a dar algo a un(a) amigo(a) para su cumpleaños?
6. Si tu amigo(a) no va a una fiesta, ¿vas tú?

PERSPECTIVAS

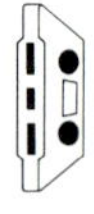

El diario de Cristóbal Colón

Para el Día de la Raza las clases de español tuvieron que leer el diario del primer viaje de Cristóbal Colón. — Columbus Day

3 de agosto

Nuestro viaje para buscar un nuevo camino a las Indias comenzó hoy. Salimos de Palos con tres carabelas: la Niña, la Pinta y la Santa María. Navegamos con viento fuerte hacia el sur. — strong / south

6 de agosto

La Pinta empezó a hacer agua y tuvimos que quedarnos en la isla de Tenerife casi un mes. De una montaña muy alta de esa isla vimos salir un gran fuego. — take on water / remain

9 de septiembre

Hoy por primera vez no pudimos ver la tierra.

17 de septiembre

Los hombres comenzaron a quejarse del largo viaje. Tuve que darles esperanzas y recordarles la promesa que hicimos de no abandonar nuestros planes. — complain / hope

6 de octubre

Los marineros de la Niña vieron unos pájaros y vimos una maravillosa lluvia de fuego en el cielo. — sailors / rain; sky

7 de octubre

Nos ayudó la corriente y encontramos mucha hierba muy verde en el agua. Esto nos hizo pensar que estamos cerca de tierra. — current / plants; land

8 de octubre

Tuvimos fuertes lluvias. Siguen las señales de tierra. Debemos estar cerca de alguna isla. No quise detenerme pues mi fin es llegar a las Indias. — signs; stop

9 de octubre

Cambió el viento. Toda la noche oímos pasar pájaros. — changed

11 de octubre

Sacamos del agua una hierba que crece en tierra. Con esta señal todos se sintieron muy alegres. — grows

12 de octubre

Dos horas después de medianoche los marineros de la Pinta gritaron ¡Tierra! ¡Tierra! cuando vieron por fin una isla. Di gracias a Dios y todos hicieron lo mismo. Luego fuimos hasta la playa. Allí puse la bandera real en tierra y tomé posesión de la isla en nombre del rey y la reina de España. — shouted; royal flag; king / queen

COMPRENSIÓN

Answer the following questions based on **El diario de Cristóbal Colón**.

1. ¿Cuándo comenzó la aventura de Colón?
2. ¿De dónde salieron y cómo viajaron?
3. ¿Qué le pasó a la Pinta?
4. ¿De qué se quejaron los marineros?
5. ¿Qué vieron los marineros de la Niña? ¿Cuándo?
6. ¿Qué señales de tierra vieron?
7. ¿Qué tiempo hizo el ocho de octubre?
8. ¿Adónde llegaron y cuándo?
9. ¿Qué hizo Colón cuando llegó?
10. ¿Cuánto tiempo estuvo Colón en el mar?

COMUNICACIÓN

A. Candidato(a) para la exploración. Would you be a good candidate for a trip similar to the one taken by Columbus? To find out, take the following test and then check the **Interpretación** at the end.

1.	¿Te gusta la aventura?	sí	no
2.	¿Te sientes bien cuando hace calor o frío?	sí	no
3.	¿Te sientes contento(a) cuando estás lejos de tu familia?	sí	no
4.	¿Puedes vivir sin televisión ni radio ni cine?	sí	no
5.	¿Insistes en seguir cuando las cosas son difíciles?	sí	no
6.	¿Puedes pasar horas y horas sin dormir ni comer?	sí	no
7.	¿Te gusta estar solo(a)?	sí	no
8.	En general, ¿eres una persona independiente?	sí	no
9.	¿Estás siempre listo(a) para algo nuevo?	sí	no
10.	¿Te fascinan las cosas peligrosas?	sí	no

Interpretación: Cada respuesta afirmativa es un punto. Suma (*add*) los puntos para ver qué clase de aventurero(a) eres.

9–10 puntos	Tienes espíritu de aventurero(a). Pero ten cuidado, eres a menudo muy impulsivo(a) y esto puede ser peligroso.
6–8 puntos	Estás listo(a) para la aventura y eres responsable, pero no sirves para las expediciones más peligrosas.
3–5 puntos	No eres muy valiente. La aventura y la exploración te interesan un poco, pero prefieres quedarte con tu familia y tus amigos.
0–2 puntos	La aventura no es para ti. En tu caso, es mejor mirar las aventuras de los otros en la televisión o en el cine.

B. Tú y la aventura. Tell which of the following you have already done. Then tell which you think you will do someday or never do.

EJEMPLO Ya piloteé un avión.
Nunca voy a escalar una montaña.
Algún día voy a bajar el Río Colorado en canoa.

1. cruzar el océano Atlántico en barco
2. hacer un viaje de 300 kilómetros o más
3. escalar una montaña
4. participar en un safari
5. explorar una selva o un bosque
6. hacer un viaje al extranjero
7. bajar un río en canoa
8. caminar durante horas por la playa
9. participar en una carrera
10. acampar durante el invierno
11. esquiar o practicar el esquí acuático
12. explorar el mundo submarino
13. saltar de un avión en paracaídas
14. salir al mar en velero
15. pilotear un avión o un barco

C. El aventurero eres tú. Imagine that you took part in an exciting or dangerous adventure. Write a short description of what happened.

D. Entrevista. Use the suggestions to interview other students in your class about what they did (or did not do) yesterday at various times.

EJEMPLO ¿Cuándo tuviste la clase de español?
Tuve la clase de español a las ocho.

Sugerencias

tener la clase de inglés
hacer ejercicios
mirar la televisión
ir a casa
hablar con unos amigos
almorzar
practicar deportes
llegar a casa
tomar el desayuno
escuchar discos
dar una caminata
venir a la escuela
acostarse
levantarse
vestirse
?

VOCABULARIO DEL CAPÍTULO

NOUNS

el automóvil car
la bandera flag
la canoa canoe
la carabela sailing ship
la carrera race
el cielo sky
la corriente current
Dios God
la esperanza hope
la expedición expedition
el fin goal
la hierba plant
el kilómetro kilometer
la lluvia rain
el marinero sailor
el mundo world
el paracaídas parachute
la reina queen
el rey king
el río river
el safari safari
la selva jungle
la señal sign
el sur south
la tierra land
el velero sailboat

ADJECTIVES

amazónico Amazon
desesperado hopeless
fuerte strong
peligroso dangerous
perdido lost
real royal
solo single
submarino underwater
venezolano Venezuelan

VERBS

abandonar to abandon, give up
bajar to go down
cambiar to change
crecer (zc) to grow
cruzar (z ⟶ c) to cross
detenerse to stop, detain oneself
escalar to climb
explorar to explore
gritar to shout
navegar to navigate, sail
pasear to go for a ride (or walk)
pilotear to pilot
quedarse to remain, stay
quejarse (de) to complain
saltar to jump
separar(se) to separate (oneself)

ADVERBS

accidentalmente accidentally
hacia toward
inmediatamente immediately
peor worse

NEGATIVES AND AFFIRMATIVES

alguien someone
nadie no one
ni . . . ni neither . . . nor
nunca never
o . . . o either . . . or
tampoco neither

EXPRESSIONS

dar la vuelta al mundo to go around the world
el Día de la Raza Columbus Day
hacer agua to take on water
tomar posesión to take possession
yo mismo(a) I myself

Capítulo de enlace

PERSPECTIVES

PRIMERA PERSPECTIVA

¿Sabes cómo es tu chico o chica ideal?

Para elegir al compañero o compañera ideal, primero debes saber cómo eres tú. Contesta el siguiente test, pero trata de usar no sólo el corazón sino también la cabeza. Así, vas a poder encontrar a alguien compatible con tu manera de ser.

elegir: choose
trata de: try to

1. Tu sitio ideal para vivir es
   - **a.** un chalet cerca de un lago.
   - **b.** una casa en la playa.
   - **c.** un apartamento en la ciudad.
2. Como regalo, ¿qué te gustaría más?
   - **a.** un anillo
   - **b.** unos patines
   - **c.** un libro de la historia del rock
3. Una persona que te interesa te llama a las cinco para invitarte a salir dos horas más tarde. Tú le dices:
   - **a.** No sé, llámame en una hora. Cuando llama otra vez, aceptas.
   - **b.** ¡Fantástico! Estoy listo(a) en una hora.
   - **c.** Lo siento. La próxima vez llámame con más anticipación.
4. Te encantaría salir a pasear en
   - **a.** una carroza antigua.
   - **b.** un velero.
   - **c.** una limosina elegantísima.

sitio: place
lago: lake
patines: skates
próxima: next
carroza: carriage

5. Tu idea de unas vacaciones fabulosas es
   a. un crucero por las islas del Caribe. — cruise
   b. una semana en una playa totalmente desierta.
   c. una visita a una ciudad cosmopolita, como Nueva York, París o Buenos Aires.
6. La primera cosa que te atrae en un(a) chico(a) es — attracts
   a. su carácter romántico.
   b. su espíritu de aventura.
   c. su inteligencia.
7. Tú y tus amigos organizan un día de campo, pero cuando llegan allí empieza a llover. Entonces,
   a. buscas un refugio en donde hacer el día de campo. — shelter
   b. no te importa estar bajo la lluvia. — under
   c. invitas a todo el mundo a tu casa.
8. En tu ropero predomina la ropa de colores — closet
   a. fríos como el azul y el verde, y los colores claros. — light
   b. cálidos como el amarillo y el rojo, y los tonos vivos. — warm
   c. Ninguno en particular. Te gustan todos. — none

Interpretación

Mayoría de respuestas A:
Vives entre las nubes. Eres una persona muy romántica. Según esto, tu chico(a) ideal debe ser romántico(a), sentimental y de ideas anticuadas. — clouds / according to; old-fashioned

Mayoría de respuestas B:
Te encanta la aventura y vivir plenamente cada momento. Así, tu chico(a) ideal debe ser un(a) fanático(a) de la vida al aire libre, las aventuras y las cosas nuevas. — fully

Mayoría de respuestas C:
Eres bastante maduro(a). Sabes lo que quieres y sabes vivir. Tu chico(a) ideal debe ser sofisticado(a), quizás mayor que tú, estable y con deseos de superación. — mature; older; self-improvement

Adaptado de la revista *Tú*, abril 1983.

COMUNICACIÓN

A. Tú, la computadora, ¿y quién? Imagine that a club in your school has developed a computer program to find out with whom you are most compatible. Answer the following questions so the computer operator can enter your personal data.

¿Cómo te llamas?
¿Dónde vives?
¿Cuántos años tienes?
¿De qué color tienes el pelo?
¿De qué color son tus ojos?
¿Cómo eres tú?
¿Cuáles son tus pasatiempos favoritos?
¿Qué deportes te gustan?
¿Qué te gusta hacer en tus ratos libres?

B. ¿Eres un buen detective? The following illustration shows Marcos Santana's room. Based on what you see, tell as much as you can about his likes, dislikes, and interests.

C. Entrevista. Answer the following questions relating to you and your school or use them to interview another student.

1. ¿Qué estudias ahora? ¿En qué año estás?
2. ¿Cuántas clases tienes cada día? ¿Cuál es la primera, la segunda, la última?
3. ¿Cuál es la clase que te gusta más? ¿Por qué?
4. ¿Cuál es la clase que te gusta menos? ¿Por qué?
5. ¿A qué hora es tu recreo? ¿Qué haces durante el recreo?
6. ¿Participas en las actividades de la escuela? ¿En cuáles?
7. ¿Eres miembro de algún club? ¿Cuál?
8. ¿Cuál es tu clase más fácil? ¿Y la más difícil?
9. ¿Cuáles son tus pasatiempos favoritos?
10. ¿Qué quieres hacer después de graduarte?

D. Amigos por correspondencia. An international pen pal organization has provided information about teenagers from different countries. Use the information provided about each student to answer the questions below.

Rosa María. Soy venezolana, estudio para secretaria bilingüe. Deseo tener correspondencia con chicos europeos de 16 años. Me pueden escribir en inglés, español o francés.	**Juan Ignacio.** Soy un joven español aficionado a la exploración submarina y a los deportes acuáticos. Me gustaría corresponder con chicas de origen hispano de 17 a 19 años.
Pedro. Soy de Chile. Soy fanático de los automóviles y del jazz. Si tú tienes los mismos intereses que yo, escríbeme.	**Inés.** Soy dominicana. Estudio música clásica y quiero visitar los Estados Unidos. Me gustaría tener correspondencia con jóvenes norteamericanos para aprender inglés bien.

1. ¿De dónde es Rosa María? ¿En qué idiomas pueden escribirle a ella?
2. ¿Es Pedro de Venezuela? ¿Cuáles son sus intereses?
3. ¿Con quién quiere Pedro tener correspondencia?
4. ¿De dónde es Juan Ignacio? ¿Qué le gusta hacer?
5. ¿A quiénes quiere escribir?
6. ¿Dónde vive Inés? ¿Qué estudia ella?
7. ¿Por qué quiere corresponder con chicos o chicas norteamericanos?

E. Escríbanme. Write your own ad for the pen pal page of a magazine. Tell something about your interests and what type of person you would like to write to.

F. Prioridades. Tell how important each of the following is for you.

Es muy importante para mí.
Es bastante importante para mí.
No es muy importante para mí.
Es poco importante para mí.

1. estar en una clase con mi(s) amigo(a)(s)
2. tomar los cursos que quiero
3. tener un trabajo para ganar dinero
4. tener profesores exigentes
5. tener tiempo libre para mis pasatiempos
6. sacar buenas notas
7. participar en las actividades de la escuela
8. poder dar mi opinión en la clase
9. vivir cerca de la escuela
10. ?

G. Entrevista. Make up questions to ask other students about their leisure activities.

EJEMPLO ¿Vas mucho a la playa?
¿Das caminatas a veces?

H. Descripción. Use the lists below to describe somebody you know or an imaginary person. Make sure to put the adjectives in the appropriate form.

La apariencia física
ser pequeño, alto, grande, gordo, delgado, guapo; tener el pelo rubio (negro, castaño); tener los ojos negros (azules, pardos, grises, verdes); vestirse bien (mal), ?

La personalidad
ser bueno, cómico, divertido, exagerado, idealista, independiente, inteligente, simpático, antipático, inteligente, malo, paciente, sentimental, serio, sofisticado, responsable, tacaño, razonable, romántico, ?

Joven español desea comunicarse con estudiante norteamericano para practicar su inglés. Llame a Joaquín 36-24-80.	Chica panameña de diecisiete años desea correspondencia para intercambiar estampillas. Luisa Aldonza, San Miguel 22

SEGUNDA PERSPECTIVA

Sugerencias para el viajero

Cuando usted viaja a otro país, usted entra en contacto con una nueva cultura, una cultura totalmente diferente. Para gozar de su viaje plenamente, recuerde siempre estas sugerencias.

gozar: enjoy

No hable mal de cómo vive la gente. Respete su manera de ser. Recuerde que cada país tiene su orgullo propio y una cultura diferente.

No hable mal ni de los héroes nacionales ni del gobierno. Nadie aprecia la opinión de los extranjeros en los asuntos políticos de su país.

aprecia: values
orgullo / propio / asuntos: pride / own / matters

Disfrute de las cosas típicas. Pruebe la comida del país. No pase su tiempo haciendo las mismas cosas que hace en casa. Esté listo para la aventura, haga cosas nuevas. Vaya a escuchar un mariachi o a ver una corrida de toros. Es más emocionante.

Disfrute de: enjoy
haciendo: doing
mariachi: Mexican band

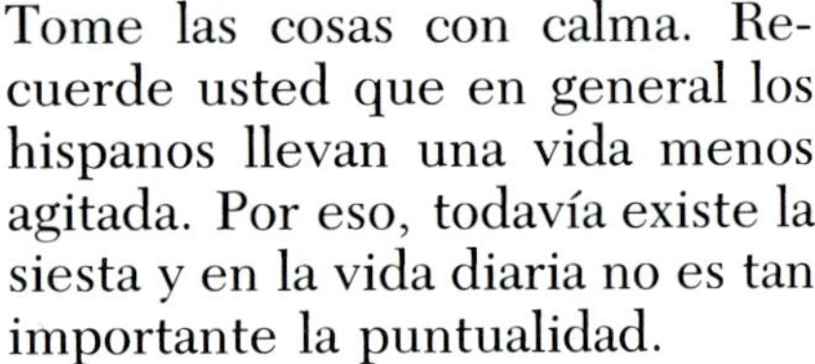
Tome las cosas con calma. Recuerde usted que en general los hispanos llevan una vida menos agitada. Por eso, todavía existe la siesta y en la vida diaria no es tan importante la puntualidad.

No haga comparaciones negativas entre las cosas de su país y las del país donde usted está de visita. Evite todo tipo de crítica. Y no diga que en su país todo es mejor. Eso no le gusta a nadie.

Basado en "Si viaja, no haga estas cosas" de *Spanish for Oral and Written Review*, 2*a* ed., de Iglesias y Meiden (New York: Holt, Rinehart and Winston, 1981).

COMPRENSIÓN

Answer the following questions. Try to add opinions and reasons of your own.

1. Si las condiciones de vida son muy diferentes de las condiciones en los Estados Unidos, ¿qué debe hacer el viajero?
2. ¿Debe el viajero criticar al gobierno de otro país? ¿Por qué?
3. ¿Qué puede hacer una persona para disfrutar de las cosas típicas? ¿Debe probar cosas nuevas?
4. ¿Hay alguna diferencia entre la vida en los países hispanos y la vida de este país? ¿Qué debe hacer el turista?
5. ¿Por qué no debe hacer comparaciones negativas entre el país extranjero y su propio país?
6. ¿Qué otras sugerencias tiene usted para el viajero?

COMUNICACIÓN

A. ¿Qué hacer? Give some advice about what one should or should not do while visiting the United States.

EJEMPLO No visite solamente las ciudades grandes.
Vaya a un partido de béisbol.

B. Estereotipos. How do you feel about some of these stereotypical statements about Americans? If you do not agree, change the statement to reflect your own opinion.

1. A los americanos les gusta comer más hamburguesas que otra comida.
2. Los americanos son más agresivos que los hispanos.
3. Para los americanos, no hay deporte más emocionante que el fútbol americano.
4. Los americanos pasan menos tiempo con su familia que con sus perros.
5. La comida americana es peor que la comida de otros países.
6. Los americanos son más ricos que el resto del mundo.
7. Los americanos llevan una vida más agitada que los latinoamericanos.
8. Los americanos respetan menos la gente que el dinero.

C. ¿Quieres probarlo? Below is a selection of typical Hispanic dishes. Tell whether or not you are willing to try them. Use the scale below in giving your answers.

1. sopa de ajo
2. plátanos con huevos
3. agua de coco
4. flan
5. camarones a la plancha
6. paella valenciana

D. El arte de regatear. A handmade hat that costs 1,000 **pesos mexicanos** may be bought for much less at an open-air market in Mexico City. Use your bargaining skills to convince the merchant to reduce his price.

VENDEDOR	Usted quiere un sombrero, ¿eh? Mire, este sombrero de Guadalajara sólo le cuesta 1,000 pesos.
USTED	________
VENDEDOR	Lo siento, 1,000 pesos es su precio—un verdadero regalo. Si va a una tienda le va a costar por lo menos tres veces más caro.
USTED	________
VENDEDOR	¡Imposible! Si le vendo el sombrero a ese precio voy a perder dinero. Pero le voy a dar el sombrero en 950 pesos . . .
USTED	________
VENDEDOR	No, no, sólo puedo venderlo por 100 pesos menos. Este es mi precio final.
USTED	________
VENDEDOR	Está bien, aquí lo tiene, deme el dinero.

E. Gestos. Can you identify what these Hispanic gestures mean? Match the pictures with the expressions.

a. ¡No, no!
b. ¡Ay, Dios mío!
c. ¡Tacaño!
d. ¡Fantástico!
e. Ten cuidado.

TERCERA PERSPECTIVA

Viaje por Andalucía

Llegaron por fin las vacaciones y salimos el grupo de quince estudiantes con nuestra profesora de español, listos para conocer Andalucía. Andalucía es una región que queda al sur de España, famosa por su música, y por ser cuna de pintores y poetas. También es rica en tradiciones e* historia; por ella pasaron los romanos, visigodos, moros y judíos.

cuna: cradle
moros / judíos: Moors / Jews

Fuimos primero a Córdoba, que fue capital de la España musulmana y uno de los centros culturales e intelectuales más importantes de Europa. Aquí sacamos muchas fotos de la Mezquita, uno de los monumentos moros más bellos de España. Pudimos también visitar el Alcázar de los Reyes Cristianos, un palacio militar, y una sinagoga antigua en el barrio judío. Fue un día muy agitado y nos acostamos temprano.

musulmana: Moslem
Mezquita: mosque
bellos: beautiful
barrio: quarter

**y* becomes *e* before *i* or *hi*

Al día siguiente tomamos el autobús a Sevilla, famosa por su belleza y ambiente romántico. El tiempo fue magnífico y vimos flores, árboles y plantas por todas partes. Lo que más nos impresionó fue su catedral gótica, una de las más grandes del mundo, y la Giralda, una torre mora desde donde vimos toda la ciudad. ¡Qué vista tan increíble! Por la noche comimos en un restaurante típico donde oímos cantar a unos gitanos y después fuimos a ver un espectáculo de flamenco. Esa noche nos divertimos muchísimo.

atmosphere / flowers / trees / Gothic
tower
view
gypsies

Pasamos los últimos días de nuestro viaje en Granada. Aquí visitamos el magnífico palacio moro de La Alhambra, la Catedral y la Capilla Real donde enterraron a los Reyes Católicos Isabel y Fernando. También tuvimos oportunidad de ir al Mercado Moro donde compramos muchos recuerdos. En total, fue un viaje maravilloso y todos regresamos a Madrid muy contentos y con deseos de volver algún día a Andalucía, tierra romántica y mágica.

Chapel
buried

COMPRENSIÓN

Answer the following questions based on **Viaje por Andalucía**.

1. ¿Quiénes fueron a Andalucía?
2. ¿Dónde queda esa región?
3. ¿Por qué es famosa Andalucía?
4. ¿A qué ciudad fueron primero?
5. ¿Qué hicieron en la Mezquita? ¿Qué más vieron en Córdoba?
6. ¿Cómo llegaron a Sevilla? ¿Cómo fue el tiempo allí?
7. ¿Qué hicieron por la noche?
8. ¿Dónde pasaron los últimos días del viaje?
9. ¿Qué compraron en Granada?
10. ¿Qué impresión tuvieron de Andalucía?

COMUNICACIÓN

A. Un viaje inolvidable. Using the questions below as a guide, tell about a trip that you took.

1. ¿Cuándo fuiste de vacaciones?
2. ¿Cómo viajaste? ¿en avión?
3. ¿Con quién(es) hiciste el viaje?
4. ¿Adónde fuiste?
5. ¿Qué visitaste y qué viste?
6. ¿Qué hiciste durante el viaje?
7. ¿Tuviste tiempo para verlo todo?
8. ¿Tuviste algún problema?

B. Concurso. The Spanish Club is sponsoring a contest for a trip to Spain. In order to win, you must write an essay describing why you want to go and what you will do there. You may want to use some of the suggestions below.

practicar el español
sacar muchas fotos
visitar monumentos
ver cosas nuevas
conocer una cultura diferente
visitar a amigos o familia
oír una tuna universitaria
probar la comida española
pasear por las grandes avenidas
visitar el museo del Prado
ver una corrida de toros
asistir a un festival de flamenco
pasar una semana en la playa

C. ¿Qué tiempo hace? The chart below indicates the temperature and rainfall of different countries in the Americas. Find out the following information on the chart. Then make comparisons.

1. ¿Dónde llueve más en mayo, en Rio de Janeiro o en Buenos Aires?
2. ¿Dónde llueve menos en mayo, en Perú o en Ecuador?
3. ¿Dónde hace más calor en julio, en las Antillas o en Nueva York?
4. ¿Dónde hace menos calor en julio, en México o en Argentina?
5. ¿Qué país tiene un clima similar al clima donde tú vives?

	¿QUE TIEMPO HACE? TEMPERATURA (C°) Y PRECIPITACION (cm)							
PAIS	CIUDAD	MAYO		JULIO		SEPTIEMBRE	
Antillas		26°	125	26°7	179	26°7	196
Argentina	Buenos Aires	15°	80	10°	95	13°	90
Bolivia	La Paz	11°2	22	9°8	5	11°8	48
Brasil	Manaus	26°6	193	26°9	61	27°9	52
	Río de Janeiro	23°5	77,5	22°	40	24°	65
Canadá	Montreal	13°	72	21°	89	15°	82
Colombia	Bogotá	17°2	161	17°3	40	17°7	94
Ecuador	Quito	13°1	130	12°9	20	13°2	81
Estados Unidos	Los Angeles	18°	70	23°	20	21°	
	Nueva York	17°	91	25°	94	20°	100
México	México	17°4	55	15°9	160	15°9	129
Perú	Lima	17°8	6	15°3	6	15°4	6

D. Itinerario. Based on Señor Alba's schedule of two business trips to South America, tell when and at what time he leaves for the following cities.

EJEMPLO Sale para Caracas el 28 de marzo a las ocho y media de la mañana.

Ciudad	Vuelo	Fecha	Hora de Salida
Caracas	21	28/3	8:30
Bogotá	103	2/4	15:00
Lima	76	9/4	9:25
Quito	92	17/4	13:50
Asunción	333	30/10	18:15
Santiago	47	5/11	10:00
Buenos Aires	159	11/11	16:38
Río de Janeiro	451	22/11	13:05

E. Y mañana, de vacaciones. Today is the last day of class. Use some of the following verbs to describe what you did today or yesterday, and what you will do beginning tomorrow.

EJEMPLO Esta mañana me levanté a las siete, pero mañana voy a dormir hasta el mediodía.

despertarse	vestirse	sentirse
levantarse	lavarse	prepararse
bañarse	acostarse	ponerse
peinarse	dormirse	divertirse

F. ¿Quién lo hizo? Ask questions to find out who in your class did the following things during the past school year.

EJEMPLO ¿Quién estuvo en otro país?

1. ¿Quién hizo un viaje por los Estados Unidos?
2. ¿Quién vio al grupo Menudo en la televisión?
3. ¿Quién comió en un restaurante mexicano?
4. ¿Quién visitó Washington, D.C.?
5. ¿Quién acampó durante el invierno?
6. ¿Quién vio una película en español?
7. ¿Quién tuvo correspondencia con un(a) amigo(a) hispano(a)?
8. ¿Quién aprendió una canción española?
9. ¿Quién fue a esquiar?
10. ¿Quién encontró a su chico(a) ideal?

Cuadro de verbos

REGULAR VERBS

Infinitive	*Present*		*Preterite*		*Commands*	
					Formal	*Familiar*
tomar	tomo tomas toma	tomamos toman	tomé tomaste tomó	tomamos tomaron	tome tomen	toma no tomes
comer	como comes come	comemos comen	comí comiste comió	comimos comieron	coma coman	come no comas
vivir	vivo vives vive	vivimos viven	viví viviste vivió	vivimos vivieron	viva vivan	vive no vivas

STEM-CHANGING VERBS

pensar (e → ie)	**pienso** **piensas** **piensa**	pensamos **piensan**	pensé pensaste pensó	pensamos pensaron	piense piensen	piensa no pienses
like pensar: cerrar, comenzar, despertarse, empezar, nevar (*only* **nieva** *used*)						
perder (e → ie)	**pierdo** **pierdes** **pierde**	perdemos **pierden**	perdí perdiste perdió	perdimos perdieron	pierda pierdan	pierde no pierdas
like perder: entender						
volver (o → ue)	**vuelvo** **vuelves** **vuelve**	volvemos **vuelven**	volví volviste volvió	volvimos volvieron	vuelva vuelvan	vuelve no vuelvas
like volver: doler, llover (*only* **llueve** *used*)						
mostrar (o → ue)	**muestro** **muestras** **muestra**	mostramos **muestran**	mostré mostraste mostró	mostramos mostraron	muestre muestren	muestra no muestres
like mostrar: acostarse, almorzar, contar, costar, encontrar(se), probarse, recordar						

Infinitive	*Present*		*Preterite*		*Commands* *Formal*	*Familiar*
jugar (u → ue)	**juego** **juegas** **juega**	jugamos **juegan**	**jugué** jugaste jugó	jugamos jugaron	juegue jueguen	juega no juegues
sentir (e → ie, i)	**siento** **sientes** **siente**	sentimos **sienten**	sentí sentiste **sintió**	sentimos **sintieron**	sienta sientan	siente no sientas
like sentir: divertirse, preferir, sentirse						
dormir (o → ue, u)	**duermo** **duermes** **duerme**	dormimos **duermen**	dormí dormiste **durmió**	dormimos **durmieron**	duerma duerman	duerme no duermas
like dormir: dormirse, morir*						
pedir (e → i, i)	**pido** **pides** **pide**	pedimos **piden**	pedí pediste **pidió**	pedimos **pidieron**	pida pidan	pide no pidas
like pedir: conseguir, repetir, seguir, servir, vestirse						

IRREGULAR VERBS

dar	**doy** das da	damos dan	**di** **diste** **dio**	**dimos** **dieron**	**dé** **den**	da no **des**
decir	**digo** **dices** **dice**	decimos **dicen**	**dije*** **dijiste** **dijo**	**dijimos** **dijeron**	diga digan	**di** no digas
estar	**estoy** estás está	estamos están	**estuve** **estuviste** **estuvo**	**estuvimos** **estuvieron**	**esté** **estén**	está no **estés**
hacer	**hago** haces hace	hacemos hacen	**hice** **hiciste** **hizo**	**hicimos** **hicieron**	haga hagan	**haz** no hagas

Infinitive	*Present*		*Preterite*		*Commands*	
					Formal	*Familiar*
ir	**voy**	**vamos**	**fui**	**fuimos**	**vaya**	**ve**
	vas		**fuiste**		**vayan**	**no vayas**
	va	**van**	**fue**	**fueron**		
oír	**oigo**	oímos	oí*	oímos	oiga	oye
	oyes		oíste		oigan	no oigas
	oye	**oyen**	**oyó**	**oyeron**		
like oír (**y** *between vowels*): creer, leer						
poder	**puedo**	podemos	**pude**	**pudimos**		
	puedes		**pudiste**			
	puede	**pueden**	**pudo**	**pudieron**		
poner	**pongo**	ponemos	**puse**	**pusimos**	ponga	**pon**
	pones		**pusiste**		pongan	no pongas
	pone	ponen	**puso**	**pusieron**		
querer	**quiero**	queremos	**quise**	**quisimos**		
	quieres		**quisiste**			
	quiere	**quieren**	**quiso**	**quisieron**		
saber	**sé**	sabemos	**supe**	**supimos**	**sepa***	sabe
	sabes		**supiste**		**sepan**	no **sepas**
	sabe	saben	**supo**	**supieron**		
salir	**salgo**	salimos	salí	salimos	salga	**sal**
	sales		saliste		salgan	no salgas
	sale	salen	salió	salieron		
ser	**soy**	**somos**	**fui**	**fuimos**	**sea**	**sé**
	eres		**fuiste**		**sean**	**no seas**
	es	**son**	**fue**	**fueron**		
tener	**tengo**	tenemos	**tuve**	**tuvimos**	tenga	**ten**
	tienes		**tuviste**		tengan	no tengas
	tiene	**tienen**	**tuvo**	**tuvieron**		
like tener: detenerse						
traer	**traigo**	traemos	**traje***	**trajimos**	traiga	trae
	traes		**trajiste**		traigan	no traigas
	trae	traen	**trajo**	**trajeron**		
venir	**vengo**	venimos	**vine**	**vinimos**	venga	**ven***
	vienes		**viniste**		vengan	no vengas
	viene	**vienen**	**vino**	**vinieron**		

IRREGULAR VERBS (continued)

Infinitive	*Present*		*Preterite*		*Commands* *Formal*	*Familiar*
ver	**veo** ves ve	vemos ven	vi viste vio	vimos vieron	vea vean	ve no veas

VERBS WITH SPELLING CHANGES

conocer	**conozco** conoces conoce	conocemos conocen	conocí conociste conoció	conocimos conocieron	**conozca** **conozcan**	conoce no **conozcas**
like conocer (**c** → **zc** before **o** or **a**): crecer, desaparecer, nacer,* parecer, reconocer*						
llegar	llego llegas llega	llegamos llegan	**llegué** llegaste llegó	llegamos llegaron	**llegue** **lleguen**	llega no **llegues**
like llegar (**g** → **gu** before **e**): jugar (ue), navegar, pagar						
buscar	busco buscas busca	buscamos buscan	**busqué** buscaste buscó	buscamos buscaron	**busque** **busquen**	busca no **busques**
like buscar (**c** → **qu** before **e**): practicar, sacar, tocar						
empezar	**empiezo** **empiezas** **empieza**	empezamos **empiezan**	**empecé** empezaste empezó	empezamos empezaron	**empiece** **empiecen**	empieza no **empieces**
like empezar (**z** → **c** before **e**): comenzar (ie), almorzar (ue)						

REFLEXIVE VERBS[†]

lavarse	me lavo te lavas se lava	nos lavamos se lavan	me lavé te lavaste se lavó	nos lavamos se lavaron	lávese* lávense	lávate no te laves

*Not taught in **¿Y tú?** May appear in **Rincones culturales.**

[†]Stem-changing reflexive verbs are listed under the appropriate model in the chart.

Vocabulario español-inglés

The **Vocabulario español-inglés** includes all vocabulary, except numbers and obvious cognates, from the **Capítulo preliminar** (P) through Chapter 12, including vocabulary from the **Rincones culturales** (RC). It does not include vocabulary from the optional **Capítulo de enlace**. The number following each entry indicates the chapter in which the word or expression is first introduced. If a word is used in the text in more than one sense, each use is given, with the appropriate chapter reference.

Adjectives are given in the masculine, with the feminine endings noted. In the case of irregular adjectives and professions, the feminine form is given in full. Idiomatic expressions are listed under the main words in each idiom. Verbs marked with an * are irregular in some forms and may be found in the verb charts.

The following abbreviations are used:

adj. adjective; *adv.* adverb; *fam.* familiar; (*f*) feminine; *inf.* infinitive; *lit.* literally; (*m*) masculine; *obj.* object; *pl.* plural; *prep.* preposition; *pron.* pronoun

A

a to, at **1**
abandonar to abandon, give up **12**
el **abogado, la abogada** lawyer **11**
el **abrazo** hug **8**
abril April **8**
abrir to open **6**
la **abuela** grandmother **4**
el **abuelo** grandfather **4**
los **abuelos** grandparents **4**
aburrido,-a boring **1**
acabar to finish **11**; **acabar de** + *inf.* to have just **9**
el **acampador, la acampadora** camper **9**
acampar to camp **8**
accidentalmente accidentally **12**
aconsejar to advise **11**
acostarse (ue)* to go to bed **10**
la **actividad** activity **8**
el **actor, la actriz** actor, actress **11**
acuático,-a water (*adj.*), aquatic **8**
además in addition, furthermore, besides **2**
adivinar to guess **12RC**
admirar to admire **8**
¿adónde? where (to)? **2**
el **aeropuerto** airport **2**
la **agencia** agency **11**
el **agente, la agente de viajes** travel agent **11**
agitado,-a hectic, agitated **8**
agosto August **8**
el **agua** (*f*) water **6**; **el agua mineral** mineral water **6**
ahí there, right there **7**
ahora now **2**
el **aire** air **8**; **al aire libre** outdoors **9**
el **ajedrez** chess **9**
el **álbum** album **4**
alegrarse (de) to be glad **3**; **¡Me alegro!** I'm glad! **3**; **¡Cuánto me alegro!** I'm so glad, happy! **3**
alegre cheerful, lively **1**
el **álgebra** (*f*) algebra **5**
algo something **3**
alguien someone **12**
algunos,-as some **8**; **algún día** someday **3**
allá there (*distant*) **10**
allí over there **7**
almorzar (ue)* to have lunch **9**
el **almuerzo** lunch **6**
altísimo,-a extremely high **9RC**
alto,-a tall **1**
amarillo,-a yellow **10**
amazónico,-a Amazon (*adj.*) **12**
el **amigo, la amiga** friend **2**
el **anillo** ring **4**
el **animal** animal **1**; **el animal doméstico** pet **11**
anoche last night **10**
antes de before **6**
antiguo,-a ancient, old **10**
antipático,-a unfriendly **1**
el **anuario** yearbook **9**
el **anuncio** commercial **7**
el **año** year **4**; **cumplir ____ años** to turn (be) ____

years old **4**; **tener ____ años** to be ____ years old **4**; **el año pasado** last year **10**
aprender (a) to learn (to) **5**
aquel, aquella that (*distant, over there*) **7**
aquí here **2**
arreglar to fix, repair **10**; **arreglar el cuarto** to straighten up one's room **2**
¡Arriba! Get up! **5**
el arroz rice **6**
el arte art **5**; **las artes** (*fine, creative*) arts **9**
la artesanía crafts **10**
el artista, la artista entertainer **11**
la asistencia social social work **11RC**
asistir (a) to attend **6**
atlético,-a athletic **9**
aumentar de peso to gain weight **6**
el autobús bus **8**
el automóvil car **12**
la avenida avenue **7**
el avión plane **8**
ayer yesterday **10**
ayudar to help **2**
azul blue **10**

B

bailar to dance **1**
el baile dance **3**
bajar to lower, lessen **6**; to go down **12**; **bajar de peso** to lose weight **6**; **bajar la voz** to lower one's voice **7**
bajo,-a short **1**
el baloncesto basketball **1**
el banco bank **2**
la banda band (*of musicians*) **7RC**
la bandera flag **12**
bañarse to take a bath **10**
barato,-a cheap **4**
el barco boat, ship **8**
basta: Ya basta. That's enough. **7**
bastante quite, fairly **1**; **bastante bien** pretty well **P**
la basura garbage **9**
el béisbol baseball **1**
la biblioteca library **2**
la bicicleta bicycle **2**; **montar bicicleta** to ride a bike, go bike riding **2**
bien fine, well **P**; **bastante bien** pretty well **P**; **está bien** okay **7**
la biología biology **5**
el bistec steak **6**
blanco,-a white **10**
la blusa blouse **10**
la boca mouth **10**
la bodega grocery store **6RC**
el boliche bowling **2**; **jugar boliche** to bowl, go bowling **2**
el bolígrafo ball-point pen **4**
bonito,-a pretty, nice **1**
el bosque woods, forest **9**
el bote small boat **3**
el brazo arm **10**
la brisa breeze **8**
bueno,-a good **1**; **bueno** okay, well **2**; **¡Qué bueno!** Good! **3**
buscar* to look for **5**

C

la cabeza head **10**; **tener dolor de cabeza** to have a headache **3**
cada each **10RC**
el café café (*coffee shop*) **2**; coffee **6**
los calcetines socks **10**
la calculadora calculator **4**
calor: Hace calor. It's hot, warm (*weather*). **3**; **tener calor** to feel (be) warm, hot **6**
la calle street **7**
la cámara camera **3**
el camarero, la camarera waiter, waitress **6**
los camarones shrimp **6**
cambiar to change **12**
caminar to walk **9**
la caminata hike **9**; **dar una caminata** to go on a hike **9**
el camino path, walk, road **9**
la camisa shirt **4**
la camiseta tee shirt **4**
el campamento de verano summer camp **8**
el campo country (*countryside*) **8**
la canción song **7**
la canoa canoe **12**
cansado,-a tired **3**
cantar to sing **1**
la cara face **10**
la carabela sailing ship **12**
¡Caramba! Wow! **7**
la carne meat **6**; **la carne asada** roast beef **6**
la carnicería butcher shop **6RC**
caro,-a expensive **4**
la carrera race **12**
el cartel poster **4**
la cartera wallet **4**
la casa house **2**; **en casa** at home **3**
casi almost **4**
castaño,-a brown (*especially hair*) **10**
el catarro cold **3**; **tener catarro** to have a cold **3**
la catedral cathedral **8**
la cebolla onion **6**
celoso,-a jealous **3**
la cena dinner, supper **6**
el centro center **3**; **el centro comercial** shopping center **10**
cerca (de) near (to) **8**
cerrar (ie)* to close **P, 6RC**
el cielo sky **12**
cien, ciento hundred **4, 7**
las ciencias science **5**
el científico, la científica scientist **5**

el cine movies, movie theater **2**
la cinta tape **4**
la cita date, appointment **3**
la ciudad city **8**
la clase class **P**
clásico,-a classical **1**
el club club **9**
el coche car **1**
la cocina cooking, cuisine **9**
cocinar to cook **2**
el cocinero, la cocinera cook **6**
colaborar (en) to collaborate (on) **9**
coleccionar to collect **9**
el coleccionista, la coleccionista collector **9**
el colegio school **5**
colonial colonial **10**
la comedia comedy **7**
comenzar (a) (ie)* to begin (to) **8**
comer to eat **4**
cómico,-a funny **4**
la comida food, meal **6**; **la comida al paso** fast food **6RC**
el comilón glutton **7**
como like **4**; since, because **8**
¿cómo? what? **P**; how? **P**; **¿Cómo se dice . . . ?** How do you say . . . ? **P**
comprar to buy **3**
compras: ir de compras to go shopping **2**
comprender to understand **5**
la computadora computer **5**
con with **3**
el concierto concert **1**
el concurso quiz show, contest **7**
la condición condition **11**
el condimento seasoning **6RC**
la conducta behavior **10RC**
conmigo with me **9**
conocer (zc)* to know **6**
conseguir (i, i)* to obtain, get **11**
conservar to conserve **9**
la consideración consideration **9**
consistir en to consist of **11**
la contabilidad bookkeeping, accounting **5**
contento,-a happy **3**
contestar to answer **8RC**
contigo with you (*fam.*) **9**
contra against **2**
el corazón heart **10**
la corbata necktie **10**
el coro chorus **9**
el correo post office **2**
correr to run, jog **9**
la corrida de toros bullfight **8**
la corriente current **12**
corto,-a short **8**
la cosa thing **8**
la costa coast **12RC**
costar (ue)* to cost **9**
crecer (zc)* to grow **12**
creer* to believe **8**
la crema cream **6RC**
cruzar* to cross **12**
el cuaderno notebook **4**
¿cuál? what?, which one? **5**
¿cuándo? when? **2**
¿cuánto,-a? how much?, (*pl.*) how many? **4**; **¡Cuánto lo siento!** I'm so sorry! **3**
el cuarto room **2**; quarter (*hour*) **5**
cuidado: tener cuidado to be careful **9**
cuidar to take care of **4**
la cultura culture **11**
el cumpleaños birthday **4**
cumplir to complete, reach **4**; **cumplir _____ años** to be (turn) _____ years old **4**
el curso course (*of study*) **11**

Ch

la chaqueta jacket **10**
el chico boy **3**
la chica girl **3**
el chocolate chocolate **6**
las chuletas de cerdo pork chops **6**

D

las damas checkers **9**
daño: hacer daño to harm **9**
dar* to give **8**; **dar un paseo** to take a walk **2**; **dar una caminata** to go on a hike **9**; **dar la vuelta al mundo** to go around the world **12**
de from **1**; of **4**
debajo de under, beneath **8**
el debate debate **9**
deber to have to, should **5**
decir* to say, tell **7**; **decir que no** to say no **7**; **decir que sí** to say yes **7**; **es decir** that is to say **11**; **¿Qué quiere decir . . . ?** What does . . . mean? **P**; **¡No me digas!** Don't tell me! You don't say! **3**
dejar to leave behind **9**
Déjalos . . . Let them . . . **7**
delgado,-a slim, thin **4**
demasiado (*adv.*) too much **9**
el dentista, la dentista dentist **11**
dentro de inside of **7**
el deporte sport **1**
deprimido,-a depressed **3**
la derecha right **8**; **a la derecha** to the right **8**
desaparecer (zc)* to disappear **7**
el desayuno breakfast **6**
descansar to rest **2**
descubrir to discover **12RC**
desde from **8**
desear to want, wish **6**
desesperado,-a hopeless **12**
el desierto desert **9RC**
desilusionado,-a disappointed **3**

despertarse (ie)* to wake up **10**
después (*adv.*) afterward, after **3**; **después de** (*prep.*) after **5**
detenerse* to stop, detain oneself **12**
detrás (de) behind **8**
di *fam. command of* **decir 9**
el **día** (*m*) day **2**; **algún día** someday **2**; **Es de día.** It's daytime. **9**; **todos los días** everyday **4**
el **Día de la Raza** Columbus Day **12**
el **diario** diary **3**
dibujar to draw **9**
los **dibujos animados** cartoons **7**
el **diccionario** dictionary **4**
diciembre December **8**
el **diente** tooth **10**
diferente different **6RC**
difícil difficult **1**
la **dificultad** difficulty **6**
el **dinero** money **1**
Dios God **12**; **¡Dios mío!** My goodness! **5**
el **disco** record **1**
la **diversión** entertainment **7RC**
divertido,-a fun, amusing **1**
divertirse (ie, i)* to have fun **11**
el **documental** documentary **7**
doler (ue)* to ache **10**
el **dolor** ache, pain **3**
el **domingo** Sunday **5**
el **dominó** dominoes **9**
¿dónde? where? **2**; **¿de dónde?** from where? **2**
dormir (ue, u)* to sleep **6**
dormirse (ue, u)* to fall asleep **10**
los **dulces** sweets, candy **6**
durante during **3**

E

el **edificio** building **10**
la **educación física** physical education **5**
el **educador, la educadora** educator **12RC**
el **ejemplo** example **1**
el **ejercicio** exercise **6**
el the (*m*) **1**
él he, it **1**; him (*after prep.*) **9**
eléctrico,-a electric **11**
ella she, it **1**; her (*after prep.*) **6**
ellas they (*f*) **1**; them (*after prep.*) **9**
ellos they (*m*) **1**; them (*after prep.*) **9**
emocionado,-a excited **3**
emocionante exciting **1**
empezar (a) (ie)* to begin (to) **8**
en in, on, at **1**
encantado,-a delighted **3**
encantar to like a lot **9**; **me encanta** I love it **7**
encima (de) on (top of), above **8**
encontrar (ue)* to find, meet **9**; **encontrarse con** to meet, come across **10**
la **energía** energy **6**
enero January **8**
el **enfermero, la enfermera** nurse **11**
enfermo,-a sick, ill **3**
enfrente de in front of **8**
enojado,-a angry **3**
la **ensalada** salad **6**
la **enseñanza** teaching **11RC**
enseñar to teach **7**
entender (ie)* to understand **8**
entero,-a entire, whole **9RC**
entonces then **2**
la **entrada** appetizer, first course (*of a meal*) **6**
entrar (en) to enter **5**
entre between **8**
el **entusiasmo** enthusiasm **9RC**
la **época** period, epoch **12RC**
el **equipo** team **2**; equipment **9**
escalar to climb **12**
escribir to write **6**
el **escritor, la escritora** writer **12RC**
escuchar to listen to **1**
la **escuela** school **1**
ese, esa (*adj.*) that **7**
eso (*pron.*) that **3**; **por eso** therefore **10RC**
el **espacio** space **7**
la **espalda** back **3**; **tener dolor de espalda** to have a backache **3**
el **español** Spanish (*language*) **P**; (*adj.*) **español,-a 12RC**
especialmente especially **2**
la **esperanza** hope **12**
esperar to wait for **5**
el **esquí acuático** water skiing **8**
esquiar to ski **1**
la **estación** season (*of year*) **8**
el **estadio** stadium **2**
los **Estados Unidos** United States **P**
la **estampilla** postage stamp **9**
estar* to be **3**; **Está bien.** Okay. **7**
este, esta this (*adj.*) **7**
estereofónico,-a stereo, **10**
esto this (*pron.*) **7**
el **estómago** stomach **10**; **tener dolor de estómago** to have a stomachache **3**
el **estudiante, la estudiante** student **5**
estudiantil student (*adj.*) **9**
estudiar to study **1**; **estudiar para** to study to be . . . **11**
el **estudio** studio **8**
los **estudios** studies **11**
europeo,-a European **10**
evitar to avoid **6**
exagerado,-a theatrical (exaggerated) **3**
el **examen** exam **1**
excelente excellent **1**
exigente demanding **9**
exigir to demand, require **11**
la **expedición** expedition **12**
la **experiencia** experience **9**

la **explicación** explanation **5**
el **explorador** (boy) scout **9**
explorar to explore **12**
extra extra **7**
el **extranjero: en el extranjero** in a foreign country, abroad **8**

F

fabuloso,-a fabulous **8**
fácil easy **1**
la **falda** skirt **10**
la **familia** family **3**
el **fanático** fan **2**; **ser fanático de** to be a fan of **2**; **¡Fantástico!** Great! **3**
fascinar to fascinate **11**
fatigoso,-a tiring **9**
favorito,-a favorite **4**
febrero February **8**
la **fecha** date **8**; **¿Cuál es la fecha de hoy? ¿Qué fecha es hoy?** What's today's date? **8**
feroz fierce **9RC**
la **fiebre** fever **8**; **tener fiebre** to have a fever **3**
la **fiesta** party **1**
la **figura** figure **7**
el **fin** end **2**; goal **12**; **en fin** all in all **8**; **el fin de semana** weekend **2**; **por fin** finally **8**
finalmente finally **5**
la **física** physics **5**
la **fogata** campfire **9**
formidable great, wonderful **1**
la **foto** (*f*) photo **2**
el **fotógrafo, la fotógrafa** photographer **2**
el **francés** French (*language*) **5**; (*adj.*) **francés, francesa** French **10**
frente a facing, opposite **8**
la **fresa** strawberry **6**
fresco: hacer fresco to be cool (*weather*) **3**
frío cold **3**; **hacer frío** to be cold (*weather*) **3**; **tener frío** to be (*feel*) cold **6**
la **fruta** fruit **6**
el **fuego** fire **9**
la **fuente** fountain **12RC**; **la fuente de la juventud** fountain of youth **12RC**
fuerte strong **12**
fundar to found **12RC**
el **fútbol** soccer **1**
el **fútbol americano** football **1**
el **futuro** future **11**
futuro,-a (*adj.*) future **5**

G

el **galeón** galleon **12RC**
ganar to earn **2**; to win **9**
la **garganta** throat **3**; **tener dolor de garganta** to have a sore throat **3**
gastar to spend (*money*) **8**
el **gato** cat **3**
general: en general generally, usually **1**
generalmente generally, usually **6RC**
el **genio, la genia** genius **4**
la **gente** people **7**
la **geografía** geography **5**
la **geometría** geometry **5**
el **gerente, la gerente** manager **11**
la **gimnasia** gymnastics **1**
el **gobernador** governor **12RC**
gordo,-a overweight **4**
el **gorila** gorilla **11**
la **grabadora** tape recorder **3**
Gracias. Thank you. **P**
graduarse to graduate **11**
grande big, large **4**
la **gripe** flu **3**; **tener gripe** to have the flu **3**
gris gray **10**
gritar to shout **12**
el **grupo** group **5**
el **guante** glove, mitt **5**
guapo,-a good-looking, handsome **1**
la **guía** (girl) scout, guide **9**
la **guitarra** guitar **1**
gustar to like **P**; **me (le) gustaría** I (she, he, you) would like **3**
gusto: mucho gusto pleased to meet you **P**; **con mucho gusto** with pleasure **6**

H

las **habichuelas** beans **6**
hablar to speak, talk **1**
hacer* to do, make **6**; **hacer gimnasia** to do gymnastics **2**; **hacer un viaje** to take a trip **8**; **hacer yoga** to practice yoga **9**; *see also* **hacer** *and expressions of weather:* **calor, fresco, frío, sol, tiempo, viento**; **hacer agua** to take on water (*naut.*) **12**
hacerse* to become (*a profession*) **11**
el **hambre** (*f*) hunger **6**; **tener hambre** to be hungry **6**
la **hamburguesa** hamburger **6RC**
hasta until **8**; **Hasta luego (mañana).** See you later (tomorrow). **P**
hay there is, there are **2**
haz *fam. command of* **hacer 9**
la **heladería** ice cream parlor **6RC**
el **helado** ice cream **6**
la **hermana** sister **4**
el **hermano** brother **4**
los **hermanos** brothers and sisters **4**
la **hierba** plant (*lit.* grass) **12**
la **hija** daughter **4**
el **hijo** son **4**
los **hijos** children **4**
hispánico,-a Hispanic **3**
hispano,-a of Hispanic origin **7RC**

los hispanos Hispanic people **6**
la historia history **5**
la historieta comic book **4**
el hombre man **10**; **el hombre de negocios** businessman **11**
la hora time, hour **5**; **¿Qué hora es?** What time is it? **5**; **es hora de** it's time to **7**
el hospital hospital **3**
hoy today **2**
el huevo egg **6**
hundirse to sink **12RC**
el huracán hurricane **12RC**

I

la idea idea **3**
ideal ideal **8**
identificar to identify **9RC**
el idioma (*m*) language **11**
la iglesia church **2**
el impermeable raincoat **10**
importa: No importa. It doesn't matter. **10**; **¡Qué importa!** Who cares! **3**
importante important **1**
impresionar to impress **10**
independiente independent **1**
la ingeniería engineering **11**
el ingeniero, la ingeniera engineer **11**; **el ingeniero, la ingeniera electricista** electrical engineer **11**
el inglés English (*language*) **4**
inmediatamente immediately **12**
el insecto insect **9**
insistir (en) to insist (on) **6**
el instituto institute **5**
el instrumento instrument **9**
inteligente intelligent **1**
el interés interest **8RC**
interesante interesting **1**
interesar to be interested in **9**
internacional international **9**
el invierno winter **8**
invitar (a) to invite **5**
ir* to go **1**; **ir a** + *inf.* to be going to **2**; **ir de compras** to go shopping **2**
la isla island **8**
la izquierda left **8**; **a la izquierda** to the left **8**

J

el jamón ham **6**
el jazz jazz (*music*) **1**
los jeans jeans **10**
joven young **4**; **los jóvenes** young people **10**
el juego electrónico video game **1**
el jueves Thursday **5**
el jugador, la jugadora player **2**
jugar (ue)* to play (*a game*) **1, 9**
el jugo juice **6**
julio July **8**
junio June **8**

K

el kilómetro kilometer **12**

L

la her, it **1**; the (*f*) **1**
el laboratorio laboratory **5**
lado: al lado de next to, beside **8**
el lápiz (*pl.* **lápices**) pencil **P**
largo,-a long **10**
lavar to wash **2**
lavarse to wash, get washed **10**; **lavarse los dientes** to brush one's teeth **10**
la lección lesson **5**
la leche milk **6**
la lechería dairy store **6RC**
leer* to read **5**
lejos (de) far (from) **8**
los lentes (eye)glasses **4**; **los lentes de sol** sunglasses **10**
levantar to lift **9**; **levantar pesas** to lift weights **9**; **levantar una tienda** to pitch a tent **9**
levantarse to get up **10**
liberar to liberate **12RC**
libre free **8**
el libro book **P**
la licencia license **11**
limpio,-a clean **9**
listo,-a ready **5**
loco,-a crazy **5**
la lucha libre wrestling **1**
luchar to fight **12RC**
el lunes Monday **5**

Ll

llamar to call **5**; **llamar por teléfono** to talk on the phone **2**
llamarse to be named **P**; **Me llamo . . .** My name is . . . **P**
la llave key **4**
llegar* to arrive **8**
llevar to carry, to take (someone, something) along **8**
llover* to rain; **estar lloviendo** to be raining **3**
la lluvia rain **12**

M

la madre mother **4**
malo,-a bad **1**
mamá mom **4**
la manera manner, way **9RC**
la mano (*f*) hand **10**
la mantequilla butter **6**
la manzana apple **6**
la mañana morning **5**; **de la mañana** in the morning (A.M.) **5**; **por la mañana** in the morning **5**; **mañana** (*adv.*) tomorrow **2**; **pasado mañana** day after tomorrow **4**

el **mapa** (*m*) map **9RC**
la **máquina de escribir** typewriter **3**
el **mar** sea **8**
el **marinero** sailor **12**
el **martes** Tuesday **5**
marzo March **8**
más more **2**; **más tarde** later **2**; **No puedo más.** I can't take it anymore. **8**; **más . . . que** more . . . than **12**
la **máscara** mask **7**; **el baile de máscaras** costume ball **7**
las **matemáticas** math **3**
maya Mayan **8**
mayo May **8**
la **mayoría** majority **6RC**
mayormente mainly **10RC**
me me **8**, to me **9**
la **mecanografía** typing **5**
media half (*hour*) **5**
la **medianoche** midnight **5**
el **médico, la médica** doctor **11**
el **mediodía** (*m*) noon **5**
mejor best **8**; better **12**
el **melón** melon **6**
menos less **5**; before the hour **5**; **por lo menos** at least **11**; **menos . . . que** less than **12**
mental mental **11**
la **mentira** lie **7**
el **menú** menu **6**
el **mercado** market **10**
la **mermelada** jam **6**
el **mes** month **8**
mexicano,-a Mexican **8**
la **mezcla** mixture **10**
mí me (*after prep.*) **9**
mi, mis my **4**
el **miedo** fear **6**; **tener miedo** to be afraid **6**
el **miembro** member **9**
el **miércoles** Wednesday **5**
mil thousand **7**
el **militar** military person **12RC**
millón: un millón (de) a million **7**
el **minuto** minute **6**
mirar to look at, watch **1**
mismo: lo mismo the same **6**; **por ti mismo,-a** for yourself **9**; **yo mismo,-a** I myself **12**
la **mochila** knapsack, backpack **4**
la **moda** style, fashion **10**; **estar a la moda** to be in style **10**; **seguir (i, i)* la moda** to keep up with the styles **10**
moderno,-a modern **9**
la **moneda** coin **9**
la **montaña** mountain **8**
montar: montar bicicleta to ride a bike, go bike riding **2**
el **monumento** monument **8**
morado,-a purple **10**
morir (ue, u)* to die **12RC**
mostrar (ue)* to show **9**
la **moto** (*f*) motorbike, motorcycle **3**
la **muchacha** girl **P**; **la muchacha guía** girl scout **9**; **el muchacho** boy **P**; **el muchacho explorador** boy scout **9**
mucho,-a a lot, much **1**
la **muela** tooth (*molar*) **3**; **tener dolor de muelas** to have a toothache **3**
la **mujer** woman **11**; **la mujer de negocios** businesswoman **11**
el **mundo** world **12**; **todo el mundo** everybody **8**
la **muñeca** doll **9**
el **museo** museum **2**
la **música** music **1**
muy very **1**

N

nacer (cz)* to be born **12RC**
nada nothing **3**; **De nada.** You're welcome. **P**; **No me gusta nada.** I don't like it at all. **1**
nadar to swim **1**
nadie no one **12**
la **naranja** orange **6**
la **nariz** nose **10**
la **natación** swimming **8**
la **naturaleza** nature **8**
navegar* to navigate, sail **12**
necesitar to need **6**
negro,-a black **10**
nervioso,-a nervous **3**
nevar(ie)* to snow; **estar nevando** to be snowing **3**
ni . . . ni neither . . . nor **6**
la **niña** child, girl **7**
el **niño** child, boy **7**
los **niños** children **7**
no no **P**; **¿No?** Isn't that so? Aren't you? etc. **1**
noche night, evening **5**; **anoche** last night **10**; **de la noche** in the evening, at night (P.M.) **5**; **de noche** at night, nighttime **6**; **esta noche** tonight **2**; **por la noche** at night **5**
norteamericano,-a American (*from U.S.*) **6RC**
nosotros,-as we **1**; us (*after prep.*) **6**
la **nota** grade, mark **8**
las **noticias** news **3**
la **novela** novel **5**; soap opera **7**
noviembre November **8**
nuestro,-a our **4**
nuevo,-a new **1**
nunca never **4, 12**

O

o or **2**
o . . . o either . . . or **12**
observar to observe **9**
octubre October **8**
ocupado,-a busy **5**
oír* to hear **7**
el **ojo** eye **7**
olvidar to forget **7**
operar to operate **11**

la opinión opinion **7**
opuesto,-a opposite **8RC**
la oreja ear **10**
el origen origin **7RC**
el oro gold **12RC**
el osito de felpa teddy bear **4**
el otoño autumn **8**
otro,-a another, other **2**
¡Oye! Hey! Listen! **2**

P

paciente patient **1**
padre father **4**
los padres parents **4**
pagar* to pay (for) **11**
el país country (*nation*) **9**
el pájaro bird **7**
el pan bread **6**
la panadería bakery **6RC**
los pantalones pants **10**
la papa potato **6**
papá dad **4**
el papel paper **P**
papi (*nickname for papá*) daddy **11**
para to, in order to **2**; for **5**
el paracaídas (*m sing.*) parachute **12**
pardo,-a brown **10**
parecer (zc)* to seem (like) **4**; **¿No te parece?** Don't you think so? **4**; **¿Qué te parece?** What do you think? **4**
el parque park **2**
participar (en) to participate (in) **9**
el partido game, match **2**
pasado,-a last **10**; **el año pasado** last year **10**; **pasado mañana** day after tomorrow **4**
el pasajero, la pasajera passenger **11**
pasar to spend (time) **4**
el pasatiempo pastime, hobby **9**
pasear to go for a ride or walk **12**
paseo: dar un paseo to take a walk **2**
el pastel pastry, cake, cookie **6**
la pastelería pastry shop **6RC**
patinar to skate **9**
patriótico,-a patriotic **9RC**
pedir (i, i)* to ask for, order **10**
peinarse to comb one's hair **10**
la película film, movie **2**; **la película de ciencia-ficción** science fiction film **7**; **la película policíaca** detective film, police show **7**
peligroso,-a dangerous **12**
el pelo hair **10**; **tomar el pelo** to kid, pull someone's leg **11**
pena: ¡Qué pena! What a shame! **3**
pensar (ie)* to think **8**; **pensar** + *inf.* to plan on, intend to **8**; **pensar en** to think about **8**
peor worse **12**
pequeño,-a small **4**
la pera pear **6**
perder (ie)* to lose, waste, miss (*a bus, plane*) **8**
perdido,-a lost **12**
perfecto,-a perfect **4**
el perfume perfume **4**
el periódico newspaper **5**
el periodista, la periodista journalist **11**
permitir to permit **6**
pero but **1**
el perro dog **3**
la persona person **1**
pesa: levantar pesas to lift weights **9**
pesadísimo,-a extremely heavy **5**
pesado,-a boring **3**; **¡Qué pesado!** What a bore! How boring! **3**
el pescado fish **6**
el piano piano **2**
el pie foot **10**
la pierna leg **10**
pilotear to pilot **12**
el piloto, la pilota, de aviación pilot **11**
el pirata pirate **12RC**
la piscina swimming pool **2**
el piso floor **7**
la pizarra chalkboard **P**
el plan plan **5**
la planta plant **9**
la plata silver **12RC**
el plátano banana **6**
el plato dish, plate **2**
la playa beach **8**
la plaza plaza, square **2**
la población population **10RC**
pobre poor **8**
pobrecito,-a poor (little) thing **5**
poco a little **4**; **un poco de** a little of **6**
poder (ue, u)* to be able, can **9**
la poesía poetry **5**
el policía, la mujer policía police officer **11**
el político politician **12RC**
el pollo chicken **6**
pon *fam. command of* **poner 9**
poner* to put, place, set **6**
ponerse* to put on (*clothing*) **10**
popular popular **1**
por for, during **3**; at, in **5**; through **10**; **por favor** please **P**; **por eso** therefore **10RC**; **por fin** finally **8**; **¿por qué?** why? **2**
porque because **3**
portugués,-a Portuguese **10RC**
posible possible **3**; **lo más posible** as much as possible **11**
el postre dessert **6**
practicar* to practice **1**
el precio price **6**
preferir (ie, i)* to prefer **8**
preguntar to ask (*a question*) **7**

el premio prize **9**
preocupado,-a worried **3**
preparar to prepare **6**
presentarse to (be) show(n) **7RC**
la primavera spring **8**
primer(o),-a first **5**; **primero** (*adv.*) first **5**
el primo, la prima cousin **4**
prisa: tener prisa to be in a hurry **6**
privado,-a private **9RC**
probablemente probably **9**
probarse (ue)* to try on **10**
el problema (*m*) problem **3**
producir (zc)* to produce **9RC**
la profesión profession **11**
profesional professional **9RC**
el profesor, la profesora teacher **P**
el programa (*m*) program **5**
la programación de computadoras computer programming **5**
el programador, la programadora de computadoras computer programmer **11**
programar to program **9**, to plan **11**
prometer to promise **5**
el pronóstico del tiempo weather forecast **7**
pronto soon **1**
el puesto job, position **11**
la pulsera bracelet **4**
el puntaje score **7**
el punto point **7**; **en punto** sharp, on the dot (*time*) **5**

Q

¿qué? what? **1**; which **2**
quedar to be located **8**; to fit **10**; **me (le) queda bien** it fits me (him, her) well **10**
quedarse to remain, stay **12**
quejarse (de) to complain **12**
querer (ie, i)* to want, wish **2**; to love **8**
querido,-a dear **1**
el queso cheese **6**
¿quién? who? **2**; **¿a quién(es)?** (to) whom? **5**; **¿de quién(es)?** whose? **4**
la química chemistry **5**
quizás maybe, perhaps **2**

R

el radio radio (*set*) **3**
la radio radio (*broadcasting*) **1**
raro,-a strange **7**
el rato short while **7**; **un rato más** a little while longer **7**; **los ratos libres** free time **9**
la raza race **10RC**; **el Día de la Raza** Columbus Day **12**
razón: tener razón to be right **6**
real royal **12**
la realidad reality **6RC**
realmente really **9RC**
recibir to receive **6**
reconocer (zc)* to recognize **7RC**
recordar (ue)* to remember **9**
el recreo recess, break **5**
el recuerdo souvenir **8**
los recursos resources
el refresco soft drink **6**
el regalo gift, present **4**
el regateo bargaining **7RC**
la regla rule **9**
regresar to return **3**
la reina queen **12**
el reloj watch, clock **3**
la relojería watch shop **7RC**
repetir (i, i)* to repeat **7**; to have a second helping **10**
el reportaje deportivo sports report **7**
representar to represent **10**
la reproducción reproduction, copy **8**
respetar to respect **9**
responder to answer **7**
la responsabilidad responsibility **11**
responsable responsible **1**
el restaurante restaurant **2**
los restos remains **12RC**
la revista magazine **4**
el rey king **12**
rico,-a rich **9RC**
el río river **9RC**, **12**
el robo robbery **7RC**
rock (*adj.*) rock (*music*) **1**
rojo,-a red **10**
el rompecabezas (*m sing.*) puzzle **4**
la ropa clothes, clothing **10**
rosado,-a pink **10**
rubio,-a blond **10**
el ruido noise **7**
las ruinas ruins **8**

S

el sábado Saturday **5**
saber* to know **6**
sacar* to take out; **sacar fotos** to take pictures **2**; **sacar músculos** to develop muscles **9**; **sacar . . . notas** to get . . . grades **8**
el safari safari **12**
sal *fam. command of* **salir 9**
salir* to leave, go out **5**
la salsa sauce **6**; type of music **2**
saltar to jump **12**
la salud health **9**
saludos regards, greetings **8**
sé *fam. command of* **ser 9**
sé: No sé. I don't know. **P**; *see* **saber**
el secretario, la secretaria secretary **11**
secundario,-a secondary **11**
la sed thirst **6**; **tener sed** to be thirsty **6**
seguir (i, i)* to follow, continue **10**; **seguir la moda** to keep up with

fashion **10**; **seguir un curso** to take a course **11**
segundo,-a second **7**
seguro,-a sure **11**
la selección selection **6**
la selva jungle **12**
la semana week **3**
sentirse (ie, i)* to feel **11**; **¡Cuánto lo siento!** I'm so sorry! **3**
la señal sign **12**
separar(se) to separate (oneself) **12**
septiembre September **8**
ser to be **1**; **¡No puede ser!** It can't be! **3**
el ser being **7**
serio,-a serious **3**; **en serio** seriously **11**
servir (i, i)* to serve **10**; **servir para** to be good for, useful **10**
si if **3**
sí yes **1**
siempre always **2**
la siesta nap **6RC**
siguiente next, following **5**; **al día siguiente** the next day **5**
el símbolo symbol **9RC**
simpático,-a nice, friendly **1**
sin without **8**
sobre about, on **2**
el sol sun **8**; **hacer sol** to be sunny **8**; **tomar el sol** to take a sunbath **8**
solamente only **7**
solo,-a alone **9**; single **12**
sólo only (*short for* **solamente**) **7**
la solución solution **6**
el sombrero hat **10**
el sonido sound **7**
la sopa soup **6**
sorprendido,-a surprised **3**
su, sus his, her, its, your (*polite*), their **4**
submarino,-a underwater **12**
el sueño dream **7**; **tener sueño** to be sleepy **6**
la suerte luck **8**; **¡Buena suerte!** Good luck! **3**
el suéter sweater **4**
el supermercado supermarket **2**
supuesto: por supuesto of course **5**
el sur south **12**

T

tacaño,-a stingy **4**
el talento talent **2**
la talla size (clothing) **10**
también also, too **1**
el tambor drum **7RC**
tampoco neither, not either **12**
tan such a, so **2**
tanto,-a so much, so many **5**; **tanto que hacer** so much to do **5**; **No es para tanto.** Big deal. **7**
la tarde afternoon, early evening **5**; **de la tarde** in the afternoon (P.M.) **5**; **por la tarde** in the afternoon **5**
tarde (*adv.*) late **2**; **más tarde** later **2**
la tarea homework **1**
la tarjeta card **3**
la tarta pie, tart **6**
el taxi taxi **10**
te you (*fam.*) **8**; to you **9**
el té tea **6**
el teatro theater **2**
el técnico, la técnica technician **10**
la tele TV (*short for* **televisión**) **1**
el teléfono telephone **2**; **por teléfono** by phone **2**
la televisión television **1**
el televisor television set **3**
temprano early **8**
ten *fam. command of* **tener 9**
tener* to have **3**; **tener _____ años** to be _____ years old **4**; **¿Qué tiene?** What's wrong with him (her)? **3**; *to express illness see* **tener** *and* **cabeza**, **catarro**, **espalda**, **estómago**, **fiebre**, **garganta**, **gripe**, **muelas**, **tos**; **tener ganas de** to feel like (*doing something*) **3**; **tener que** to have to (*do something*) **3**; **tener cuidado** to be careful **9**; *see also* **calor**, **frío**, **hambre**, **miedo**, **prisa**, **razón**, **sed**, **sueño**
el tenis tennis **1**
la tensión tension **8**
el tesoro treasure **12RC**
ti you (*after prep.*) **9**; **ti mismo,-a** yourself **9**
la tía aunt **4**
el tiempo weather **3**; **¿Qué tiempo hace?** What's the weather like? **3**; **Hace buen (mal) tiempo.** It's nice (nasty) out. **3**; time (*in a general sense*) **6**
la tienda store **2**; tent **9**
la tierra land **12**
el tigre tiger **11**
el tío uncle **4**
los tíos aunt(s) and uncle(s) **4**
típico,-a typical, characteristic **8**
el título title **9RC**
el tocadiscos (*sing.*) record player **3**
tocar* to play (*an instrument, radio, etc.*) **2**
todavía still, yet **3**
todo (*pron.*) everything **9**; **todos** everyone **3**
todo,-a (*adj.*) all **1**; **todos los días** every day **4**; **todo el mundo** everyone, everybody **8**
tomar to take, have (*eat, drink*) **6**; **tomar el sol** to take a sunbath **8**; **tomar el pelo** to kid, pull

someone's leg **11**; **tomar posesión** to take possession **12**
el tomate tomato **6**
la tontería nonsense **3**
la tortilla omelet **6**
la tos cough **3**; **tener tos** to have a cough **3**
el total total **7**
trabajar to work **1**
el trabajo work, job **8**
traer* to bring **6**
el traje de baño swimsuit **10**
el transistor transistor **10**
el tren train **8**
la trompeta trumpet **7RC**
tropical tropical **8**
tu, tus your (*fam.*) **4**
tú you (*fam.*) **1**
el turista, la turista tourist **2**
turístico,-a tourist (*adj.*) **12RC**

U

último,-a last **7**
un, una a, an, one **2**
la universidad university **4**
usar to use, wear **10**
usted, ustedes you (*polite*) **1**
la uva grape **6**

V

las vacaciones vacation **1**; **estar de vacaciones** to be on vacation **3**
vamos a + *inf.* Let's . . . **2**
las variedades variety show **7**
veces *see* **vez**
el vegetal vegetable **6**
el velero sailboat **12**
el vendedor, la vendedora salesperson **7**
venezolano,-a Venezuelan **12**
venir* to come **10**
la venta sale **10**; **en venta** on sale **10**
ver* to see **5**
el verano summer **8**
veras: ¿De veras? Really? **3**
la verdad truth **5**; **¿verdad?** right? **1**
verde green **10**
el vestido dress **10**
vestirse (i, i)* to get dressed **10**
el veterinario, la veterinaria veterinarian **11**
la vez (*pl.* **veces**) time, instance **7**; **a veces** sometimes **4**; **muchas veces** often; **otra vez** again **3**; **pocas veces** rarely **4**; **la primera (última) vez** the first (last) time **7**
viajar to travel **2**
el viaje trip **8**; **hacer un viaje** to take a trip **8**
la vida life **8**
viejo,-a old **1**
el viento wind **3**; **hacer viento** to be windy **3**
el viernes Friday **5**
la visita visit **3**
visitar to visit **2**
vivir to live **6**
el volibol volleyball **1**
volver (ue)* to return **9**
la voz (*pl.* **voces**) voice **7**
la vuelta: dar la vuelta al mundo to go around the world **12**

Y

y and **1**
ya already, yet **4**; **Ya basta.** That's enough. **7**; **ya no** no longer, not anymore **3**
yo I **1**; **yo mismo,-a** I myself **12**
el yoga (*m*) yoga **9**

Z

el zapato shoe **10**
la zona zone, district **10**
el zoológico zoo **10**

English-Spanish Vocabulary

This vocabulary includes items in the **Vocabularios del capítulo** as well as in the **Introducciones**, **Exploraciones**, and **Perspectivas**. It does not include definite articles, numbers, vocabulary from the **Rincones culturales** or from the **Capítulo de enlace**.

A

a, an un, una **2**
to **abandon** abandonar **2**
able: to be able poder (ue, u)* **9**
about sobre **2**
above encima (de) **8**
abroad en el extranjero **8**
accidentally accidentalmente **12**
accounting la contabilidad **5**
ache el dolor **3**
to **ache** doler (ue)* **10**
activity la actividad **8**
actor el actor **11**
actress la actriz **11**
to **admire** admirar **8**
to **advise** aconsejar **11**
afraid: to be afraid tener miedo **6**
after después de **5**
afternoon: in the afternoon por la tarde **5**
afterward después **5**
again otra vez **3**
against contra **2**
agency la agencia **11**
agitated agitado,-a **8**
air el aire **8**
airport el aeropuerto **2**
album el álbum **4**
algebra el álgebra (*f*) **5**
all todos **3**; **all in all** en fin **8**; **I don't like it at all!** ¡No me gusta nada! **1**
almost casi **4**
alone solo,-a **9**; **Leave them alone!** ¡Déjalos! **4**
to **allow** permitir **6**
alphabet el alfabeto **P**
already ya **4**
also también **1, 12**
always siempre **2, 12**
amateur (*adj.*) aficionado,-a **2**
Amazon (*adj.*) amazónico,-a **12**; (*n.*) el Amazonas **12**
amusing divertido,-a **1**
ancient antiguo,-a **10**
angry enojado,-a **3**
animal el animal **1**
another otro,-a **1**
to **answer** contestar **P**; responder **7**
anymore: not anymore ya no **3**
appetizer la entrada **6**
apple la manzana **6**
April abril **8**
aquatic acuático,-a **8**
arm el brazo **10**
around: to go around the world dar la vuelta al mundo **12**
to **arrive** llegar* **8**
art el arte **5**
arts las artes **9**
to **ask** (*a question*) preguntar **7**; **to ask for** pedir (i, i)* **10**
asleep: to fall asleep dormirse (ue, u)* **10**
athletic atlético,-a **8**
athletics el atletismo **8**
to **attend** asistir (a) **6**
August agosto **8**
aunt la tía; **aunt(s) and uncle(s)** los tíos **4**
autumn el otoño **8**
avenue la avenida **7**
to **avoid** evitar **6**

B

backache: to have a backache tener dolor de espalda **3**
backpack la mochila **4**
bad malo,-a **1**; **to be bad** (*weather*) hacer mal tiempo **3**
ball: costume ball el baile de máscaras **7**
ball-point pen el bolígrafo **4**
banana el plátano **6**
bank el banco **2**
baseball el béisbol **P**
basketball el baloncesto **P**
bath: to take a bath bañarse **10**
to **be** ser* **1**; estar* **3**; quedar (*location*) **8**; **It can't be!** ¡No puede ser! **3**; *see also weather expressions*
beach la playa **8**
beans las habichuelas **6**
bear: teddy bear el osito de felpa **4**
because porque **3**
to **become** (+ *a profession*) hacerse* **11**
bed: to go to bed acostarse (ue)* **10**
beef: roast beef la carne asada **6**
before antes de **5**
to **begin** comenzar (ie)* (a) **8**; empezar (ie)* (a) **8**

behind detrás de **8**
being el ser **7**
to **believe** creer* **8**; **I don't believe it!** ¡No lo creo! **5**
beneath debajo de **8**
beside al lado de **8**
besides además **2**
best mejor **8**; **the best** el, la mejor **8**
better (*adv.*) mejor **8, 12**
between entre **8**
bicycle la bicicleta **2**
big grande **4**
bike la bicicleta **2**; **to ride a bike** montar bicicleta **2**
biology la biología **5**
bird el pájaro **7**
birthday el cumpleaños **4**
black negro,-a **10**
blond (*hair*) rubio,-a **10**
blouse la blusa **10**
blue azul **10**
board (*chalkboard*) la pizarra **P**
boat el bote **3**; el barco **8**
book el libro **1**; **comic book** la historieta **4**
bookkeeping la contabilidad **5**
bore: What a bore! ¡Qué pesado! **3**
bored aburrido,-a **1**
boring aburrido,-a **1**; **How boring!** ¡Qué pesado! **3**
bowling el boliche **2**; **to go bowling** jugar boliche **2**
boy el muchacho **P**; el chico **3**; el niño **7**
boy scout el (muchacho) explorador **9**
bracelet la pulsera **4**
bread el pan **6**
break (*recess*) el recreo **5**
breakfast el desayuno **6**
breeze la brisa **8**
to **bring** traer* **6**
brother el hermano **4**; **brothers and sisters** los hermanos **4**
brown pardo,-a **10**; (*hair*) castaño,-a **10**
to **brush: to brush one's teeth** lavarse los dientes **10**
building el edificio **10**
bullfight la corrida de toros **8**
bus el autobús **8**
businessman el hombre de negocios **11**
businesswoman la mujer de negocios **11**
busy ocupado,-a **5**
but pero **1**
butter la mantequilla **6**
to **buy** comprar **3**

C

café (*restaurant*) el café **2**
cake el pastel **6**
calculator la calculadora **4**
to **call** llamar **5**
camera la cámara **3**
camp: summer camp el campamento de verano **8**
to **camp** acampar **8**
camper el acampador, la acampadora **9**
campfire la fogata **9**
can poder (ue, u)* **9**
candy los dulces **6**
canoe la canoa **12**
car el coche **1**; el automóvil **12**
card la tarjeta **3**
care: Who cares! ¡Qué importa! **3**; **to take care of** cuidar **4**
careful: to be careful tener cuidado **9**
cheese el queso **6**
chemistry la química **5**
chess el ajedrez **9**
chicken el pollo **6**
child el niño, la niña **7**
children los hijos **4**; los niños **7**
chocolate el chocolate **6**
chorus el coro **9**
church la iglesia **2**
city la ciudad **8**
class la clase **P**
classical clásico,-a **1**
clean limpio,-a **9**
to **climb** escalar **12**
clock el reloj **3**
close (to) cerca (de) **8**
to **close** cerrar (ie)* **P**
clothes la ropa **10**
clothing la ropa **10**
club el club **9**
coffee el café **6**
coin la moneda **9**
cold frío **3**; **to be cold** (*weather*) hacer frío **3**; **to have a cold** tener catarro **3**; **to be** (*feel*) **cold** tener frío **6**
to **collect** coleccionar **9**
collector el, la coleccionista **9**
colonial colonial **10**
Columbus Day el Día de la Raza **12**
to **comb** (*one's hair*) peinarse **10**
to **come** venir* **10**
comedy la comedia **7**
comic book la historieta **4**
commercial (*TV*) el anuncio **7**
to **complain** quejarse (de) **12**
completely completamente **7**
computer la computadora **5**
computer programmer el programador, la programadora de computadoras **11**
computer programming la programación de computadoras **5**
concert el concierto **1**
condition la condición **11**
to **conserve** conservar **9**
consideration la consideración **9**
to **consist of** consistir en **11**
to **continue** seguir (i, i)* **10**
cook el cocinero, la cocinera **6**
to **cook** cocinar **6**
cookie el pastel **6**
cooking la cocina **9**
cool fresco,-a **3**; **to be cool**

(*weather*) hacer fresco **3**
copy la reproducción **8**
corner la esquina **8**; **on the corner of** en la esquina de **8**
costume ball el baile de máscaras **7**
to cost costar (ue)* **9**
cough la tos **3**; **to have a cough** tener tos **3**
to count contar (ue)* **9**
country (*countryside*) el campo **8**; (*nation*) el país **9**; **in a foreign country** en el extranjero **8**
course (*school*) el curso **11**; **to take a course** seguir un curso **11**; **of course** por supuesto **5**
cousin el primo, la prima **4**
crafts la artesanía **10**
crazy loco,-a **5**
to cross cruzar* **12**
cuisine la cocina **9**
culture la cultura **11**
current la corriente **12**
customer el, la cliente **4**

D

Dad papi **11**
dance el baile **3**
to dance bailar **1**
dangerous peligroso,-a **12**
dark-haired moreno,-a **4**
date la fecha **8**; **What's today's date?** ¿Cuál es la fecha de hoy? **8**; ¿Qué fecha es hoy? **8**
daughter la hija **4**
day el día (*m*) **2**; **someday** algún día **2**; **every day** todos los días **4**; **the next day** al día siguiente **5**
daytime: It's daytime. Es de día. **9**
deal: Big deal! ¡No es para tanto! **7**
dear querido,-a **1**
debate el debate **9**
December diciembre **8**
delighted encantado,-a **3**
to demand exigir **11**
demanding exigente **9**
dentist el, la dentista **11**
depressed deprimido,-a **3**
dessert el postre **6**
detective film la película policíaca **7**
dictionary el diccionario **4**
difficult difícil **1**
difficulty la dificultad **6**
dinner la cena **6**
to disappear desaparecer (zc)* **7**
disappointed desilusionado,-a **3**
dish el plato **2**
district la zona **10**
to do hacer* **2**; **What are we going to do?** ¿Qué vamos a hacer? **2**; **so much to do** tanto que hacer **5**
doctor el médico, la médica **11**
documentary el documental **7**
dog el perro **3**
doll la muñeca **9**
dollar el dólar **P**
domino, dominoes el dominó **9**
dot: on the dot (*time*) en punto **5**
to draw dibujar **9**
dream el sueño **7**
dress el vestido **10**
dressed: to get dressed vestirse (ie, i)* **10**
during durante **5**

E

each cada **10**
ear la oreja **10**
early temprano **8**
to earn ganar **2**
easy fácil **1**
to eat comer **4**
egg el huevo **6**
either . . . or o . . . o **12**
electric eléctrico,-a **11**
electronic electrónico,-a **7**
energy la energía **6**
engineer el ingeniero, la ingeniera **11**; **electrical engineer** el ingeniero, la ingeniera electricista **11**
engineering la ingeniería **11**
English (*language*) el inglés **4**
enough: That's enough. Ya basta. **7**
to enter entrar (en) **5**
entertainer el, la artista **11**
equipment el equipo **9**
especially especialmente **2**
European europeo,-a **10**
evening: in the evening por la tarde **5**
every: every day todos los días **4**
everybody todo el mundo **8**
everyone todos **3**; todo el mundo **8**
everything todo **9**
exam el examen **1**
example el ejemplo **1**
excellent excelente **1**
excited emocionado,-a **3**
exciting emocionante **1**
exercise el ejercicio **6**
expedition la expedición **12**
expensive caro,-a **4**
experience la experiencia **9**
explanation la explicación **5**
to explore explorar **12**
eye el ojo **7**
eyeglasses los lentes **4**

F

fabulous fabuloso,-a **8**
face la cara **10**
facing frente a **8**
fairly bastante **1**
fall (*season*) el otoño **8**
family la familia **3**
fan: to be a fan of ser fanático de **2**
fantastic fantástico,-a **3**
far (from) lejos (de) **8**

to fascinate fascinar **11**
fashion la moda **10**
father el padre, el papá **4**
favorite favorito,-a **4**
fear el miedo **6**
February febrero **8**
to feel sentirse (ie, i)* **11**; **to feel like** (*doing something*) tener ganas de + *inf.* **3**
fever la fiebre **3**
fewer menos **5**
fifteen: fifteen-year-old girl la quinceañera **4**
figure la figura **7**
film la película **2**; **science fiction film** la película de ciencia-ficción **7**; **detective film** la película policíaca **7**
finally finalmente **5**; por fin **8**
to find encontrar (ue)* **9**; **to find oneself** encontrarse con **10**
fine bien, muy bien **P**
to finish acabar **11**
fire el fuego **9**
first primero (*adv.*) **5**; primer(o),-a (*adj.*) **7**
fish el pescado **6**
to fit: It fits me (him, her) well. Me (le) queda bien. **10**
to fix arreglar **11**
flag la bandera **12**
floor el piso **7**
flu la gripe **3**; **to have the flu** tener gripe **3**
to follow seguir (i, i)* **10**
following siguiente **5**
food la comida **6**
foot el pie **10**
football el fútbol americano **P**
for para **2**, **5**; por **3**
foreign: in a foreign country en el extranjero **8**
forest el bosque **9**
to forget olvidar **7**
free libre **8**; **free time** los ratos libres **9**
French (*language*) el francés **5**; (*adj.*) francés, francesa **10**
fried frito,-a **6**
friend el amigo, la amiga **2**
friendly simpático,-a **1**
from de **1**; desde **8**
front: in front of en frente de **8**
fruit la fruta **6**
fun: to have fun divertirse (ie, i)* **11**
fun (*adj.*) divertido,-a **1**
funny cómico,-a **4**
furthermore además **2**
future el futuro **11**
future (*adj.*) futuro,-a **5**

G

to gain weight aumentar de peso **6**
game el juego **1**; **video game** el juego electrónico **1**; (*match*) el partido **2**
garbage la basura **9**
genius el genio, la genia **4**
geography la geografía **5**
geometry la geometría **5**
to get: to get . . . grades sacar . . . notas **8**
to get up levantarse **10**; **Get up!** ¡Arriba! **5**
gift el regalo **4**
girl la muchacha **P**; la chica **3**; la niña **7**
girl scout la (muchacha) guía **9**
to give dar* **8**
to give up abandonar **12**
glad: I'm so glad! ¡Cuánto me alegro! **3**
glasses los lentes **4**
glove (*mitt*) el guante **5**
glutton el comilón **7**
to go ir* **1**; **Let's go!** ¡Vámonos! **3**
to go down bajar **12**
goal el fin **11**
God Dios **12**
going: to be going to ir a + *inf.* **2**
to go out salir* (de) **6**
good bueno,-a **1**; **Good!** ¡Qué bueno! **3**; **Good morning.** Buenos días. **P**; **Good afternoon.** Buenas tardes. **P**; **Good night.** Buenas noches. **P**; **Good luck!** ¡Buena suerte! **3**; **to be good for** servir para **10**; **It looks good on me.** Me queda bien. **10**
good-bye hasta mañana **P**; hasta luego **P**
good-looking guapo,-a **1**
goodness: My goodness! ¡Dios mío! **5**
gorilla el gorila **11**
grade la nota **8**; **to get . . . grades** sacar . . . notas **8**
to graduate graduarse **11**
grandfather el abuelo **4**
grandmother la abuela **4**
grandparents los abuelos **4**
grapes las uvas **6**
gray gris **10**
great formidable **1**; **Great!** ¡Qué bueno! **3**; ¡Fantástico! **3**
green verde **10**
greetings saludos **8**
group el grupo **4**
to grow crecer (zc)* **12**
guitar la guitarra **1**
gymnastics la gimnasia **P**; **to do gymnastics** hacer gimnasia **2**

H

hair el pelo **10**; **to comb one's hair** peinarse **10**
half past (*the hour*) . . . y media **5**
ham el jamón **6**
hand la mano (*f*) **10**
happy contento,-a **3**
to harm hacer daño **9**
hat el sombrero **10**

to have tener* 3; **What does he/she have?** (*illness*) ¿Qué tiene? 3; **to have** (*eat or drink*) **something** tomar 6
to have just acabar de + *inf.* 9; **to have to do** (*something*) tener que + *inf.* 3; deber 5
he él 1
head la cabeza 10
headache: to have a headache tener dolor de cabeza 3
health la salud 9
to hear oír* 7
heart el corazón 10
heavy: very heavy pesadísimo 5
hectic agitado,-a 8
hello hola **P**
to help ayudar 2; **to help at home** ayudar en casa 2
helping: to have a second helping repetir (i, i)* 10
her (*obj. pron.*) la 7; (*after prep.*) ella 3; (*poss. adj.*) su, sus 4
here aquí 2
Hey! ¡Oye! 2
hike la caminata 9
him lo 7; él (*after prep.*) 3
his su, sus 4
Hispanic hispánico,-a 3; **Hispanic people** los hispanos 6
history la historia 5
hobby el pasatiempo 9
home la casa 2; **at home** en casa 3
homework la tarea 1
hope la esperanza 12
hopeless desesperado,-a 12
hospital el hospital 3
hot: to be (*feel*) **hot** tener calor 6; **to be hot** (*weather*) hacer calor 6
hotel el hotel 2
hour la hora 5; **after the hour** y 5; **before the hour** menos 5
house la casa 3
how cómo **P**; (*interrog.*) ¿cómo? **P**; **How are you?** ¿Cómo estás? **P**; ¿Cómo está? **P**; **How do you say . . . ?** ¿Cómo se dice . . . ? **P**; **How's everything?** ¿Qué tal? **P**; **How many?** ¿Cuántos,-as . . . ? 4; **How much . . . ?** ¿Cuánto,-a . . . ? 4
hug el abrazo 8
hundred cien 4; ciento 7
hungry: to be hungry tener hambre 6
hurry: to be in a hurry tener prisa 6
to hurt doler (ue)* 10

I

I yo 1; **I myself** yo mismo,-a 12
ice cream el helado 6
idea la idea 3
ideal ideal 8
if si 3
ill enfermo,-a 3
immediately inmediatamente 12
important importante 1
to impress impresionar 10
inexpensive barato,-a 4
insect el insecto 9
inside dentro de 7
to insist (on) insistir (en) 6
institute el instituto 5
instrument el instrumento 9
intelligent inteligente 1
to intend pensar* + *inf.* 8
to interest: It interests me (him/her). Me (le) interesa 9
interesting interesante 1
international internacional 9
to invite invitar (a) 5
island la isla 8
it lo, la 7
its su, sus 4

J

jacket la chaqueta 10
jam la mermelada 6
January enero 8
jazz (*music*) el jazz 1
jealous celoso,-a 3
jeans los jeans 10
job el trabajo 8; el puesto 11
to jog correr 9
journalist el, la periodista 11
juice el jugo 6
July julio 8
to jump saltar 12
June junio 8
jungle la selva 12
just: to have just acabar de + *inf.* 9

K

to keep up (*with styles*) seguir* la moda 10
key la llave 4
to kid (*someone*) tomar(le) el pelo 11
kilometer el kilómetro 12
kind: What kind of . . . ? ¿Qué clase de . . . ? 6
king el rey 12
knapsack la mochila 4
to know saber* 6; conocer (zc)* 6

L

laboratory el laboratorio 5
land la tierra 12
language el idioma (*m*) 11
last último,-a 7; pasado,-a (*past*) 10; **last year** el año pasado 10
late tarde 2
later más tarde 2; después 5; **See you later.** Hasta luego. **P**
lawyer el abogado, la abogada 11

to learn (to) aprender (a) **5**
least: at least por lo menos **11**
to leave salir* (de) **5**; **to leave on a trip** salir de viaje **8**
left (*direction*) la izquierda **8**
leg la pierna **10**; **to pull someone's leg** tomar(le) el pelo **11**
less menos **5**; **less . . . than** menos que **12**
lesson la lección **5**
let: Let's . . . Vamos a . . . **2**; **Let them . . .** ¡Déjalos! **7**
library la biblioteca **2**
license la licencia **11**
lie la mentira **7**
life la vida **8**
to lift levantar **9**; **to lift weights** levantar pesas **9**
like (*prep.*) como **4**
to like gustar **P**; **I like . . .** Me gusta(n) . . . **P**; **I don't like it at all.** No me gusta nada. **1**; **I (he, she) would like** Me (le) gustaría . . . **3**; **to like a lot** encantar **9**
to listen escuchar **P**; **Listen!** ¡Oye! **2**
little poco **4**; **a little (bit) of** un poco de **6**
to live vivir **6**
lively alegre **1**
long largo,-a **10**
longer: no longer ya no **3**
to look at mirar **P**; **Look!** ¡Mira! **3**
to look for buscar* **5**
to lose perder (ie)* **8**; **to lose weight** bajar de peso **6**
lost perdido,-a **12**
to love querer* **8**; encantar **7**
to lower bajar **7**
lot: a lot mucho **1**
luck suerte **8**; **good luck** buena suerte **3**
lunch el almuerzo **6**
lunch: to have lunch almorzar (ue)* **9**

M

magazine la revista **4**
to make hacer* **6**
man el hombre **10**
manager el, la gerente **11**
many muchos,-as **1**; **how many?** ¿cuántos,-as? **4**; **so many** tantos,-as **4**
March marzo **8**
market el mercado **10**
mask la máscara **7**
match (*game*) el partido **2**
math las matemáticas **3**
matter: it doesn't matter no importa **10**; **What's the matter with him (her)?** ¿Qué tiene? **3**
May mayo **8**
Mayan maya (*adj., m/f*) **8**
maybe quizás **2**
me me **P**
meal la comida **6**
mean: What does . . . mean? ¿Qué quiere decir . . . ? **P**
meat la carne **6**
to meet encontrar (ue)* **9**; encontrarse con **10**
melon el melón **6**
member el miembro **9**
mental mental **11**
menu el menú **6**
Mexican mexicano,-a **8**
midnight la medianoche **5**
milk la leche **6**
million un millón (de) **7**
mineral water el agua mineral **6**
to miss (*a plane, bus*) perder (ie)* **8**
mitt el guante **5**
mixture la mezcla **10**
modern moderno,-a **9**
month el mes **8**
monument el monumento **8**
more más **2**; **I can't take it any more.** No puedo más. **8**; **more . . . than** más que **12**
mother la madre **4**; la mamá **4**
morning la mañana **5**; **in the morning** por la mañana **5**; **A.M.** de la mañana **5**
motorbike, motorcycle la moto (*f*) **3**
mountain la montaña **8**
mouth la boca **10**
movie theater el cine **2**
movies el cine **2**; (*film*) la película **2**
much mucho,-a **1**; **how much?** ¿cuánto,-a? **4**; **so much to do** tanto que hacer **5**
muscles los músculos **9**; **to develop muscles** sacar músculos **9**
museum el museo **2**
music la música **P**
my mi, mis **4**
myself: I myself yo mismo,-a **12**

N

name: first name el nombre **P**; **last name** el apellido **P**; **nickname** el apodo **P**; **My name is . . .** Me llamo . . . **P**
nasty: to be nasty (*weather*) hacer mal tiempo **3**
nation el país **9**
nature la naturaleza **8**
to navigate navegar* **12**
near (to) cerca (de) **8**
necktie la corbata **10**
to need necesitar **6**
neither tampoco **12**
neither . . . nor ni . . . ni **6, 12**
nervous nervioso,-a **3**
never nunca **4**
nevertheless sin embargo **10**
new nuevo,-a **1**
news las noticias **3**; **sports**

news el reportaje deportivo **7**
newspaper el periódico **5**
next siguiente **5**
next to al lado de **8**
nice simpático,-a **1**; bonito,-a **1**; **It's nice weather.** Hace buen tiempo. **3**; **Nice to meet you.** Mucho gusto. **P**
night la noche **5**; **at night** por la noche **5**; **last night** anoche **10**
nighttime de noche **6**
no no **P**; **to say no** decir que no **7**
nobody nadie **12**
noise el ruido **7**
nonsense: What nonsense! ¡Qué tontería! **3**
noon el mediodía (*m*) **5**
no one nadie **12**
nose la nariz **10**
notebook el cuaderno **4**
nothing nada **3, 12**
novel la novela **5**
November noviembre **8**
now ahora **2**
number el número **P**
nurse el enfermero, la enfermera **11**

O

to **observe** observar **9**
to **obtain** conseguir (i,i)* **11**
October octubre **8**
often muchas veces **4**
Oh! ¡Ay! **3**
Okay regular **P**; bueno **2**; Está bien. **7**
old viejo,-a **1**; antiguo,-a **10**; **to turn (be) ____ years old** cumplir ____ años **4**; **to be ____ years old** tener ____ años **4**
omelet la tortilla **6**
on sobre **2**; **on top of** encima de **8**
one uno, una **P**
only (*adv.*) solamente **4**; sólo **7**
to **open** abrir **6**
to **operate** operar **11**
opinion la opinión **7**
opposite frente a **8**
or o **6**
orange la naranja **6**
to **order** pedir (i,i)* **10**
other otro,-a **2**; **others** otros **2**
our nuestro,-a nuestros,-as **4**
outdoors al aire libre **9**
over there allí **7**; allá **10**
overweight gordo,-a **4**

P

pain el dolor **3**
pants los pantalones **10**
paper el papel **P**
parachute el paracaídas (*m, sing.*) **12**
parents los padres **4**
park el parque **2**
to **participate (in)** participar (en) **9**
party la fiesta **1**; **fifteenth birthday party** la fiesta de los quince **4**
passenger el pasajero, la pasajera **11**
past pasado,-a **10**
pastime el pasatiempo **9**
pastry los pasteles **6**
path el camino **9**
to **pay (for)** pagar* **11**
pear la pera **6**
pen (*ball-point*) el bolígrafo **4**
pencil el lápiz (*pl.* lápices) **P**
people la gente **7**
perfect perfecto,-a **4**
perfume el perfume **4**
perhaps quizás **2**
to **permit** permitir **6**
person la persona **2**
personal particular **5**
pet el animal doméstico **11**
phone el teléfono **2**; **to talk on the phone** hablar por teléfono **2**
photo la foto (*f*) **3**
photographer el fotógrafo, la fotógrafa **2**
physical education la educación física **5**
physics la física **5**
piano el piano **2**
pictures: to take pictures sacar* fotos **2**
pie la tarta **6**
pilot el piloto, la pilota (de aviación) **11**
to **pilot** pilotear **12**
pink rosado,-a **10**
to **place** poner* **6**
plan el plan **5**
to **plan** programar **11**
to **plan on** pensar* + *inf.* **8**
plane el avión **8**
plant la planta **9**; la hierba **12**
plate el plato **2**
to **play** (*a game*) jugar (ue)* **1**; (*an instrument, radio, record*) tocar* **2**
player el jugador, la jugadora **2**
plaza la plaza **2**
please por favor **P**
pleasure: with pleasure con mucho gusto **6**
poetry la poesía **5**
point el punto **7**
police officer el policía, la mujer policía **11**
police show la película policíaca **7**
pool la piscina **2**
poor pobre **8**; **the poor things** los pobres **4**; **poor little thing** pobrecito,-a **5**
popular popular **1**
pork chop la chuleta de cerdo **6**
position el puesto **11**
possession: to take possession tomar posesión **11**

Q

R

S

de compras **2**; **shopping center** el centro comercial **10**
short (*stature*) bajo,-a **1**; (*length*) corto,-a **8**
should deber **5**
to shout gritar **11**
to show mostrar (ue)* **9**
shrimp los camarones **6**
sick enfermo,-a **3**
sign la señal **12**
since como **8**
to sing cantar **1**
single solo **12**
sister la hermana **4**; **brothers and sisters** los hermanos **4**
size (*clothing*) la talla **10**
to skate patinar **9**
to ski esquiar **1**
skirt la falda **10**
sky el cielo **12**
to sleep dormir (ue, u)* **6**; **to go to sleep** dormirse **10**
sleepy: to be sleepy tener sueño **6**
slim delgado,-a **4**
small pequeño,-a **4**
to snow nevar (ie)* **3**; **to be snowing** estar nevando **3**
so (*adv.*) tan **2**
soap opera la novela **7**
soccer el fútbol **P**
socks los calcetines **10**
soft drink el refresco **6**
solution la solución **6**
some algunos,-as **8**
someday algún día **2**
someone alguien **12**
something algo **3, 12**
sometimes a veces **4**
son el hijo **4**
song la canción **7**
soon pronto **1**
sorry: I'm so sorry! ¡Cuánto lo siento! **3**
sound el sonido **7**
soup la sopa **6**
south el sur **12**
souvenir el recuerdo **8**
space el espacio **7**
Spanish (*language*) español, **P**; (*adj.*) español,-a **12RC**
to speak hablar **1**
to spend (*time*) pasar **4**; (*money*) gastar **8**
sport el deporte **1**
sports news el reportaje deportivo **7**
spring la primavera **8**
square la plaza **2**
stadium el estadio **2**
stamp la estampilla **9**
to stay quedarse **12**
steak el bistec **6**
stereo el tocadiscos (*m, sing.*) **3**; (*adj.*) estereofónico,-a **10**
still todavía **3**
stingy tacaño,-a **4**
stomach el estómago **10**
stomachache: to have a stomachache tener dolor de estómago **3**
to stop detenerse* **12**
store la tienda **2**
straight: Go straight ahead. Siga derecho. **8**
to straighten up arreglar **2**; **to straighten up one's room** arreglar el cuarto **2**; **Go straight ahead.** Siga derecho. **8**
strange raro,-a **7**
strawberries las fresas **6**
street la calle **7**
strong fuerte **12**
student el, la estudiante **5**
student (*adj.*) estudiantil **9**
studies los estudios **11**
studio el estudio **8**
to study estudiar **P**; **to study to be . . .** estudiar para . . . **11**
style la moda **10**; **to keep up with the styles** seguir la moda **10**; **to be in style** estar a la moda **10**
such a tan **2**
summer el verano **8**
sunbath: to take a sunbath tomar el sol **8**
sunglasses los lentes de sol **10**
sunny: to be sunny hacer sol **3**
supermarket el supermercado **2**
supper la cena **6**
sure seguro,-a **11**
surprised sorprendido,-a **3**
sweater el suéter **4**
sweets los dulces **6**
to swim nadar **1**
swimming la natación **8**
swimming pool la piscina **2**
swimsuit el traje de baño **10**

T

to take: to take (*along*) llevar **8**; **to take pictures** sacar fotos **2**; **I can't take it any more.** No puedo más. **8**; **to take a course** seguir* un curso **11**
talent el talento **2**
to talk hablar **1**
tall alto,-a **1**
tape (*cassette*) la cinta **4**
tape recorder la grabadora **3**
tart la tarta **6**
taxi el taxi **10**
tea el té **6**
to teach enseñar **7**
teacher el profesor, la profesora **P**
team el equipo **2**
technician el técnico, la técnica **10**
teddy bear el osito de felpa **4**
tee shirt la camiseta **4**
teeth los dientes **10**; **to brush one's teeth** lavarse los dientes **10**
telephone el teléfono **2**
television la televisión **P**; **television set** el televisor **3**
to tell decir* **7**; **¡Don't tell me!** ¡No me digas! **3**
tennis el tenis **P**
tension la tensión **8**

tent la tienda **9**; **to pitch a tent** levantar una tienda **9**
thank you gracias **P**
that (*adj.*) ese, esa **7**; (*over there*) aquel, aquella **7**
that (*pron.*) eso **3**
theater el teatro **2**
their su, sus **4**
them los, las **7**; ellos, ellas (*after prep.*) **9**
then pues **P**; entonces **2**
there ahí **7**; allá **10**; **right there** ahí **7**; **over there** allí **7**
there is, there are hay **2**
these (*adj.*) estos, estas **7**
they ellos (*m*), ellas (*f*) **1**
thin delgado,-a **4**
thing la cosa **8**; **the poor things** los pobres **4**; **poor little thing** pobrecito,-a **5**
to think pensar (ie)* **8**; **to think about** (*someone or something*) pensar en **8**; **What do you think?** ¿Qué te parece? **4**; **I think so.** Creo que sí. **Don't you think so?** ¿No te parece? **4**
third tercero,-a **7**
thirst la sed **6**
thirsty: to be thirsty tener sed **6**
this (*pron.*) esto **7**; **What's this?** ¿Qué es esto? **7**
this (*adj.*) este, esta **7**
those (*adj.*) esos, esas **7**; (*over there*) aquellos, aquellas **7**
thousand mil **7**
throat la garganta **3**; **to have a sore throat** tener dolor de garganta **3**
through por **10**
tiger el tigre **11**
time (*hour*) la hora **5**; (*moment*) el tiempo **6**; (*instance*) la vez **7**; **What time is it?** ¿Qué hora es? **5**; **it's time to** es hora de **7**; **free time** los ratos libres **8**; **the first (last) time** la primera (última) vez **7**; **on time** puntual **1**
tired cansado,-a **3**
tiring fatigoso,-a **9**
to a **1**
today hoy **2**
tomato el tomate **6**
tomorrow mañana **P**; **See you tomorrow.** Hasta mañana. **P**; **day after tomorrow** pasado mañana **4**
tonight esta noche **2**
too también **1**
too much demasiado **9**
tooth el diente **10**, la muela **3**
toothache: to have a toothache tener dolor de muelas **3**
top: on top of encima de **8**
total el total **7**
tourist el, la turista **2**
train el tren **8**
transistor el transistor **10**
to travel viajar **2**
travel agent el, la agente de viajes **11**
trip: to take a trip hacer un viaje **8**; **to leave on a trip** salir de viaje **8**; **to take a trip around the world** dar la vuelta al mundo **12**
tropical tropical **8**
truth la verdad **5**
to try on probarse (ue)* **10**
to turn . . . (*direction*) doblar **8**
typewriter la máquina de escribir **3**
typical típico,-a **8**
typing la mecanografía **5**

U

uncle el tío **4**; **aunt(s) and uncle(s)** los tíos **4**
under debajo de **8**
to understand comprender **5**; entender (ie)* **8**
underwater submarino,-a **12**
unfriendly antipático,-a **1**
United States los Estados Unidos **P**
university la universidad **4**
until hasta **P, 8**
up: Get up! ¡Arriba! **5**; **to get up** levantarse **10**
us (*obj. pron.*) nos, (*obj. prep.*) nosotros,-as **9**
to use usar **10**
useful: to be useful servir para **10**

V

vacation las vacaciones (*used in pl.*) **3**; **to be on vacation** estar de vacaciones **3**
variety show las variedades **7**
vegetables los vegetales **6**
Venezuelan venezolano,-a **12**
very muy **1**
veterinarian el veterinario, la veterinaria **11**
visit la visita **3**
to visit visitar **2**
voice la voz **7**; **Lower your voice.** Baja la voz. **7**
volleyball el volibol **P**

W

to wait for esperar **5**
waiter el camarero **6**
waitress la camarera **6**
to wake up despertarse (ie)* **10**
walk (*noun*) el paseo **2**; **to take a walk** dar un paseo **2**; **to go for a walk** pasear **12**
wallet la cartera **4**
to want querer (ie, i)* **2**; desear **6**
warm: to be warm (*weather*) hacer calor **3**; (*feel warm*) tener calor **6**

to **wash** (*something*) lavar **2**; (*oneself*) lavarse **10**
to **waste** perder (ie)* **8**
watch el reloj **3**
to **watch** mirar **P**
water el agua (*f*) **6**; **mineral water** el agua mineral **6**; **to take on water** (*ship*) hacer agua **12**
water (*adj.*) acuático,-a **8**
waterskiing el esquí acuático **8**
we nosotros, nosotras **1**
to **wear** usar **10**
weather el tiempo **3**; **How's the weather?** ¿Qué tiempo hace? **3**; **It's good weather.** Hace buen tiempo. **3**; **The weather is bad.** Hace mal tiempo. **3**; **What will the weather be like?** ¿Qué tiempo va a hacer? **3**; **weather report** (*forecast*) el pronóstico del tiempo **7**
week la semana **3**
weekend el fin de semana **2**
weight: to gain weight aumentar de peso **6**; **to lose weight** bajar de peso **6**
weights las pesas **9**; **to lift weights** levantar pesas **9**
welcome: You're welcome. De nada. **P**
well pues **P**; bueno **2**; **very well** muy bien **P**; **pretty well** bastante bien **P**
what? ¿qué? (*adj.*) **1**; (*pron.*) **2**; ¿cuál? **5**
when? ¿cuándo? **2**
where? ¿dónde? **2**; **where from?** ¿de dónde? **2**; **where to?** ¿adónde? **2**
which? ¿qué? **2**; **which one?** ¿cuál? **5**
while mientras **P**; **a little while longer** un rato más **7**
white blanco,-a **10**
who? ¿quién? **2**
whom? ¿a quién(es)? **5**
whose? ¿de quién(es)? **4**
why ¿por qué? **2**
wind el viento **3**; **to be windy** hacer viento **3**
winter el invierno **8**
to **wish** querer (ie, i)* **2**; desear **6**
with con **3**
without sin **8**
woman la mujer **11**; **businesswoman** la mujer de negocios **11**
wonderful formidable **1**; fantástico **3**
woods el bosque **9**
work el trabajo **8**
to **work** trabajar **1**
to **work on** colaborar **9**
worried preocupado,-a **3**
world el mundo **12**; **to go around the world** dar la vuelta al mundo **12**
worse peor **12**
Wow! ¡Caramba! **7**
wrestling la lucha libre **P**
to **write** escribir **6**
wrong: What's wrong with him (her)? ¿Qué tiene? **3**; **to be wrong** no tener razón **6**

Y

year el año **4**; **to be (turn) _____ years old** cumplir _____ años **4**; **to be _____ years old** tener _____ años **4**
yearbook al anuario **9**
yellow amarillo,-a **10**
yes sí **P**; **to say no** decir que no **7**; **to say yes** decir que sí **7**
yesterday ayer **10**
yet pero **1**; todavía **3**; ya **4**
yoga el yoga (*m*) **9**
you (*familiar*) tú **1**; (*polite*) usted **1**; (*plural*) ustedes **1**
young joven **4**; **young people** los jóvenes **10**
your (*fam.*) tu, tus **4**; (*polite*) su, sus **4**
yourself: for yourself (*fam.*) por ti mismo,-a **9**

Z

zone la zona **10**
zoo el zoológico **10**

Index

PHOTO CREDITS

Abbreviations used: *t*=top; *c*=center; *b*=bottom; *l*=left; *r*=right; *i*=inset

All photos by Russell Dian except as noted below.

Capítulo preliminar
x: *tl*, © Kenn Duncan; *bl*, HRW Photo by Robert Royal; *c*, Jeff Rotman. **1:** *tl*, © Richard Steedman/The Stock Market; *tr*, *bl*, Slim Aarons; *bc*, © 1982 Joel Gordon. **19:** Morton Beebe.

Capítulo uno
22: *b*, Owen Franken. **25:** Estadio del Rayo Vallecano. **29:** *l*, Mitchell B. Reibel/Sports Photo File; *ct*, Irv Glaser/Gamma-Liaison; *cb*, Andrew Rakoczy; *r*, Henry Grossman. **34:** Katherine A. Lambert. **37:** HRW Photo by Tor Eigeland. **44:** Courtesy Ribbon Publications; Cortesia de **GeoMundo revista mensual,** Photo by Roberto Redondo, Copyright Editorial America, S.A.; Replica Publishing Inc. **45:** Victor Englebert.

Capítulo dos
47: HRW Photo by Robert Royal. **48:** Cindy Karp/Black Star 1983. **54:** Courtesy CBS Records; *l*, © Joseph F. Viesti. **57:** both HRW Photos by Robert Royal. **58:** *lt*, *b*, Roberto Redondo/Fotolaminados de P.R. Inc.; *br*, HRW Photo by Roberto Redondo. **59:** *t*, Roberto Redondo/Fotolaminados de P.R.; *b*, Susan McCartney/Photo Researchers. **63:** Tor Eigeland. **66:** Teatro de la Ciudad. **67:** Courtesy Madison Square Garden.

Capítulo tres
71: © Joel Gordon 1982. **77:** *r*, HRW Photo by Robert Royal. **80:** Robert Royal. **82:** *tl*, Robert Royal; all other photos, Antonio Suarez/Wheeler Pictures. **92:** © François Grohier/Photo Researchers. **94:** Owen Franken.

Capítulo cuatro
98: HRW Photo by Alejandro Betancourt M. **102:** Marilyn Perez-Abreu. **104:** HRW Photo by Alejandro Betancourt M. **108:** Courtesy INOSA. **109:** William Clark/Fotowest. **112:** *l*, From the MGM release *At the Circus* © 1939 Loew's Incorporated. Renewed 1966 Metro-Goldwyn-Mayer Inc.; *r* from the MGM release *A Day at the Races* © 1937 Metro-Goldwyn-Mayer Corporation. Renewed 1964 © Metro-Goldwyn-Mayer, Inc. **113:** From left to right: The Columbia Information Service; Courtesy Aeroméxico; Courtesy Museo de Arte Abstracto Español; Courtesy National Gallery of Art, Washington, D.C.

Capítulo cinco
124: HRW Photo by Tor Eigeland. **127:** Courtesy Columbia Pictures International Corporation. **131:** *l*, Kathy Kayser; *r*, Courtesy New York State Department of Commerce. **135:** Courtesy Colegio San Ignacio, San Juan, Puerto Rico. **136:** Courtesy CCC, Spain. **137:** *l*, Owen Franken; *tr*, HRW Photo by Robert Royal; *br*, Cameramann International Ltd.

Capítulo seis
145: © Richard Steedman/The Stock Market. **152:** HRW Photo by Robert Royal. **153:** Courtesy Restaurante Antigua Casa Sobrino de Botin. **155:** *bl*, HRW Photo by Robert Royal; *br*, HRW Photo by Tor Eigeland. **159:** *t*, HRW Photo by Tor Eigeland; *c*, HRW Photo by Lee Boltin; *b*, HRW Photo by Lucy Barber. **162:** Cameramann International Ltd. **163:** all HRW Photos by Tor Eigeland. **167:** *b*, HRW Photo by Tor Eigeland. **168:** *Club de Gourmets, Cocina y Hogar*, a monthly magazine edited by Hymsa (Spain).

Capítulo siete
171: © Kenn Duncan. **172:** HRW Photo by Yoav Levy. **175:** Courtesy CBS Records. **176:** Courtesy *Antena TV*, Spain. **177:** Loren A. McIntyre. **178, 179:** Courtesy *TelePublicaciones*, South America. **184:** *bl*, Loren A. McIntyre; *br*, Victor Englebert. **189:** Courtesy HOTASA. **190:** Orquestra Filarmonica de la Ciudad de México; Rolling, S.A.; Jardines Neptuno; Castell Comte d'Altaz. **192:** *l*, Courtesy Twentieth Century-Fox; *r*, Courtesy of LUCASFILM LTD. **193:** both, Courtesy Twentieth Century-Fox.

Capítulo ocho
195: Slim Aarons. **196:** *t*, Luis Villota/The Stock Market. **197:** Nick Nicholson. **203:** Joachim Messerschmidt/Bruce Coleman Incorporated. **208:** Courtesy Plaza de Toros Monumental, Barcelona. **209:** *tr*, Luis Villota/The Stock Market; *cl*, David Maenza/The Image Bank; *br*, Carl Frank/Photo Researchers. **216:** *l*, Courtesy Consejo Nacional de Turismo de México; *cl* & *r*, Courtesy Patronato Municipal de Turismo de Madrid; *cr*, Courtesy Iberia Lineas Aereas Internacionales de España. **218:** *tl*, Cameramann International Ltd.; *br*, Vince Streano/The Stock Market. **219:** *tr*, Robert Frerck/Odyssey Productions; *c*, Morton Beebe; *br*, Andrew Rakoczy.

Capítulo nueve
223: Slim Aarons. **224:** *t*, HRW Photo by Yoav Levy. **225:** *b*, HRW Photo by Lee Boltin. **231:** HRW Photo by Robert Royal. **235:** Katherine A. Lambert. **237:** *tl*, © Robert Rattner; *tr* © Loren McIntyre 1981/Woodfin Camp; *bl*, Loren A. McIntyre; *br*, John Dominis/Wheeler Pictures. **240:** Courtesy Ministerio de Transportes Y Turismo, España; Festivales de España, Repertorio Español, New York. **243:** Ministerio de Transportes Y Turismo, España. **245:** © Bob Adelman. **246:** HRW Photo by Alejandro Betancourt M. **247:** *tl*, *br*, HRW Photos by Alejandro Betancourt M.; *tr*, Asociación de Scouts de México, Courtesy World Scout Bureau; *bl*, © Joseph F. Viesti. **248:** World Association of Girl Guides and Girl Scouts; HRW Photo by Alejandro Betancourt M.

Capítulo diez
251: HRW Photo by Robert Royal. **254:** Galerias Preciados, Photo by Augusto Robert. **258:** *l*, HRW Photo by Tor Eigeland. **261:** Cameramann International Ltd. **268:** *tl*, Carmen Cavazos; *tr*, © Norman Prince. **272:** *tl*, Robert Frerck/Odyssey Productions; *tr*, © Richard Steedman/The Stock Market; *bl*, © Andrew Rakoczy; *br*, © Vince Streano/The Stock Market. **273:** © Robert Frerck/Odyssey Productions.

Capítulo once
278: HRW Photo by Yoav Levy. **284:** *l*, © MCMLXXX Peter Menzel; *r*, David Woo/Stock Boston. **288:** AFHA, Barcelona. **291:** Marilyn Perez-Abreu. **295:** Richard Steedman/The Stock Market. **299:** *t*, Felipe Andrade/Aeroperu Airways. **300:** *l*, © Bettina Cirone 1980/Photo Researchers; *c*, © 1981 John McGrail/Wheeler Pictures; *r*, Bob Adelman. **301:** *tl*, © 1982 Bernard Pierre Wolff/Photo Researchers; *r*, © Peter Menzel.

Capítulo doce
303: Jeff Rotman; **304:** © Loren A. McIntyre. **305:** Venezuelan Government Tourist Office. **309:** Courtesy Federacion Española de Esquí, Madrid, España, and Oficina de Baqueira-Beret, Barcelona. **313:** NASA. **314:** *lt*, *bl*, *rc*, © Loren A. McIntyre; *lc*, *br*, *rb*, Venezuelan Tourist Office, NY; *rt*, Cameramann International Ltd. **317:** HRW Photo by Alejandro Betancourt M. **319:** *tl*, *tr*, *bl*, New York Public Library; *br*, Culver Pictures. **322:** *l*, Warren Bolster/Sports Illustrated; TIME Inc.; *r*, Loren A. McIntyre/Woodfin Camp. **323:** © Enrico Ferorelli/Wheeler Pictures. **324:** Theodore DeBry, *ca* 1590. Rare Books and Manuscript Division, NY Public Library, Astor, Lenox, and Tilden Foundation. **326:** From Ptolemaeus, Basileae, 1540. **318:** Nautical Orly. **327:** El Descubrimiento; *El Tiempo*.

Capítulo de enlace
339: *l*, *br*, Courtesy Spanish National Tourist Office, New York City; *tr*, HRW Photo by Jan Lukas. **340:** *tl*, Victor Englebert; *bl*, Michael Kuh; *tr*, HRW Photo by Vincent P. Duggan; *br*, © 1979 Gail Mooney/PhotoUnique. **341:** *c*, Courtesy El patronato provincial de Turismo y el centro de iniciativas turisticas de Sevilla; *b*, Courtesy Jefatura Provincial de Turismo, Madrid.

PHOTO IDENTIFICATION

Capítulo preliminar
x: *tl*, Alvin Ailey American Dance Theatre, "The Stack Up"; *bl*, Pacha Disco, Madrid, Spain. **x-1:** *cb*, Academia Cristo Rey, Ponce, Puerto Rico. **1:** *tl*, Mexico; *tr*, Costa Brava, Spain; *bl*, Basque country, Spain; *bc*, Peruvian girls in New York City; *br*, Torre de L'Oro, Seville, Spain. **2:** *t*, New York, N.Y.; *b*, N.Y. Public Library, New York, N.Y. **4:** Ponce, P.R. **5:** *t*, Colegio San Ignacio, San Juan, P.R.; *b*, Ponce, P.R. **15:** *tl*, *br*, Academia Cristo Rey, Ponce, P.R.; *tr*, Colegio San Ignacio, San Juan, P.R.; *bl*, Guadalajara Restaurant, New York, N.Y. **16:** *t*, Academia Cristo Rey, Ponce, P.R.; *b*, Avenida de los Toreros, Madrid, Spain. **17:** *t*, Madrid, Spain; *c*, Brooklyn, N.Y.; *b*, Retiro Park, Madrid, Spain. **19:** Uxmal ruins, Mexico.

Capítulo uno
21: Ponce, P.R. **22:** *t*, New York, N.Y.; *b*, Cartagena, Colombia. **34:** Puente Alto, Chile. **37:** Statue of Christopher Columbus, Ramblas, Barcelona, Spain. **39:** Seville, Spain. **42:** Brooklyn, N.Y. **45:** La Puerta Trujillo, Venezuela.

Capítulo dos
47: Pacha Disco, Madrid, Spain. **48:** Mexico City. **50:** Madrid, Spain. **54:** *br*, Barcelona, Spain. **57:** *l*, Prado Museum, Madrid, Spain; *r*, Plaza de España, Madrid, Spain. **58:** *tl*, University of San Juan, San Juan, P.R.; *bl*, El Yunque, P.R.; *cr*, Old San Juan, P.R.; *br*, El Morro Castle, San Juan, P.R. **59:** *tl*, Phosphorescent Bay, La Parguera, P.R.; *bl*, Luquillo Beach, P.R.; *r*, La Plaza de Cristóbal Colón, Mayagüez, P.R. **63:** Sitges, Spain. (Safety helmets are not required at resorts in Spain.) **64:** María Luisa Park, Seville, Spain. **68:** San Cristóbal, Old San Juan, P.R.

Capítulo tres
71: Peruvian girls in New York, N.Y. **77:** *l*, Seville, Spain; *r*, Post Office Building, Madrid, Spain. **80:** World Cup Playoffs, Madrid, Spain. **82:** *all*, World Cup Playoffs. **92:** Patagonian Andes Ice Cap, Lake Pingo, Paine National Park, Chile. **93:** A New York City school. **94:** San Sebastián, Spain.

Capítulo cuatro
97: Arcos de la Frontera, Spain. **98:** Sanborn's, Mexico City. **102:** Seville Cathedral, Seville, Spain. **104:** Mexico City. **107:** María Luisa Park, Seville, Spain. **109:** Santa Fe, New Mexico. **118, 119:** A Cuban family residing in the U.S.

Capítulo cinco
121: Academia Cristo Rey, Ponce, P.R. **122:** Colegio San Ignacio, San Juan, P.R. **124:** San Pedro del Ribes, Spain. **137:** *l*, Saint George's School, Quilmes, Argentina; *tr*, Instituto Nacional de Bachillerato, Madrid, Spain; *bl*, Oruro, Bolivia. **140:** Students from the Instituto Nacional de Bachillerato, Madrid, Spain. **143:** Colegio Central Presbiteriano, Mayagüez, P.R.

Capítulo seis
145: Guadalajara, Mexico. **152:** Madrid, Spain. **155:** *t*, *bl*, Madrid, Spain; *br*, Sitges, Spain. **159:** *t*, San Pedro del Ribes, Spain. **162:** Ajijic, Jalisco, Mexico. **163:** *tl*, San Pedro del Ribes, Spain; *tr*, *bl*, *br*, Sitges, Spain. **167:** Sitges, Spain.

Capítulo siete
171: "The Stack Up," Alvin Ailey American Dance Theater. **172:** New York, N.Y. **177:** Quito TV, Quito, Ecuador. **184:** *l*, Chipaya, Bolivia; *r*, near Potosí, Bolivia. **187:** *l* and *r*, the Rastro, Madrid, Spain.

Capítulo ocho
195: Costa Brava, Spain. **196:** Torremolinos, Costa del Sol, Spain. **197:** Bariloche, Argentina. **203:** Argentina. **208:** *l*, Escuela Taurina de Madrid; *r*, Savir, Barcelona, Spain. **209:** *tr*, Spain; *cl*, *or* Caracas, Venezuela. **211:** Madrid, Spain. **218:** *tl* and *br*, Mexico City. **219:** *t*, Chichén Itzá ruins, Mexico; *c*, Uxmal ruins, Mexico; *b*, El Castillo, Chichén Itzá, Mexico.

Capítulo nueve
223: Basque country, Spain. **224:** *t*, Bronx, N.Y.; *b*, Joffrey School, New York, N.Y. **225:** *t*, Horace Mann School, Riverdale, N.Y.; *c*, Croton, N.Y. **231:** Gimnasio Samurai, Roland Burger's Judo Class, Madrid, Spain. **235:** Costa Rica. **237:** *tl*, the Pampas, Argentina; *bl*, Atacama Desert, Chile; *tr*, Andean Mountains, near Chuma, Bolivia; *br*, Amazon jungle. **241:** *both*, Madrid, Spain. **243:** Spain. **244:** New York, N.Y. **245:** Old San Juan, P.R. **246–247:** Mexico. **248:** *r*, Casa de Campo, Madrid, Spain. **249:** Mexico.

Capítulo diez
251: Madrid, Spain. **258:** *l*, Sueca, Spain; *r*, Arcos de la Frontera, Spain. **261:** Caracas, Venezuela. **266:** *l* and *r*, Boutique Victorio Lucchino, Seville, Spain. **268:** *t*, *l* to *r*, Mexico, Spain, Guatemala; *b*, *l* to *r*, Uruguay, Puerto Rico, Cuba. **272:** *tl*, Patzcuaro, Mexico; *tr*, Mexico; *bl*, Guadalajara, Mexico; *br*, Coyoacán, Guadalajara, Mexico. **273:** Plaza de las Tres Culturas, Mexico City.

Capítulo once
277: Time Magazine's VISTA System, Electronic Art Dept., New York, N.Y. **278:** Samuel Gompers Vocational and Technical High School, Bronx, N.Y. **280:** *l*, New York, N.Y.; *r*, Westchester County, N.Y. **284:** *l*, Mexico City. **291:** the Alhambra, Granada, Spain. **295:** Cuernavaca, Mexico. **298:** San Diego Zoo. **299:** *t*, Miami, Fla.; *b*, New York, N.Y. **300:** *l*, Seville, Spain; *c*, V.A. Medical Center, Palo Alto, Cal.; *r*, San Juan, P.R. **301:** *tl*, Bogotá School for the Deaf, Bogotá, Colombia; *bl*, Westchester County, N.Y.; *r*, Guadalajara, Mexico.

Capítulo doce
304: Orinoco River, Venezuela. **313:** Ed White over Mexico, Gemini Mission #4. **314:** *all*, Venezuela; *lt*, Orinoco River; *lb*, Sucre; *cl*, Salto Angel; *cr*, Mérida; *rt*, Caracas; *rc*, Cumaná; *br*, Canaima. **317:** Mural, by Diego Rivera, Del Prado Hotel, Mexico City. **322:** *l*, Flat Island, Indian Ocean, near Mozambique; *r*, Andes, Colombia. **323:** West Virginia.

Capítulo de enlace
329: Torre del Oro, Seville, Spain. **339:** *all*, Cordoba, Spain: *l*, La Mezquita, interior; *tr*, La Mezquita, exterior; *br*, Jewish Quarter street scene. **340:** *tl*, Seville, Spain; *bl*, Seville Cathedral from Patio de Naranjos; Cathedral tower, La Giralda; *tr*, the Alhambra, Granada, Spain; *br*, *Los Gallos*, Seville, Spain. **343:** Bridge at Plaza de España, Seville, Spain.